ISS 325:
War and Revolution in the 21st Century

ISS 325:
WAR AND REVOLUTION IN THE 21ST CENTURY

PREPARED FOR
PROFESSOR BARRY STEIN

MICHIGAN STATE UNIVERSITY
2002

WITH SELECTIONS FROM:
FOREIGN AFFAIRS
THE ATLANTIC MONTHLY
THE NATIONAL INTEREST

A FOREIGN AFFAIRS CUSTOM ANTHOLOGY

CONTENTS

THE COMING ANARCHY

by ROBERT D. KAPLAN

How scarcity, crime, overpopulation, tribalism, and disease are rapidly destroying the social fabric of our planet

THE Minister's eyes were like egg yolks, an aftereffect of some of the many illnesses, malaria especially, endemic in his country. There was also an irrefutable sadness in his eyes. He spoke in a slow and creaking voice, the voice of hope about to expire. Flame trees, coconut palms, and a ballpoint-blue Atlantic composed the background. None of it seemed beautiful, though. "In forty-five years I have never seen things so bad. We did not manage ourselves well after the British departed. But what we have now is something worse—the revenge of the poor, of the social failures, of the people least able to bring up children in a modern society." Then he referred to the recent coup in the West African country Sierra Leone. "The boys who took power in Sierra Leone come from houses like this." The Minister jabbed his finger at a corrugated metal shack teeming with children. "In three months these boys confiscated all the official Mercedes, Volvos, and BMWs

Right: outside Monrovia, Liberia, civilian victims of civil war, dumped near the airport. Far right: government troops in Sierra Leone reoccupy a rebel position

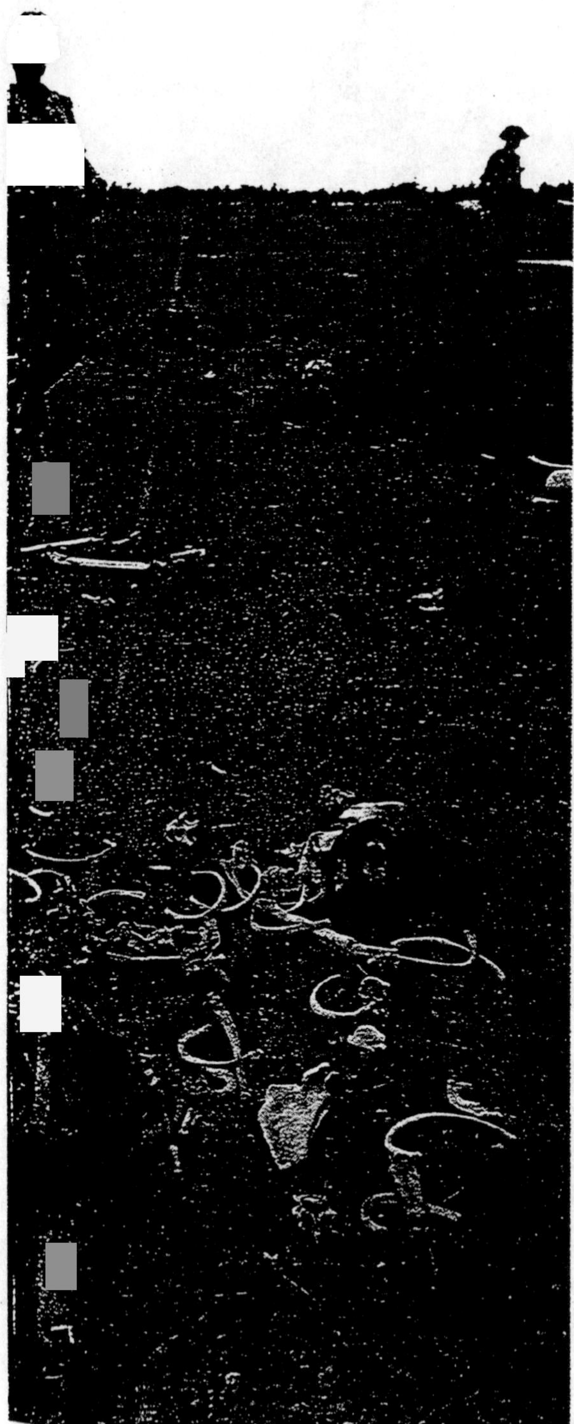

PATRICK ROBERT/SYGMA

and willfully wrecked them on the road." The Minister mentioned one of the coup's leaders, Solomon Anthony Joseph Musa, who shot the people who had paid for his schooling, "in order to erase the humiliation and mitigate the power his middle-class sponsors held over him."

Tyranny is nothing new in Sierra Leone or in the rest of West Africa. But it is now part and parcel of an increasing lawlessness that is far more significant than any coup, rebel incursion, or episodic experiment in democracy. Crime was what my friend—a top-ranking African official whose life would be threatened were I to identify him more precisely—really wanted to talk about. Crime is what makes West Africa a natural point of departure for my report on what the political character of our planet is likely to be in the twenty-first century.

The cities of West Africa at night are some of the unsafest places in the world. Streets are unlit; the police often lack gasoline for their vehicles; armed burglars, carjackers, and muggers proliferate. "The government in Sierra Leone has

MIKE GOLDWATER-NETWORK/MATRIX

no writ after dark," says a foreign resident, shrugging. When I was in the capital, Freetown, last September, eight men armed with AK-47s broke into the house of an American man. They tied him up and stole everything of value. Forget Miami: direct flights between the United States and the Murtala Muhammed Airport, in neighboring Nigeria's largest city, Lagos, have been suspended by order of the U.S. Secretary of Transportation because of ineffective security at the terminal and its environs. A State Department report cited the airport for "extortion by law-enforcement and immigration officials." This is one of the few times that the U.S. government has embargoed a foreign airport for reasons that are linked purely to crime. In Abidjan, effectively the capital of the Côte d'Ivoire, or Ivory Coast, restaurants have stick- and gun-wielding guards who walk you the fifteen feet or so between your car and the entrance, giving you an eerie taste of what American cities might be like in the future. An Italian ambassador was killed by gunfire when robbers invaded an Abidjan restaurant. The family of the Nigerian ambassador

SIERRA LEONE IS A MICROCOSM OF WHAT IS OCCURRING IN WEST AFRICA AND MUCH OF THE UNDER-DEVELOPED WORLD: THE WITHERING AWAY OF CENTRAL GOVERNMENTS, THE RISE OF TRIBAL AND REGIONAL DOMAINS, THE UNCHECKED SPREAD OF DISEASE, AND THE GROWING PERVA-SIVENESS OF WAR.

was tied up and robbed at gunpoint in the ambassador's residence. After university students in the Ivory Coast caught bandits who had been plaguing their dorms, they executed them by hanging tires around their necks and setting the tires on fire. In one instance Ivorian policemen stood by and watched the "necklacings," afraid to intervene. Each time I went to the Abidjan bus terminal, groups of young men with restless, scanning eyes surrounded my taxi, putting their hands all over the windows, demanding "tips" for carrying my luggage even though I had only a rucksack. In cities in six West African countries I saw similar young men everywhere—hordes of them. They were like loose molecules in a very unstable social fluid, a fluid that was clearly on the verge of igniting.

"You see," my friend the Minister told me, "in the villages of Africa it is perfectly natural to feed at any table and lodge in any hut. But in the cities this communal existence no longer holds. You must pay for lodging and be invited for food. When young men find out that their relations cannot put them up, they become lost. They join other migrants and slip gradually into the criminal process."

"In the poor quarters of Arab North Africa," he continued, "there is much less crime, because Islam provides a social anchor: of education and indoctrination. Here in West Africa we have a lot of superficial Islam and superficial Christianity. Western religion is undermined by animist beliefs not suitable to a moral society, because they are based on irrational spirit power. Here spirits are used to wreak vengeance by one person against another, or one group against another." Many of the atrocities in the Liberian civil war have been tied to belief in *juju* spirits, and the BBC has reported, in its magazine *Focus on Africa*, that in the civil fighting in adjacent Sierra Leone, rebels were said to have "a young woman with them who would go to the front naked, always walking backwards and looking in a mirror to see where she was going. This made her invisible, so that she could cross to the army's positions and there bury charms . . . to improve the rebels' chances of success."

Finally my friend the Minister mentioned polygamy. Designed for a pastoral way of life, polygamy continues to thrive in sub-Saharan Africa even though it is increasingly uncommon in Arab North Africa. Most youths I met on the road in West Africa told me that they were from "extended" families, with a mother in one place and a father in another. Translated to an urban environment, loose family structures are largely responsible for the world's highest birth rates and the explosion of the HIV virus on the continent. Like the communalism and animism, they provide a weak shield against the corrosive social effects of life in cities. In those cities African culture is being redefined while desertification and deforestation—also tied to overpopulation—drive more and more African peasants out of the countryside.

A PREMONITION OF THE FUTURE

WEST Africa is becoming *the* symbol of worldwide demographic, environmental, and societal stress, in which criminal anarchy emerges as the real "strategic" danger. Disease, overpopulation, unprovoked crime, scarcity of resources, refugee migrations, the increasing erosion of nation-states and international borders, and the empowerment of private armies, security firms, and international drug cartels are now most tellingly demonstrated through a West African prism. West Africa provides an appropriate introduction to the issues, often extremely unpleasant to discuss, that will soon confront our civilization. To remap the political earth the way it will be a few decades hence—as I intend to do in this article—I find I must begin with West Africa.

There is no other place on the planet where political maps are so deceptive—where, in fact, they tell such lies—as in West Africa. Start with Sierra Leone. According to the map, it is a nation-state of defined borders, with a government in control of its territory. In truth the Sierra Leonian government, run by a twenty-seven-year-old army captain, Valentine Strasser, controls Freetown by day and by day also controls part of the rural interior. In the government's territory the national army is an unruly rabble threatening drivers and passengers at most checkpoints. In the other part of the country units of two separate armies from the war in Liberia have taken up residence, as has an army of Sierra Leonian rebels. The government force fighting the rebels is full of renegade commanders who have aligned themselves with disaffected village chiefs. A pre-modern formlessness governs the battlefield, evoking the wars in medieval Europe prior to the 1648 Peace of Westphalia, which ushered in the era of organized nation-states.

As a consequence, roughly 400,000 Sierra Leonians are internally displaced, 280,000 more have fled to neighboring Guinea, and another 100,000 have fled to Liberia, even as

400,000 Liberians have fled to Sierra Leone. The third largest city in Sierra Leone, Gondama, is a displaced-persons camp. With an additional 600,000 Liberians in Guinea and 250,000 in the Ivory Coast, the borders dividing these four countries have become largely meaningless. Even in quiet zones none of the governments except the Ivory Coast's maintains the schools, bridges, roads, and police forces in a manner necessary for functional sovereignty. The Koranko ethnic group in northeastern Sierra Leone does all its trading in Guinea. Sierra Leonian diamonds are more likely to be sold in Liberia than in Freetown. In the eastern provinces of Sierra Leone you can buy Liberian beer but not the local brand.

THIS PAGE AND OPPOSITE: BETTY PRESS/WOODFIN CAMP

In Sierra Leone, as in Guinea, as in the Ivory Coast, as in Ghana, most of the primary rain forest and the secondary bush is being destroyed at an alarming rate. I saw convoys of trucks bearing majestic hardwood trunks to coastal ports. When Sierra Leone achieved its independence, in 1961, as much as 60 percent of the country was primary rain forest. Now six percent is. In the Ivory Coast the proportion has fallen from 38 percent to eight percent. The deforestation has led to soil erosion, which has led to more flooding and more mosquitoes. Virtually everyone in the West African interior has some form of malaria.

Sierra Leone is a microcosm of what is occurring, albeit in a more tempered and gradual manner, throughout West Africa and much of the underdeveloped world: the withering away of central governments, the rise of tribal and regional domains, the unchecked spread of disease, and the growing pervasiveness of war. West Africa is reverting to the Africa of the Victorian atlas. It consists now of a series of coastal trading posts, such as Freetown and Conakry, and an interior that, owing to violence, volatility, and disease, is again becoming, as Graham Greene once observed, "blank" and "unexplored." However, whereas Greene's vision implies a certain romance, as in the somnolent and charmingly seedy Freetown of his celebrated novel *The Heart of the Matter*, it is Thomas Malthus, the philosopher of demographic doomsday, who is now the prophet of West Africa's future. And West Africa's future, eventually, will also be that of most of the rest of the world.

CONSIDER "Chicago." I refer not to Chicago, Illinois, but to a slum district of Abidjan, which the young toughs in the area have named after the American city. ("Washington" is another poor section of Abidjan.) Although Sierra Leone is widely regarded as beyond salvage, the Ivory Coast has been considered an African success story, and Abidjan has been called "the Paris of West Africa." Success, however, was built on two artificial factors: the high price of cocoa, of which the Ivory Coast is the world's leading producer, and the talents of a French expatriate community, whose members have helped run the government and the private sector. The expanding cocoa economy made the Ivory Coast a magnet for migrant workers from all over West Africa: between a third and a half of the country's population is now non-Ivorian, and the figure could be as high as 75 percent in Abidjan. During the 1980s cocoa prices fell and the French began to leave. The skyscrapers of the Paris of West Africa are a façade. Perhaps 15 percent of Abidjan's population of three million people live in shantytowns like Chicago and Washington, and the vast majority live in places that are not much better. Not all of these places appear on any of the readily available maps. This is another indication of how political maps are the products of tired conventional wisdom and, in the Ivory Coast's case, of an elite that will ultimately be forced to relinquish power.

Chicago, like more and more of Abidjan, is a slum in the bush: a checkerwork of corrugated zinc roofs and walls made of cardboard and black plastic wrap. It is located in a gully teeming with coconut palms and oil palms, and is ravaged by flooding. Few residents have easy access to electricity, a sewage system, or a clean water supply. The crumbly red

The press of population. Right: doing the wash in lagoon in Abidjan, the Iv. Coast. Left: the nearly impassable downtown of Lagos, Nigeria.

laterite earth crawls with foot-long lizards both inside and outside the shacks. Children defecate in a stream filled with garbage and pigs, droning with malarial mosquitoes. In this stream women do the washing. Young unemployed men spend their time drinking beer, palm wine, and gin while gambling on pinball games constructed out of rotting wood and rusty nails. These are the same youths who rob houses in more prosperous Ivorian neighborhoods at night. One man I met, Damba Tesele, came to Chicago from Burkina Faso in 1963. A cook by profession, he has four wives and thirty-two children, not one of whom has made it to high school. He has

seen his shanty community destroyed by municipal authorities seven times since coming to the area. Each time he and his neighbors rebuild. Chicago is the latest incarnation.

Fifty-five percent of the Ivory Coast's population is urban, and the proportion is expected to reach 62 percent by 2000. The yearly net population growth is 3.6 percent. This means that the Ivory Coast's 13.5 million people will become 39 million by 2025, when much of the population will consist of urbanized peasants like those of Chicago. But don't count on the Ivory Coast's still existing then. Chicago, which is more indicative of Africa's and the Third World's demographic present—and even more of the future—than any idyllic junglescape of women balancing earthen jugs on their heads, illustrates why the Ivory Coast, once a model of Third World success, is becoming a case study in Third World catastrophe.

President Félix Houphouët-Boigny, who died last December at the age of about ninety, left behind a weak cluster of political parties and a leaden bureaucracy that discourages foreign investment. Because the military is small and the non-Ivorian population large, there is neither an obvious force to maintain order nor a sense of nationhood that would lessen the need for such enforcement. The economy has been shrinking since the mid-1980s. Though the French are working assiduously to preserve stability, the Ivory Coast faces a possibility worse than a coup: an anarchic implosion of criminal violence—an urbanized version of what has already happened in Somalia. Or it may become an African Yugoslavia, but one without mini-states to replace the whole.

Because the demographic reality of West Africa is a countryside draining into dense slums by the coast, ultimately the region's rulers will come to reflect the values of these shanty-towns. There are signs of this already in Sierra Leone—

and in Togo, where the dictator Etienne Eyadema, in power since 1967, was nearly toppled in 1991, not by democrats but by thousands of youths whom the London-based magazine *West Africa* described as "Soweto-like stone-throwing adolescents." Their behavior may herald a regime more brutal than Eyadema's repressive one.

The fragility of these West African "countries" impressed itself on me when I took a series of bush taxis along the Gulf of Guinea, from the Togolese capital of Lomé, across Ghana, to Abidjan. The 400-mile journey required two full days of driving, because of stops at two border crossings and an additional eleven customs stations, at each of which my fellow passengers had their bags searched. I had to change money twice and repeatedly fill in currency-declaration forms. I had to bribe a Togolese immigration official with the equivalent of eighteen dollars before he would agree to put an exit stamp on my passport. Nevertheless, smuggling across these borders is rampant. *The London Observer* has reported that in 1992 the equivalent of $856 million left West Africa for Europe in the form of "hot cash" assumed to be laundered drug money. International cartels have discovered the utility of weak, financially strapped West African regimes.

The more fictitious the actual sovereignty, the more severe border authorities seem to be in trying to prove otherwise. Getting visas for these states can be as hard as crossing their borders. The Washington embassies of Sierra Leone and Guinea—the two poorest nations on earth, according to a 1993 United Nations report on "human development"—asked for letters from my bank (in lieu of prepaid round-trip tickets) and also personal references, in order to prove that I had sufficient means to sustain myself during my visits. I was reminded of my visa and currency hassles while traveling to the communist states of Eastern Europe, particularly East Germany and Czechoslovakia, before those states collapsed.

Ali A. Mazrui, the director of the Institute of Global Cultural Studies at the State University of New York at Binghamton, predicts that West Africa—indeed, the whole continent—is on the verge of large-scale border upheaval. Mazrui writes,

> In the 21st century France will be withdrawing from West Africa as she gets increasingly involved in the affairs [of Europe]. France's West African sphere of influence will be filled by Nigeria—a more natural hegemonic power. . . . It will be under those circumstances that Nigeria's own boundaries are likely to expand to incorporate the Republic of Niger (the Hausa link), the Republic of Benin (the Yoruba link) and conceivably Cameroon.

THE future could be more tumultuous, and bloodier, than Mazrui dares to say. France *will* withdraw from former colonies like Benin, Togo, Niger, and the Ivory Coast, where it has been propping up local currencies. It will do so not only because its attention will be diverted to new challenges in Europe and Russia but also because younger French officials lack the older generation's emotional ties to the ex-colonies. However, even as Nigeria attempts to expand, it, too, is likely to split into several pieces. The State Department's Bureau of Intelligence and Research recently made the following points in an analysis of Nigeria:

> Prospects for a transition to civilian rule and democratization are slim. . . . The repressive apparatus of the state security service . . . will be difficult for any future civilian government to control. . . . The country is becoming increasingly ungovernable. . . . Ethnic and regional splits are deepening, a situation made worse by an increase in the number of states from 19 to 30 and a doubling in the number of local governing authorities; religious cleavages are more serious; Muslim fundamentalism and evangelical Christian militancy are on the rise; and northern Muslim anxiety over southern [Christian] control of the economy is intense . . . the will to keep Nigeria together is now very weak.

Given that oil-rich Nigeria is a bellwether for the region—its population of roughly 90 million equals the populations of all the other West African states combined—it is apparent that Africa faces cataclysms that could make the Ethiopian and Somalian famines pale in comparison. This is especially so because Nigeria's population, including that of its largest city, Lagos, whose crime, pollution, and overcrowding make it the cliché par excellence of Third World urban dysfunction, is set to double during the next twenty-five years, while the country continues to deplete its natural resources.

Part of West Africa's quandary is that although its population belts are horizontal, with habitation densities increasing as one travels south away from the Sahara and toward the tropical abundance of the Atlantic littoral, the borders erected by European colonialists are vertical, and therefore at cross-purposes with demography and topography. Satellite photos depict the same reality I experienced in the bush taxi: the Lomé-Abidjan coastal corridor—indeed, the entire stretch of coast from Abidjan eastward to Lagos—is one burgeoning megalopolis that by any rational economic and geographical standard should constitute a single sovereignty, rather than the five (the Ivory Coast, Ghana, Togo, Benin, and Nigeria) into which it is currently divided.

As many internal African borders begin to crumble, a more impenetrable boundary is being erected that threatens to isolate the continent as a whole: the wall of disease. Merely to visit West Africa in some degree of safety, I spent about $500 for a hepatitis B vaccination series and other disease prophylaxis. Africa may today be more dangerous in this regard than it was in 1862, before antibiotics, when the explorer Sir Richard Francis Burton described the health situation on the continent as "deadly, a Golgotha, a Jehannum." Of the approximately 12 million people worldwide whose blood is HIV-positive, 8 million are in Africa. In the capital of the Ivory Coast, whose modern road system only helps to spread the disease, 10 percent of the population is HIV-positive. And war and refugee movements help the virus break through to more-remote areas of Africa. Alan Greenberg, M.D., a representative of the Centers for Disease Control in Abidjan, explains that in Africa the HIV virus and tuberculosis are now "fast-forwarding each other." Of the approximately 4,000 newly diagnosed tuberculosis patients in Abidjan, 45 percent were also found to be HIV-positive. As African birth rates soar and slums proliferate, some experts worry that viral mutations and hybridizations might, just conceivably, result in a form of the AIDS virus that is easier to catch than the present strain.

It is malaria that is most responsible for the disease wall that threatens to separate Africa and other parts of the Third World from more-developed regions of the planet in the twenty-first century. Carried by mosquitoes, malaria, unlike AIDS, is easy to catch. Most people in sub-Saharan Africa have recurring bouts of the disease throughout their entire lives, and it is mutating into increasingly deadly forms. "The great gift of Malaria is utter apathy," wrote Sir Richard Burton, accurately portraying the situation in much of the Third World today. Visitors to malaria-afflicted parts of the planet are protected by a new drug, mefloquine, a side effect of which is vivid, even violent, dreams. But a strain of cerebral malaria resistant to mefloquine is now on the offensive. Consequently, defending oneself against malaria in Africa is becoming more and more like defending oneself against violent crime. You engage in "behavior modification": not going out at dusk, wearing mosquito repellent all the time.

IT IS MALARIA THAT IS MOST RESPONSIBLE FOR THE DISEASE WALL THAT THREATENS TO SEPARATE AFRICA AND OTHER PARTS OF THE THIRD WORLD FROM MORE-DEVELOPED REGIONS OF THE PLANET IN THE TWENTY-FIRST CENTURY. IT IS MUTATING INTO INCREASINGLY DEADLY FORMS.

And the cities keep growing. I got a general sense of the future while driving from the airport to downtown Conakry, the capital of Guinea. The forty-five-minute journey in heavy traffic was through one never-ending shantytown: a nightmarish Dickensian spectacle to which Dickens himself would never have given credence. The corrugated metal shacks and scabrous walls were coated with black slime. Stores were built out of rusted shipping containers, junked cars, and jumbles of wire mesh. The streets were one long puddle of floating garbage. Mosquitoes and flies were everywhere. Children, many of whom had protruding bellies, seemed as numerous as ants. When the tide went out, dead rats and the skeletons of cars were exposed on the mucky beach. In twenty-eight years Guinea's population will double if growth goes on at current rates. Hardwood logging continues at a madcap speed, and people flee the Guinean countryside for Conakry. It seemed to me that here, as elsewhere in Africa and the Third World, man is challenging nature far beyond its limits, and nature is now beginning to take its revenge.

AFRICA may be as relevant to the future character of world politics as the Balkans were a hundred years ago, prior to the two Balkan wars and the First World War. Then the threat was the collapse of empires and the birth of nations based solely on tribe. Now the threat is more elemental: *nature unchecked*. Africa's immediate future could be very bad. The coming upheaval, in which foreign embassies are shut down, states collapse, and contact with the outside world takes place through dangerous, disease-ridden coastal trading posts, will loom large in the century we are entering. (Nine of twenty-one U.S. foreign-aid missions to be closed over the next three years are in Africa—a prologue to a consolidation of U.S. embassies themselves.) Precisely because much of Africa is set to go over the edge at a time when the Cold War has ended, when environmental and demographic stress in other parts of the globe is becoming critical, and when the post–First World War system of nation-states—not just in the Balkans but perhaps also in the Middle East—is about to be toppled, Africa suggests what war, borders, and ethnic politics will be like a few decades hence.

To understand the events of the next fifty years, then, one must understand environmental scarcity, cultural and racial clash, geographic destiny, and the transformation of war. The order in which I have named these is not accidental. Each concept except the first relies partly on the one or ones before it, meaning that the last two—new approaches to mapmaking and to warfare—are the most important. They are also the least understood. I will now look at each idea, drawing upon the work of specialists and also my own travel experiences in various parts of the globe besides Africa, in order to fill in the blanks of a new political atlas.

THE ENVIRONMENT AS A HOSTILE POWER

FOR a while the media will continue to ascribe riots and other violent upheavals abroad mainly to ethnic and religious conflict. But as these conflicts multiply, it will become apparent that something else is afoot, making more and more places like Nigeria, India, and Brazil ungovernable.

Mention "the environment" or "diminishing natural resources" in foreign-policy circles and you meet a brick wall of skepticism or boredom. To conservatives especially, the very terms seem flaky. Public-policy foundations have contributed to the lack of interest, by funding narrowly focused environmental studies replete with technical jargon which foreign-affairs experts just let pile up on their desks.

It is time to understand "the environment" for what it is: *the* national-security issue of the early twenty-first century. The political and strategic impact of surging populations, spreading disease, deforestation and soil erosion, water depletion, air pollution, and, possibly, rising sea levels in critical, overcrowded regions like the Nile Delta and Bangladesh—developments that will prompt mass migrations and, in turn, incite group conflicts—will be the core foreign-policy challenge from which most others will ultimately emanate, arousing the public and uniting assorted interests left over from the Cold War. In the twenty-first century water will be in dangerously short supply in such diverse locales as Saudi Arabia, Central Asia, and the southwestern United States. A war could erupt between Egypt and Ethiopia over Nile River water. Even in Europe tensions have arisen between Hungary and Slovakia over the damming of the Danube, a classic case of how environmental disputes fuse with ethnic and historical ones. The political scientist and erstwhile Clinton adviser Michael Mandelbaum has said, "We have a foreign policy today in the shape of a doughnut—lots of peripheral interests but nothing at the center." The environment, I will argue, is part of a terrifying array of problems that will define a new threat to our security, filling the hole in Mandelbaum's doughnut and allowing a post–Cold War foreign policy to emerge inexorably by need rather than by design.

OUR Cold War foreign policy truly began with George F. Kennan's famous article, signed "X," published in *Foreign Affairs* in July of 1947, in which Kennan argued for a "firm and vigilant containment" of a Soviet Union that was imperially, rather than ideologically, motivated. It may be that our post–Cold War foreign policy will one day be seen to have had its beginnings in an even bolder and more detailed piece of written analysis: one that appeared in the journal *International Security*. The article, published in the fall of 1991 by Thomas Fraser Homer-Dixon, who is the head of the Peace and Conflict Studies Program at the University of

Toronto, was titled "On the Threshold: Environmental Changes as Causes of Acute Conflict." Homer-Dixon has, more successfully than other analysts, integrated two hitherto separate fields—military-conflict studies and the study of the physical environment.

In Homer-Dixon's view, future wars and civil violence will often arise from scarcities of resources such as water, cropland, forests, and fish. Just as there will be environmentally driven wars and refugee flows, there will be environmentally induced praetorian regimes—or, as he puts it, "hard regimes." Countries with the highest probability of acquiring hard regimes, according to Homer-Dixon, are those that are threatened by a declining resource base yet also have "a history of state [read 'military'] strength." Candidates include Indonesia, Brazil, and, of course, Nigeria. Though each of these nations has exhibited democratizing tendencies of late, Homer-Dixon argues that such tendencies are likely to be superficial "epiphenomena" having nothing to do with long-term processes that include soaring populations and shrinking raw materials. Democracy is problematic; scarcity is more certain.

Indeed, the Saddam Husseins of the future will have more, not fewer, opportunities. In addition to engendering tribal strife, scarcer resources will place a great strain on many peoples who never had much of a democratic or institutional tradition to begin with. Over the next fifty years the earth's population will soar from 5.5 billion to more than nine billion. Though optimists have hopes for new resource technologies and free-market development in the global village, they fail to note that, as the National Academy of Sciences has pointed out, 95 percent of the population increase will be in the poorest regions of the world, where governments now—just look at Africa—show little ability to function, let alone to implement even marginal improvements. Homer-Dixon writes, ominously, "Neo-Malthusians may underestimate human adaptability in *today's* environmental-social system, but as time passes their analysis may become ever more compelling."

While a minority of the human population will be, as Francis Fukuyama would put it, sufficiently sheltered so as to enter a "post-historical" realm, living in cities and suburbs in which the environment has been mastered and ethnic animosities have been quelled by bourgeois prosperity, an increasingly large number of people will be stuck in history, living in shantytowns where attempts to rise above poverty, cultural dysfunction, and ethnic strife will be doomed by a lack of water to drink, soil to till, and space to survive in. In the developing world environmental stress will present people with a choice that is increasingly among totalitarianism (as in Iraq), fascist-tending mini-states (as in Serb-held Bosnia), and road-warrior cultures (as in Somalia). Homer-Dixon concludes that "as environmental degradation proceeds, the size of the potential social disruption will increase."

Left: El Playón, El Salvador, repository of garbage and death-squad victims. Right: Rio de Janeiro (top) and Shanghai, crowded and still growing.

Tad Homer-Dixon is an unlikely Jeremiah. Today a boyish thirty-seven, he grew up amid the sylvan majesty of Vancouver Island, attending private day schools. His speech is calm, perfectly even, and crisply enunciated. There is nothing in his background or manner that would indicate a bent toward pessimism. A Canadian Anglican who spends his summers canoeing on the lakes of northern Ontario, and who talks about the benign mountains, black bears, and Douglas firs of his youth, he is the opposite of the intellectually

MICHAEL ENDE-FOCUS/MATRIX; OPPOSITE: DONNA DECESARE/IMPACT VISUALS

GREG GIRARD/CONTACT

severe neoconservative, the kind at home with conflict scenarios. Nor is he an environmentalist who opposes development. "My father was a logger who thought about ecologically safe forestry before others," he says. "He logged, planted, logged, and planted. He got out of the business just as the issue was being polarized by environmentalists. They hate changed ecosystems. But human beings, just by carrying seeds around, change the natural world." As an only child whose playground was a virtually untouched wilderness and seacoast, Homer-Dixon has a familiarity with the natural world that permits him to see a reality that most policy analysts—children of suburbia and city streets—are blind to.

"We need to bring nature back in," he argues. "We have to stop separating politics from the physical world—the climate, public health, and the environment." Quoting Daniel Deudney, another pioneering expert on the security aspects of the environment, Homer-Dixon says that "for too long we've been prisoners of 'social-social' theory, which assumes there are only social causes for social and political changes, rather than natural causes, too. This social-social mentality emerged with the Industrial Revolution, which separated us from nature. But nature is coming back with a vengeance, tied to population growth. It will have incredible security implications.

"Think of a stretch limo in the potholed streets of New York City, where homeless beggars live. Inside the limo are the air-conditioned post-industrial regions of North America, Europe, the emerging Pacific Rim, and a few other isolated places, with their trade summitry and computer-information highways. Outside is the rest of mankind, going in a completely different direction."

WE are entering a bifurcated world. Part of the globe is inhabited by Hegel's and Fukuyama's Last Man, healthy, well fed, and pampered by technology. The other, larger, part is inhabited by Hobbes's First Man, condemned to a life that is "poor, nasty, brutish, and short." Although both parts will be threatened by environmental stress, the Last Man will be able to master it; the First Man will not.

The Last Man will adjust to the loss of underground water tables in the western United States. He will build dikes to save Cape Hatteras and the Chesapeake beaches from rising sea levels, even as the Maldive Islands, off the coast of India, sink into oblivion, and the shorelines of Egypt, Bangladesh, and Southeast Asia recede, driving tens of millions of people inland where there is no room for them, and thus sharpening ethnic divisions.

Homer-Dixon points to a world map of soil degradation in his Toronto office. "The darker the map color, the worse the degradation," he explains. The West African coast, the Middle East, the Indian subcontinent, China, and Central America have the darkest shades, signifying all manner of degradation, related to winds, chemicals, and water problems. "The worst degradation is generally where the population is highest. The population is generally highest where the soil is the best. So we're degrading earth's best soil."

China, in Homer-Dixon's view, is the quintessential example of environmental degradation. Its current economic "success" masks deeper problems. "China's fourteen percent growth rate does not mean it's going to be a world power. It means that coastal China, where the economic growth is taking place, is joining the rest of the Pacific Rim. The disparity with inland China is intensifying." Referring to the environmental research of his colleague, the Czech-born ecologist Vaclav Smil, Homer-Dixon explains how the per capita availability of arable land in interior China has rapidly declined at the same time that the quality of that land has been destroyed by deforestation, loss of topsoil, and salinization. He mentions the loss and contamination of water supplies, the exhaustion of wells, the plugging of irrigation systems and reservoirs with eroded silt, and a population of 1.54 billion by the year 2025: it is a misconception that China has gotten its population under control. Large-scale population movements are under way, from inland China to coastal China and from villages to cities, leading to a crime surge like the one in Africa and to growing regional disparities and conflicts in a land with a strong tradition of warlordism and a weak tradition of central government—again as in Africa. "We will probably see the center challenged and fractured, and China will not remain the same on the map," Homer-Dixon says.

Environmental scarcity will inflame existing hatreds and affect power relationships, at which we now look.

SKINHEAD COSSACKS, JUJU WARRIORS

IN the summer, 1993, issue of *Foreign Affairs*, Samuel P. Huntington, of Harvard's Olin Institute for Strategic Studies, published a thought-provoking article called "The Clash of Civilizations?" The world, he argues, has been moving during the course of this century from nation-state conflict to ideological conflict to, finally, cultural conflict. I would add that as refugee flows increase and as peasants continue migrating to cities around the world—turning them into sprawling villages—national borders will mean less, even as more power will fall into the hands of less educated, less sophisticated groups. In the eyes of these uneducated but newly empowered millions, the real borders are the most tangible and intractable ones: those of culture and tribe. Huntington writes, "First, differences among civilizations are not only real; they are basic," involving, among other things, history, language, and religion. "Second ... interactions between peoples of different civilizations are increasing; these increasing interactions intensify civilization consciousness." Economic modernization is not necessarily a panacea, since it fuels individual and group ambitions while weakening traditional loyalties to the state. It is worth noting, for example, that it is precisely the wealthiest and fastest-developing city in India, Bombay, that has seen the worst intercommunal violence between Hindus and Muslims. Consider that Indian cities, like African and Chinese ones, are ecological time bombs—Delhi and Calcutta, and also Beijing, suffer the worst air quality of any cities in the world—and it is apparent how surging populations, environmental degradation, and ethnic conflict are deeply related.

Huntington points to interlocking conflicts among Hindu, Muslim, Slavic Orthodox, Western, Japanese, Confucian, Latin American, and possibly African civilizations: for instance, Hindus clashing with Muslims in India, Turkic Muslims clashing with Slavic Orthodox Russians in Central Asian cities, the West clashing with Asia. (Even in the United States, African-Americans find themselves besieged by an influx of competing Latinos.) Whatever the laws, refugees find a way to crash official borders, bringing their passions with them, meaning that Europe and the United States will be weakened by cultural disputes.

Because Huntington's brush is broad, his specifics are vulnerable to attack. In a rebuttal of Huntington's argument the Johns Hopkins professor Fouad Ajami, a Lebanese-born Shi'ite who certainly knows the world beyond suburbia, writes in the September-October, 1993, issue of *Foreign Affairs*,

> The world of Islam divides and subdivides. The battle lines in the Caucasus . . . are not coextensive with civilizational fault lines. The lines follow the interests of states. Where Huntington sees a civilizational duel between Armenia and Azerbaijan, the Iranian state has cast religious zeal . . . to the wind . . . in that battle the Iranians have tilted toward Christian Armenia.

True, Huntington's hypothesized war between Islam and Orthodox Christianity is not borne out by the alliance network in the Caucasus. But that is only because he has misidentified *which* cultural war is occurring there. A recent visit to Azerbaijan made clear to me that Azeri Turks, the world's most secular Shi'ite Muslims, see their cultural identity in terms not of religion but of their Turkic race. The Armenians, likewise, fight the Azeris not because the latter are Muslims but because they are Turks, related to the same Turks who massacred Armenians in 1915. Turkic culture (secular and based on languages employing a Latin script) is battling Iranian culture (religiously militant as defined by Tehran, and wedded to an Arabic script) across the whole swath of Central Asia and the Caucasus. The Armenians are, therefore, natural allies of their fellow Indo-Europeans the Iranians.

Huntington is correct that the Caucasus is a flashpoint of cultural and racial war. But, as Ajami observes, Huntington's plate tectonics are too simple. Two months of recent travel throughout Turkey revealed to me that although the Turks are developing a deep distrust, bordering on hatred, of fellow-Muslim Iran, they are also, especially in the shantytowns that are coming to dominate Turkish public opinion, revising their group identity, increasingly seeing themselves as Muslims being deserted by a West that does little to help besieged Muslims in Bosnia and that attacks Turkish Muslims in the streets of Germany.

CHRISTOPHER MORRIS/BLACK STAR

In Bosnia, the former Yugoslavia, compatriots add one more victim of civil war to a mass grave

In other words, the Balkans, a powder keg for nation-state war at the beginning of the twentieth century, could be a powder keg for cultural war at the turn of the twenty-first: between Orthodox Christianity (represented by the Serbs and a classic Byzantine configuration of Greeks, Russians, and Romanians) and the House of Islam. Yet in the Caucasus that House of Islam is falling into a clash between Turkic and Iranian civilizations. Ajami asserts that this very subdivision, not to mention all the divisions within the Arab world, indicates that the West, including the United States, is not threatened by Huntington's scenario. As the Gulf War demonstrated, the West has proved capable of playing one part of the House of Islam against another.

True. However, whether he is aware of it or not, Ajami is describing a world even more dangerous than the one Huntington envisions, especially when one takes into account Homer-Dixon's research on environmental scarcity. Outside the stretch limo would be a rundown, crowded planet of skinhead Cossacks and *juju* warriors, influenced by the worst refuse of Western pop culture and ancient tribal hatreds, and battling over scraps of overused earth in guerrilla

conflicts that ripple across continents and intersect in no discernible pattern—meaning there's no easy-to-define threat. Kennan's world of one adversary seems as distant as the world of Herodotus.

Most people believe that the political earth since 1989 has undergone immense change. But it is minor compared with what is yet to come. The breaking apart and remaking of the atlas is only now beginning. The crack-up of the Soviet empire and the coming end of Arab-Israeli military confrontation are merely prologues to the really big changes that lie ahead. Michael Vlahos, a long-range thinker for the U.S. Navy, warns, "We are not in charge of the environment and the world is not following us. It is going in many directions. Do not assume that democratic capitalism is the last word in human social evolution."

Before addressing the questions of maps and of warfare, I want to take a closer look at the interaction of religion, culture, demographic shifts, and the distribution of natural resources in a specific area of the world: the Middle East.

THE PAST IS DEAD

BUILT on steep, muddy hills, the shantytowns of Ankara, the Turkish capital, exude visual drama. Altindag, or "Golden Mountain," is a pyramid of dreams, fashioned from cinder blocks and corrugated iron, rising as though each shack were built on top of another, all reaching awkwardly and painfully toward heaven—the heaven of wealthier Turks who live elsewhere in the city. Nowhere else on the planet have I found such a poignant architectural symbol of man's striving, with gaps in house walls plugged with rusted cans, and leeks and onions growing on verandas assembled from planks of rotting wood. For reasons that I will explain, the Turkish shacktown is a psychological universe away from the African one.

To see the twenty-first century truly, one's eyes must learn a different set of aesthetics. One must reject the overly stylized images of travel magazines, with their inviting photographs of exotic villages and glamorous downtowns. There are far too many millions whose dreams are more vulgar, more real—whose raw energies and desires will overwhelm the visions of the elites, remaking the future into something frighteningly new. But in Turkey I learned that shantytowns are not all bad.

Slum quarters in Abidjan terrify and repel the outsider. In Turkey it is the opposite. The closer I got to Golden Mountain the better it looked, and the safer I felt. I had $1,500 worth of Turkish lira in one pocket and $1,000 in traveler's checks in the other, yet I felt no fear. Golden Mountain was a real neighborhood. The inside of one house told the story: The architectural bedlam of cinder block and sheet metal and cardboard walls was deceiving. Inside was a *home*—order, that is, bespeaking dignity. I saw a working refrigerator, a television, a wall cabinet with a few books and lots of family pictures, a few plants by a window, and a stove. Though the streets become rivers of mud when it rains, the floors inside this house were spotless.

Other houses were like this too. Schoolchildren ran along with briefcases strapped to their backs, trucks delivered cooking gas, a few men sat inside a café sipping tea. One man sipped beer. Alcohol is easy to obtain in Turkey, a secular state where 99 percent of the population is Muslim. Yet there is little problem of alcoholism. Crime against persons is infinitesimal. Poverty and illiteracy are watered-down versions of what obtains in Algeria and Egypt (to say nothing of West Africa), making it that much harder for religious extremists to gain a foothold.

My point in bringing up a rather wholesome, crime-free slum is this: its existence demonstrates how formidable is the fabric of which Turkish Muslim culture is made. A culture this strong has the potential to dominate the Middle East once again. Slums are litmus tests for innate cultural strengths and weaknesses. Those peoples whose cultures can harbor extensive slum life without decomposing will be, relatively speak-

SADDAM HUSSEINS OF THE FUTURE WILL HAVE MORE, NOT FEWER, OPPORTUNITIES. IN ADDITION TO ENGENDERING TRIBAL STRIFE, SCARCER RESOURCES WILL PLACE A GREAT STRAIN ON MANY PEOPLES WHO NEVER HAD MUCH OF A DEMOCRATIC OR INSTITUTIONAL TRADITION TO BEGIN WITH.

ing, the future's winners. Those whose cultures cannot will be the future's victims. Slums—in the sociological sense—do not exist in Turkish cities. The mortar between people and family groups is stronger here than in Africa. Resurgent Islam and Turkic cultural identity have produced a civilization with natural muscle tone. Turks, history's perennial nomads, take disruption in stride.

The future of the Middle East is quietly being written inside the heads of Golden Mountain's inhabitants. Think of an Ottoman military encampment on the eve of the destruction of Greek Constantinople in 1453. That is Golden Mountain. "We brought the village here. But in the village we worked harder—in the field, all day. So we couldn't fast during [the holy month of] Ramadan. Here we fast. Here we are more religious." Aishe Tanrikulu, along with half a dozen other women, was stuffing rice into vine leaves from a crude plastic bowl. She asked me to join her under the shade of a piece of sheet metal. Each of these women had her hair covered by a kerchief. In the city they were encountering television for the first time. "We are traditional, religious people. The programs offend us," Aishe said. Another woman complained about the schools. Though her children had educational options unavailable in the village, they had to compete with wealthier, secular Turks. "The kids from rich families with connections—they get all the places." More opportunities, more tensions, in other words.

My guidebook to Golden Mountain was an untypical one: *Tales From the Garbage Hills*, a brutally realistic novel by a Turkish writer, Latife Tekin, about life in the shantytowns, which in Turkey are called *gecekondus* ("built in a night"). "He listened to the earth and wept unceasingly for water, for work and for the cure of the illnesses spread by the garbage and the factory waste," Tekin writes. In the most revealing passage of *Tales From the Garbage Hills* the squatters are told "about a certain 'Ottoman Empire' . . . that where they now lived there had once been an empire of this name." This history "confounded" the squatters. It was the first they had heard of it. Though one of them knew "that his grandfather and his dog died fighting the Greeks," nationalism and an encompassing sense of Turkish history are the province of the Turkish middle and upper classes, and of foreigners like me who feel required to have a notion of "Turkey."

But what did the Golden Mountain squatters know about the armies of Turkish migrants that had come before their own—namely, Seljuks and Ottomans? For these recently urbanized peasants, and their counterparts in Africa, the Arab world, India, and so many other places, the world is new, to adapt V. S. Naipaul's phrase. As Naipaul wrote of urban refugees in *India: A Wounded Civilization*, "They saw themselves at the beginning of things: unaccommodated men making a claim on their land for the first time, and out of chaos evolving their own philosophy of community and self-help. For them the past was dead; they had left it behind in the villages."

Everywhere in the developing world at the turn of the twenty-first century these new men and women, rushing into the cities, are remaking civilizations and redefining their identities in terms of religion and tribal ethnicity which do not coincide with the borders of existing states.

IN Turkey several things are happening at once. In 1980, 44 percent of Turks lived in cities; in 1990 it was 61 percent. By the year 2000 the figure is expected to be 67 percent. Villages are emptying out as concentric rings of *gecekondu* developments grow around Turkish cities. This is the real political and demographic revolution in Turkey and elsewhere, and foreign correspondents usually don't write about it.

Whereas rural poverty is age-old and almost a "normal" part of the social fabric, urban poverty is socially destabilizing. As Iran has shown, Islamic extremism is the psychological defense mechanism of many urbanized peasants threatened with the loss of traditions in pseudo-modern cities where their values are under attack, where basic services like water and electricity are unavailable, and where they are assaulted by a physically unhealthy environment. The American ethnologist and orientalist Carleton Stevens Coon wrote in 1951 that Islam "has made possible the optimum survival and happiness of millions of human beings in an increasingly impoverished environment over a fourteen-hundred-year period." Beyond its stark, clearly articulated message, Islam's very militancy makes it attractive to the downtrodden. It is the one religion that is prepared to *fight*. A political era driven by environmental stress, increased cultural sensitivity, unregulated urbanization, and refugee migrations is an era divinely created for the spread and intensification of Islam, already the world's fastest-growing religion. (Though Islam is spreading in West Africa, it is being hobbled by syncretization with animism: this makes new converts less apt to become anti-Western extremists, but it also makes for a weakened version of the faith, which is less effective as an antidote to crime.)

In Turkey, however, Islam is painfully and awkwardly forging a consensus with modernization, a trend that is less apparent in the Arab and Persian worlds (and virtually invisible in Africa). In Iran the oil boom—because it put development and urbanization on a fast track, making the culture shock more intense—fueled the 1978 Islamic Revolution. But Turkey, unlike Iran and the Arab world, has little oil. Therefore its development and urbanization have been more gradual. Islamists have been integrated into the parliamentary system for decades. The tensions I noticed in Golden Mountain are natural, creative ones: the kind immigrants face the world

THIS PAGE AND OPPOSITE: AXEL KOESTER/IMPACT VISUALS

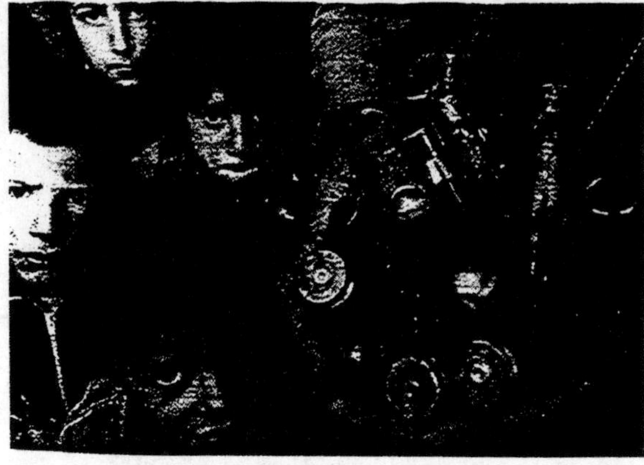

over. While the world has focused on religious perversity in Algeria, a nation rich in natural gas, and in Egypt, parts of whose capital city, Cairo, evince worse crowding than I have seen even in Calcutta, Turkey has been living through the Muslim equivalent of the Protestant Reformation.

Resource distribution is strengthening Turks in another way vis-à-vis Arabs and Persians. Turks may have little oil, but their Anatolian heartland has lots of water—the most important fluid of the twenty-first century. Turkey's Southeast Anatolia Project, involving twenty-two major dams and irrigation systems, is impounding the waters of the Tigris and Euphrates rivers. Much of the water that Arabs and perhaps Israelis will need to drink in the future is controlled by Turks. The project's centerpiece is the mile-wide, sixteen-story Atatürk Dam, upon which are emblazoned the words of modern Turkey's founder: "*Ne Mutlu Turkum Diyene*" ("Lucky is the one who is a Turk").

Unlike Egypt's Aswan High Dam, on the Nile, and Syria's Revolution Dam, on the Euphrates, both of which were built largely by Russians, the Atatürk Dam is a predominantly Turkish affair, with Turkish engineers and companies in charge. On a recent visit my eyes took in the immaculate offices and their gardens, the high-voltage electric grids and phone switching stations, the dizzying sweep of giant humming transformers, the poured-concrete spillways, and the prim unfolding suburbia, complete with schools, for dam employees. The emerging power of the Turks was palpable.

Erduhan Bayindir, the site manager at the dam, told me that "while oil can be shipped abroad to enrich only elites, water has to be spread more evenly within the society. . . . It is true, we can stop the flow of water into Syria and Iraq for up to eight months without the same water overflowing our dams, in order to regulate their political behavior."

Power is certainly moving north in the Middle East, from the oil fields of Dhahran, on the Persian Gulf, to the water plain of Harran, in southern Anatolia—near the site of the Atatürk Dam. But will the nation-state of Turkey, as presently constituted, be the inheritor of this wealth?

I very much doubt it.

THE LIES OF MAPMAKERS

WHEREAS West Africa represents the least stable part of political reality outside Homer-Dixon's stretch limo, Turkey, an organic outgrowth of two Turkish empires that ruled Anatolia for 850 years, has been among the most stable. Turkey's borders were established not by colonial powers but in a war of independence, in the early 1920s. Kemal Atatürk provided Turkey with a secular nation-building myth that most Arab and African states, burdened by artificially drawn borders, lack. That lack will leave many Arab states defenseless against a wave of Islam that will eat away at their legitimacy and frontiers in coming years. Yet even as regards Turkey, maps deceive.

It is not only African shantytowns that don't appear on urban maps. Many shantytowns in Turkey and elsewhere are also missing—as are the considerable territories controlled by guerrilla armies and urban mafias. Traveling with Eritrean guerrillas in what, according to the map, was northern Ethiopia, traveling in "northern Iraq" with Kurdish guerrillas, and staying in a hotel in the Caucasus controlled

Opposite page: Kurds in Turkey defy the governme by kindling ritual fires. Above: a Kurdish guerrill fighter; Kurdish childre with spent shells.

by a local mafia—to say nothing of my experiences in West Africa—led me to develop a healthy skepticism toward maps, which, I began to realize, create a conceptual barrier that prevents us from comprehending the political crack-up just beginning to occur worldwide.

Consider the map of the world, with its 190 or so countries, each signified by a bold and uniform color: this map, with which all of us have grown up, is generally an invention of modernism, specifically of European colonialism. Modernism, in the sense of which I speak, began with the rise of nation-states in Europe and was confirmed by the death of feudalism at the end of the Thirty Years' War—an event that was interposed between the Renaissance and the Enlightenment, which together gave birth to modern science. People were suddenly flush with an enthusiasm to categorize, to define. The map, based on scientific techniques of measurement, offered a way to classify new national organisms, making a jigsaw puzzle of neat pieces without transition zones between them. "Frontier" is itself a modern concept that didn't exist in the feudal mind. And as European nations carved out far-flung domains at the same time that print technology was making the reproduction of maps cheaper, cartography came into its own as a way of creating facts by ordering the way we look at the world.

In his book *Imagined Communities: Reflections on the Origin and Spread of Nationalism*, Benedict Anderson, of Cornell University, demonstrates that the map enabled colonialists to think about their holdings in terms of a "totalizing classificatory grid. . . . It was bounded, determinate, and therefore—in principle—countable." To the colonialist, country maps were the equivalent of an accountant's ledger books. Maps, Anderson explains, "shaped the grammar" that would make possible such questionable concepts as Iraq, Indonesia, Sierra Leone, and Nigeria. The state, recall, is a purely Western notion, one that until the twentieth century applied to countries covering only three percent of the earth's land area. Nor is the evidence compelling that the state, as a governing ideal, can be successfully transported to areas outside the industrialized world. Even the United States of America, in the words of one of our best living poets, Gary Snyder, consists of "arbitrary and inaccurate impositions on what is really here."

Yet this inflexible, artificial reality staggers on, not only in the United Nations but in various geographic and travel publications (themselves by-products of an age of elite touring which colonialism made possible) that still report on and photograph the world according to "country." Newspapers, this magazine, and this writer are not innocent of the tendency.

According to the map, the great hydropower complex emblemized by the Atatürk Dam is situated in Turkey. Forget the map. This southeastern region of Turkey is populated almost completely by Kurds. About half of the world's 20 million Kurds live in "Turkey." The Kurds are predominant in an ellipse of territory that overlaps not only with Turkey but also with Iraq, Iran, Syria, and the former Soviet Union. The Western-enforced Kurdish enclave in northern Iraq, a consequence of the 1991 Gulf War, has already exposed the fictitious nature of that supposed nation-state.

On a recent visit to the Turkish-Iranian border, it occurred to me what a risky idea the nation-state is. Here I was on the legal fault line between two clashing civilizations, Turkic and Iranian. Yet the reality was more subtle: as in West Africa, the border was porous and smuggling abounded, but here the people doing the smuggling, on both sides of the border, were Kurds. In such a moonscape, over which peoples have migrated and settled in patterns that obliterate borders, the end of the Cold War will bring on a cruel process of natural selection among existing states. No longer will these states be so firmly propped up by the West or the Soviet Union. Because the Kurds overlap with nearly everybody in the Middle East, on account of their being cheated out of a state in the post–First World War peace treaties, they are emerging, in effect, as *the* natural selector—the ultimate reality check. They have destabilized Iraq and may continue to disrupt states that do not offer them adequate breathing space, while strengthening states that do.

THE SAVAGERY OF THE FIGHTING POINTS TO A TRUTH THAT WE LACK THE STOMACH TO CONTEMPLATE: A LARGE NUMBER OF PEOPLE ON THIS PLANET, TO WHOM THE COMFORT AND STABILITY OF A MIDDLE-CLASS LIFE IS UTTERLY UNKNOWN, FIND WAR AND A BARRACKS EXISTENCE A STEP UP.

Because the Turks, owing to their water resources, their growing economy, and the social cohesion evinced by the most crime-free slums I have encountered, are on the verge of big-power status, and because the 10 million Kurds within Turkey threaten that status, the outcome of the Turkish-Kurdish dispute will be more critical to the future of the Middle East than the eventual outcome of the recent Israeli-Palestinian agreement.

AMERICA'S fascination with the Israeli-Palestinian issue, coupled with its lack of interest in the Turkish-Kurdish one, is a function of its own domestic and ethnic obsessions, not of the cartographic reality that is about to transform the Middle East. The diplomatic process involving Israelis and Palestinians will, I believe, have little effect on the early- and mid-twenty-first-century map of the region. Israel, with a 6.6 percent economic growth rate based increasingly on high-tech exports, is about to enter Homer-Dixon's stretch limo, fortified by a well-defined political community that is an organic outgrowth of history and ethnicity. Like prosperous and peaceful Japan on the one hand, and war-torn and poverty-wracked Armenia on the other, Israel is a classic national-ethnic organism. Much of the Arab world, however, will undergo alteration, as Islam spreads across artificial frontiers, fueled by mass migrations into the cities and a soaring birth rate of more than 3.2 percent. Seventy percent of the Arab population has been born since 1970—youths with little historical memory of anticolonial independence struggles, postcolonial attempts at nation-building, or any of the Arab-Israeli wars. The most distant recollection of these youths will be the West's humiliation of colonially invented Iraq in 1991. Today seventeen out of twenty-two Arab states have a declining gross national product; in the next twenty years, at current growth rates, the population of many Arab countries will double. These states, like most African ones, will be ungovernable through conventional secular ideologies. The Middle East analyst Christine M. Helms explains,

> Declaring Arab nationalism "bankrupt," the political "disinherited" are not rationalizing the failure of Arabism . . . or reformulating it. Alternative solutions are not contemplated. They have simply opted for the political paradigm at the other end of the political spectrum with which they are familiar—Islam.

Like the borders of West Africa, the colonial borders of Syria, Iraq, Jordan, Algeria, and other Arab states are often contrary to cultural and political reality. As state control mechanisms wither in the face of environmental and demographic stress, "hard" Islamic city-states or shantytown-states are likely to emerge. The fiction that the impoverished city of Algiers, on the Mediterranean, controls Tamanrasset, deep in the Algerian Sahara, cannot obtain forever. Whatever the outcome of the peace process, Israel is destined to be a Jewish ethnic fortress amid a vast and volatile realm of Islam. In that realm, the violent youth culture of the Gaza shantytowns may be indicative of the coming era.

The destiny of Turks and Kurds is far less certain, but far more relevant to the kind of map that will explain our future world. The Kurds suggest a geographic reality that cannot be shown in two-dimensional space. The issue in Turkey is not simply a matter of giving autonomy or even independence to

PATRICK ROBERT/SYGMA

Kurds in the southeast. This isn't the Balkans or the Caucasus, where regions are merely subdividing into smaller units, Abkhazia breaking off from Georgia, and so on. Federalism is not the answer. Kurds are found everywhere in Turkey, including the shanty districts of Istanbul and Ankara. Turkey's problem is that its Anatolian land mass is the home of two cultures and languages, Turkish and Kurdish. Identity in Turkey, as in India, Africa, and elsewhere, is more complex and subtle than conventional cartography can display.

A NEW KIND OF WAR

To appreciate fully the political and cartographic implications of postmodernism—an epoch of themeless juxtapositions, in which the classificatory grid of nation-states is going to be replaced by a jagged-glass pattern of city-states, shanty-states, nebulous and anarchic regionalisms—it is necessary to consider, finally, the whole question of war.

"Oh, what a relief to fight, to fight enemies who defend themselves, enemies who are awake!" André Malraux wrote in *Man's Fate*. I cannot think of a more suitable battle cry for many combatants in the early decades of the twenty-first century. The intense savagery of the fighting in such diverse cultural settings as Liberia, Bosnia, the Caucasus, and Sri Lanka—to say nothing of what obtains in American inner cities—indicates something very troubling that those of us inside the stretch limo, concerned with issues like middle-class entitlements and the future of interactive cable television, lack the stomach to contemplate. It is this: a large number of people on this planet, to whom the comfort and stability of a middle-class life is utterly unknown, find war and a barracks existence a step up rather than a step down.

"Just as it makes no sense to ask 'why people eat' or 'what they sleep for,'" writes Martin van Creveld, a military historian at the Hebrew University in Jerusalem, in *The Transformation of War*, "so fighting in many ways is not a means but an end. Throughout history, for every person who has expressed his horror of war there is another who found in it the most marvelous of all the experiences that are vouchsafed to man, even to the point that he later spent a lifetime boring his descendants by recounting his exploits." When I asked Pentagon officials about the nature of war in the twenty-first century, the answer I frequently got was "Read Van Creveld." The top brass are enamored of this historian not because his writings justify their existence but, rather, the opposite: Van Creveld warns them that huge state military machines like the Pentagon's are dinosaurs about to go extinct, and that something far more terrible awaits us.

The degree to which Van Creveld's *Transformation of War* complements Homer-Dixon's work on the environment, Huntington's thoughts on cultural clash, my own realizations in traveling by foot, bus, and bush taxi in more than sixty countries, and America's sobering comeuppances in intractable-culture zones like Haiti and Somalia is startling. The book begins by demolishing the notion that men don't like to fight. "By compelling the senses to focus themselves on the here and now," Van Creveld writes, war "can cause a man to take his leave of them." As anybody who has had experience with Chetniks in Serbia, "technicals" in Somalia, Tontons Macoutes in Haiti, or soldiers in Sierra Leone can tell you, in places where the Western Enlightenment has not penetrated and where there has always been mass poverty, people find liberation in violence. In Afghanistan and elsewhere, I vicariously experienced this phenomenon: worrying about mines and ambushes frees you from worrying about mundane details of daily existence. If my own experience is too subjective, there is a wealth of data showing the sheer frequency of war, especially in the developing world since the Second World War. Physical aggression is a part

In Liberia, summary justic meted out against a soldier (above) and suspected thieves (below right). Abo right: a scene in Vukovar, the former Yugoslavia.

of being human. Only when people attain a certain economic, educational, and cultural standard is this trait tranquilized. In light of the fact that 95 percent of the earth's population growth will be in the poorest areas of the globe, the question is not whether there will be war (there will be a lot of it) but what kind of war. And who will fight whom?

Debunking the great military strategist Carl von Clausewitz, Van Creveld, who may be the most original thinker on war since that early-nineteenth-century Prussian, writes, "Clausewitz's ideas . . . were wholly rooted in the fact that, ever since 1648, war had been waged overwhelmingly by states." But, as Van Creveld explains, the period of nation-states and, therefore, of state conflict is now ending, and with it the clear "threefold division into government, army, and people" which state-directed wars enforce. Thus, to see the future, the first step is to look back to the past immediately prior to the birth of modernism—the wars in medieval Europe which began during the Reformation and reached their culmination in the Thirty Years' War.

Van Creveld writes,

> In all these struggles political, social, economic, and religious motives were hopelessly entangled. Since this was an age when armies consisted of mercenaries, all were also attended by swarms of military entrepreneurs. . . . Many of them paid little but lip service to the organizations for whom they had contracted to fight. Instead, they robbed the countryside on their own behalf. . . .
>
> Given such conditions, any fine distinctions . . . between armies on the one hand and peoples on the other were bound to break down. Engulfed by war, civilians suffered terrible atrocities.

BACK then, in other words, there was no "politics" as we have come to understand the term, just as there is less and less "politics" today in Liberia, Sierra Leone, Somalia, Sri Lanka, the Balkans, and the Caucasus, among other places.

Because, as Van Creveld notes, the radius of trust within tribal societies is narrowed to one's immediate family and guerrilla comrades, truces arranged with one Bosnian commander, say, may be broken immediately by another Bosnian commander. The plethora of short-lived ceasefires in the Balkans and the Caucasus constitute proof that we are no longer in a world where the old rules of state warfare apply. More evidence is provided by the destruction of medieval monuments in the Croatian port of Dubrovnik: when cultures, rather than states, fight, then cultural and religious monuments are weapons of war, making them fair game.

Also, war-making entities will no longer be restricted to a specific territory. Loose and shadowy organisms such as Islamic terrorist organizations suggest why borders will mean increasingly little and sedimentary layers of tribalistic identity and control will mean more. "From the vantage point of the present, there appears every prospect that religious . . . fanaticisms will play a larger role in the motivation of armed conflict" in the West than at any time "for the last 300 years," Van Creveld writes. This is why analysts like Michael Vlahos are closely monitoring religious cults. Vlahos says, "An ideology that challenges us may not take familiar form, like the old Nazis or Commies. It may not even engage us initially in ways that fit old threat markings." Van Creveld concludes, "Armed conflict will be waged by men on earth, not robots in space. It will have more in common with the struggles of primitive tribes than with large-scale conventional war." While another military historian, John Keegan, in his new book *A History of Warfare*, draws a more benign portrait of primitive man, it is important to point out that what Van Creveld really means is *re-primitivized* man: warrior societies operating at a time of unprecedented resource scarcity and planetary overcrowding.

Van Creveld's pre-Westphalian vision of worldwide low-intensity conflict is not a superficial "back to the future" scenario. First of all, technology will be used toward primitive ends. In Liberia the guerrilla leader Prince Johnson didn't

CHRISTOPHER MORRIS/BLACK STAR

PATRICK ROBERT/SYGMA

just cut off the ears of President Samuel Doe before Doe was tortured to death in 1990—Johnson made a video of it, which has circulated throughout West Africa. In December of 1992, when plotters of a failed coup against the Strasser regime in Sierra Leone had their ears cut off at Freetown's Hamilton Beach prior to being killed, it was seen by many to be a copycat execution. Considering, as I've explained earlier, that the Strasser regime is not really a government and that Sierra Leone is not really a nation-state, listen closely to Van Creveld: "Once the legal monopoly of armed force, long claimed by the state, is wrested out of its hands, existing distinctions between war and crime will break down much as is already the case today in . . . Lebanon, Sri Lanka, El Salvador Peru, or Colombia."

If crime and war become indistinguishable, then "national defense" may in the future be viewed as a local concept. As crime continues to grow in our cities and the ability of state governments and criminal-justice systems to protect their citizens diminishes, urban crime may, according to Van Creveld, "develop into low-intensity conflict by coalescing along racial, religious, social, and political lines." As small-scale violence multiplies at home and abroad, state armies will continue to shrink, being gradually replaced by a booming private security business, as in West Africa, and by urban mafias, especially in the former communist world, who may be better equipped than municipal police forces to grant physical protection to local inhabitants.

Future wars will be those of communal survival, aggravated or, in many cases, caused by environmental scarcity. These wars will be subnational, meaning that it will be hard for states and local governments to protect their own citizens physically. This is how many states will ultimately die. As state power fades—and with it the state's ability to help weaker groups within society, not to mention other states—peoples and cultures around the world will be thrown back upon their own strengths and weaknesses, with fewer equalizing mechanisms to protect them. Whereas the distant future will probably see the emergence of a racially hybrid, globalized man, the coming decades will see us more aware of our differences than of our similarities. To the average person, political values will mean less, personal security more. The belief that we are all equal is liable to be replaced by the overriding obsession of the ancient Greek travelers: Why the differences between peoples?

LESTER SLOAN/WOODFIN CAMP

THE LAST MAP

IN *Geography and the Human Spirit,* Anne Buttimer, a professor at University College, Dublin, recalls the work of an early-nineteenth-century German geographer, Carl Ritter, whose work implied "a divine plan for humanity" based on regionalism and a constant, living flow of forms. The map of the future, to the extent that a map is even possible, will represent a perverse twisting of Ritter's vision. Imagine cartography in three dimensions, as if in a hologram. In this hologram would be the overlapping sediments of group and other identities atop the merely two-dimensional color markings of city-states and the remaining nations, themselves confused in places by shadowy tentacles, hovering overhead, indicating the power of drug cartels, mafias, and private security agencies. Instead of borders, there would be moving "centers" of power, as in the Middle Ages. Many of these layers would be in motion. Replacing fixed and abrupt lines on a flat space would be a shifting pattern of buffer entities, like the Kurdish and Azeri buffer entities between Turkey and Iran, the Turkic Uighur buffer entity between Central Asia and Inner China (itself distinct from coastal China), and the Latino buffer entity replacing a precise U.S.-Mexican border. To this protean cartographic hologram one must add other factors, such as migrations of populations, explosions of birth rates, vectors of disease. Henceforward the map of the world will never be static. This future map—in a sense, the "Last Map"—will be an ever-mutating representation of chaos.

The Indian subcontinent offers examples of what is happening. For different reasons, both India and Pakistan are increasingly dysfunctional. The argument over democracy in these places is less and less relevant to the larger issue of governability. In India's case the question arises, Is one unwieldy bureaucracy in New Delhi the best available mechanism for promoting the lives of 866 million people of diverse languages, religions, and ethnic groups? In 1950, when the Indian population was much less than half as large and nation-building idealism was still strong, the argument for democracy was more impressive than it is now. Given that in 2025 India's population could be close to 1.5 billion, that much of its economy rests on a shrinking natural-resource base, including dramatically declining water levels, and that communal violence and urbanization are spiraling upward, it is difficult to imagine that the Indian state will survive the next century. India's oft-trumpeted Green Revolution has been achieved by overworking its croplands and depleting its watershed. Norman Myers, a British development consultant, worries that Indians have "been feeding themselves today by borrowing against their children's food sources."

Pakistan's problem is more basic still: like much of Africa, the country makes no geographic or demographic sense. It was founded as a homeland for the Muslims of the subcontinent, yet there are more subcontinental Muslims outside Pakistan than within it. Like Yugoslavia, Pakistan is a patchwork of ethnic groups, increasingly in violent conflict with one another. While the Western media gushes over the fact that the country has a woman Prime Minister, Benazir Bhutto, Karachi is becoming a subcontinental version of Lagos. In eight visits to Pakistan, I have never gotten a sense of a cohesive national identity. With as much as 65 percent of its land dependent on intensive irrigation, with wide-scale deforestation, and with a yearly population growth of 2.7 percent (which ensures that the amount of cultivated land per rural inhabitant will plummet), Pakistan is becoming a more and more desperate place. As irrigation in the Indus River basin intensifies to serve two growing populations, Muslim-Hindu strife over falling water tables may be unavoidable.

Arson and looting in Los Angeles after the acquittal of police officers in the Rodney King case

"India and Pakistan will probably fall apart," Homer-Dixon predicts. "Their secular governments have less and less legitimacy as well as less management ability over people and resources." Rather than one bold line dividing the subcontinent into two parts, the future will likely see a lot of thinner lines and smaller parts, with the ethnic entities of Pakhtunistan and Punjab gradually replacing Pakistan in the space between the Central Asian plateau and the heart of the subcontinent.

None of this even takes into account climatic change, which, if it occurs in the next century, will further erode the capacity of existing states to cope. India, for instance, receives 70 percent of its precipitation from the monsoon cycle, which planetary warming could disrupt.

Not only will the three-dimensional aspects of the Last Map be in constant motion, but its two-dimensional base may change too. The National Academy of Sciences reports that

> as many as one billion people, or 20 per cent of the world's population, live on lands likely to be inundated or dramatically changed by rising waters. . . . Low-lying countries in the developing world such as Egypt and Bangladesh, where rivers are large and the deltas extensive and densely populated, will be hardest hit. . . . Where the rivers are dammed, as in the case of the Nile, the effects . . . will be especially severe.

Egypt could be where climatic upheaval—to say nothing of the more immediate threat of increasing population—will incite religious upheaval in truly biblical fashion. Natural catastrophes, such as the October, 1992, Cairo earthquake, in which the government failed to deliver relief aid and slum residents were in many instances helped by their local mosques, can only strengthen the position of Islamic factions. In a statement about greenhouse warming which could refer to any of a variety of natural catastrophes, the environmental expert Jessica Tuchman Matthews warns that many of us underestimate the extent to which political systems, in affluent societies as well as in places like Egypt, "depend on the underpinning of natural systems." She adds, "The fact that one can move with ease from Vermont to Miami has nothing to say about the consequences of Vermont acquiring Miami's climate."

Indeed, it is not clear that the United States will survive the next century in exactly its present form. Because America is a multi-ethnic society, the nation-state has always been more fragile here than it is in more homogeneous societies like Germany and Japan. James Kurth, in an article published in *The National Interest* in 1992, explains that whereas nation-state societies tend to be built around a mass-conscription army and a standardized public school system, "multicultural regimes" feature a high-tech, all-volunteer army (and, I would add, private schools that teach competing values), operating in a culture in which the international media and entertainment industry has more influence than the "national political class." In other words, a nation-state is a place where everyone has been educated along similar lines, where people take their cue from national leaders, and where everyone (every male, at least) has gone through the crucible of military service, making patriotism a simpler issue. Writing about his immigrant family in turn-of-the-century Chicago, Saul Bellow states, "The country took us over. It *was* a country then, not a collection of 'cultures.'"

During the Second World War and the decade following it, the United States reached its apogee as a classic nation-state. During the 1960s, as is now clear, America began a slow but unmistakable process of transformation. The signs hardly need belaboring: racial polarity, educational dysfunction, social fragmentation of many and various kinds. William Irwin Thompson, in *Passages About Earth: An Exploration of the New Planetary Culture*, writes, "The educational system that had worked on the Jews or the Irish could no longer work on the blacks; and when Jewish teachers in New York tried to take black children away from their parents exactly in the way they had been taken from theirs, they were shocked to encounter a violent affirmation of negritude."

Issues like West Africa could yet emerge as a new kind of foreign-policy issue, further eroding America's domestic peace. The spectacle of several West African nations collapsing at once could reinforce the worst racial stereotypes here at home. That is another reason why Africa matters. We must not kid ourselves: the sensitivity factor is higher than ever. The Washington, D.C., public school system is already experimenting with an Afrocentric curriculum. Summits between African leaders and prominent African-Americans are becoming frequent, as are Pollyanna-ish prognostications about multiparty elections in Africa that do not factor in crime, surging birth rates, and resource depletion. The Congressional Black Caucus was among those urging U.S. involvement in Somalia and in Haiti. At the *Los Angeles Times* minority staffers have protested against, among other things, what they allege to be the racist tone of the newspaper's Africa coverage, allegations that the editor of the "World Report" section, Dan Fisher, denies, saying essentially that Africa should be viewed through the same rigorous analytical lens as other parts of the world.

Africa may be marginal in terms of conventional late-twentieth-century conceptions of strategy, but in an age of cultural and racial clash, when national defense is increasingly local, Africa's distress will exert a destabilizing influence on the United States.

This and many other factors will make the United States less of a nation than it is today, even as it gains territory following the peaceful dissolution of Canada. Quebec, based on the bedrock of Roman Catholicism and Francophone ethnicity, could yet turn out to be North America's most cohesive and crime-free nation-state. (It may be a smaller Quebec, though, since aboriginal peoples may lop off northern parts of the province.) "Patriotism" will become increasingly regional as people in Alberta and Montana discover that they have far more in common with each other than they do with Ottawa or Washington, and Spanish-speakers in the Southwest discover a greater commonality with Mexico City. (*The Nine Nations of North America*, by Joel Garreau, a book about the continent's regionalization, is more relevant now than when it was published, in 1981.) As Washington's influence wanes, and with it the traditional symbols of American patriotism, North Americans will take psychological refuge in their insulated communities and cultures.

RETURNING from West Africa last fall was an illuminating ordeal. After leaving Abidjan, my Air Afrique flight landed in Dakar, Senegal, where all passengers had to disembark in order to go through another security check, this one demanded by U.S. authorities before they would permit the flight to set out for New York. Once we were in New York, despite the midnight hour, immigration officials at Kennedy Airport held up disembarkation by conducting quick interrogations of the aircraft's passengers—this was in addition to all the normal immigration and customs procedures. It was apparent that drug smuggling, disease, and other factors had contributed to the toughest security procedures I have ever encountered when returning from overseas.

Then, for the first time in over a month, I spotted businesspeople with attaché cases and laptop computers. When I had left New York for Abidjan, all the businesspeople were boarding planes for Seoul and Tokyo, which departed from gates near Air Afrique's. The only non-Africans off to West Africa had been relief workers in T-shirts and khakis. Although the borders within West Africa are increasingly unreal, those separating West Africa from the outside world are in various ways becoming more impenetrable.

But Afrocentrists are right in one respect: we ignore this dying region at our own risk. When the Berlin Wall was falling, in November of 1989, I happened to be in Kosovo, covering a riot between Serbs and Albanians. The future was in Kosovo, I told myself that night, not in Berlin. The same day that Yitzhak Rabin and Yasser Arafat clasped hands on the White House lawn, my Air Afrique plane was approaching Bamako, Mali, revealing corrugated-zinc shacks at the edge of an expanding desert. The real news wasn't at the White House, I realized. It was right below.

The End of History?

Francis Fukuyama

IN WATCHING the flow of events over the past decade or so, it is hard to avoid the feeling that something very fundamental has happened in world history. The past year has seen a flood of articles commemorating the end of the Cold War, and the fact that "peace" seems to be breaking out in many regions of the world. Most of these analyses lack any larger conceptual framework for distinguishing between what is essential and what is contingent or accidental in world history, and are predictably superficial. If Mr. Gorbachev were ousted from the Kremlin or a new Ayatollah proclaimed the millennium from a desolate Middle Eastern capital, these same commentators would scramble to announce the rebirth of a new era of conflict.

And yet, all of these people sense dimly that there is some larger process at work, a process that gives coherence and order to the daily headlines. The twentieth century saw the developed world descend into a paroxysm of ideological violence, as liberalism contended first with the remnants of absolutism, then bolshevism and fascism, and finally an updated Marxism that threatened to lead to the ultimate apocalypse of nuclear war. But the century that began full of self-confidence in the ultimate triumph of Western liberal democracy seems at its close to be returning full circle to where it started: not to an "end of ideology" or a convergence between capitalism and socialism, as earlier predicted, but to an unabashed victory of economic and political liberalism.

The triumph of the West, of the Western *idea*, is evident first of all in the total exhaustion of viable systematic alternatives to Western liberalism. In the past decade, there have been unmistakable changes in the intellectual climate of the world's two largest communist countries, and the beginnings of significant reform movements in both. But this phenomenon extends beyond high politics and it can be seen also in the ineluctable spread of consumerist Western culture in such diverse contexts as the peasants' markets and color television sets now omnipresent throughout China, the cooperative restaurants and clothing stores opened in the past year in Moscow, the Beethoven piped into Japanese department stores, and the rock music enjoyed alike in Prague, Rangoon, and Tehran.

Francis Fukuyama is deputy director of the State Department's policy planning staff and former analyst at the RAND Corporation. This article is based on a lecture presented at the University of Chicago's John M. Olin Center for Inquiry Into the Theory and Practice of Democracy. The author would like to pay special thanks to the Olin Center and to Nathan Tarcov and Allan Bloom for their support in this and many earlier endeavors. The opinions expressed in this article do not reflect those of the RAND Corporation or of any agency of the U.S. government.

Supplement to the National Interest

What we may be witnessing is not just the end of the Cold War, or the passing of a particular period of postwar history, but the end of history as such: that is, the end point of mankind's ideological evolution and the universalization of Western liberal democracy as the final form of human government. This is not to say that there will no longer be events to fill the pages of *Foreign Affairs*'s yearly summaries of international relations, for the victory of liberalism has occurred primarily in the realm of ideas or consciousness and is as yet incomplete in the real or material world. But there are powerful reasons for believing that it is the ideal that will govern the material world *in the long run.* To understand how this is so, we must first consider some theoretical issues concerning the nature of historical change.

I

THE NOTION of the end of history is not an original one. Its best known propagator was Karl Marx, who believed that the direction of historical development was a purposeful one determined by the interplay of material forces, and would come to an end only with the achievement of a communist utopia that would finally resolve all prior contradictions. But the concept of history as a dialectical process with a beginning, a middle, and an end was borrowed by Marx from his great German predecessor, Georg Wilhelm Friedrich Hegel.

For better or worse, much of Hegel's historicism has become part of our contemporary intellectual baggage. The notion that mankind has progressed through a series of primitive stages of consciousness on his path to the present, and that these stages corresponded to concrete forms of social organization, such as tribal, slave-owning, theocratic, and finally democratic-egalitarian societies, has become inseparable from the modern understanding of man. Hegel was the first philosopher to speak the language of modern social science, insofar as man for him was the product of his concrete historical and social environment and not, as earlier natural right theorists would have it, a collection of more or less fixed "natural" attributes. The mastery and transformation of man's natural environment through the application of science and technology was originally not a Marxist concept, but a Hegelian one. Unlike later historicists whose historical relativism degenerated into relativism *tout court,* however, Hegel believed that history culminated in an absolute moment—a moment in which a final, rational form of society and state became victorious.

It is Hegel's misfortune to be known now primarily as Marx's precursor, and it is our misfortune that few of us are familiar with Hegel's work from direct study, but only as it has been filtered through the distorting lens of Marxism. In France, however, there has been an effort to save Hegel from his Marxist interpreters and to resurrect him as the philosopher who most correctly speaks to our time. Among those modern French interpreters of Hegel, the greatest was certainly Alexandre Kojève, a brilliant Russian emigre who taught a highly influential series of seminars in Paris in the 1930s at the *Ecole Practique des Hautes Etudes.*[1] While largely unknown in the United States, Kojève had a major impact on the intellectual life of the continent. Among his students ranged such future luminaries as Jean-Paul Sartre on the Left and Raymond Aron on the Right; postwar existentialism borrowed many of its basic categories from Hegel via Kojève.

Kojève sought to resurrect the Hegel of the *Phenomenology of Mind,* the Hegel who proclaimed history to be at an end in 1806. For as early as this Hegel saw in Napoleon's defeat of the Prussian monarchy at the Battle of Jena the victory of the ideals of the French Rev-

[1] Kojève's best-known work is his *Introduction à la lecture de Hegel* (Paris: Editions Gallimard, 1947), which is a transcript of the *Ecole Practique* lectures from the 1930s. This book is available in English entitled *Introduction to the Reading of Hegel* arranged by Raymond Queneau, edited by Allan Bloom, and translated by James Nichols (New York: Basic Books, 1969).

go to 26

of moral values underlying any society as well.

Hegel's view of the relationship between the ideal and the real or material worlds was an extremely complicated one, beginning with the fact that for him the distinction between the two was only apparent.[5] He did not believe that the real world conformed or could be made to conform to ideological preconceptions of philosophy professors in any simple-minded way, or that the "material" world could not impinge on the ideal. Indeed, Hegel the professor was temporarily thrown out of work as a result of a very material event, the Battle of Jena. But while Hegel's writing and thinking could be stopped by a bullet from the material world, the hand on the trigger of the gun was motivated in turn by the ideas of liberty and equality that had driven the French Revolution.

For Hegel, all human behavior in the material world, and hence all human history, is rooted in a prior state of consciousness—an idea similar to the one expressed by John Maynard Keynes when he said that the views of men of affairs were usually derived from defunct economists and academic scribblers of earlier generations. This consciousness may not be explicit and self-aware, as are modern political doctrines, but may rather take the form of religion or simple cultural or moral habits. And yet this realm of consciousness *in the long run* necessarily becomes manifest in the material world, indeed creates the material world in its own image. Consciousness is cause and not effect, and can develop autonomously from the material world; hence the real subtext underlying the apparent jumble of current events is the history of ideology.

Hegel's idealism has fared poorly at the hands of later thinkers. Marx reversed the priority of the real and the ideal completely, relegating the entire realm of consciousness—religion, art, culture, philosophy itself—to a "superstructure" that was determined entirely by the prevailing material mode of production. Yet another unfortunate legacy of Marxism is our tendency to retreat into materialist or utilitarian explanations of political or historical phenomena, and our disinclination to believe in the autonomous power of ideas. A recent example of this is Paul Kennedy's hugely successful *The Rise and Fall of the Great Powers*, which ascribes the decline of great powers to simple economic overextension. Obviously, this is true on some level: an empire whose economy is barely above the level of subsistence cannot bankrupt its treasury indefinitely. But whether a highly productive modern industrial society chooses to spend 3 or 7 percent of its GNP on defense rather than consumption is entirely a matter of that society's political priorities, which are in turn determined in the realm of consciousness.

The materialist bias of modern thought is characteristic not only of people on the Left who may be sympathetic to Marxism, but of many passionate anti-Marxists as well. Indeed, there is on the Right what one might label the *Wall Street Journal* school of deterministic materialism that discounts the importance of ideology and culture and sees man as essentially a rational, profit-maximizing individual. It is precisely this kind of individual and his pursuit of material incentives that is posited as the basis for economic life as such in economic textbooks.[6] One small example will illustrate the problematic character of such materialist views.

Max Weber begins his famous book, *The Protestant Ethic and the Spirit of Capitalism*, by noting the different economic performance of

[5]Indeed, for Hegel the very dichotomy between the ideal and material worlds was itself only an apparent one that was ultimately overcome by the self-conscious subject; in his system, the material world is itself only an aspect of mind.

[6]In fact, modern economists, recognizing that man does not always behave as a *profit*-maximizer, posit a "utility" function, utility being either income or some other good that can be maximized: leisure, sexual satisfaction, or the pleasure of philosophizing. That profit must be replaced with a value like utility indicates the cogency of the idealist perspective.

go to 28

olution, and the imminent universalization of the state incorporating the principles of liberty and equality. Kojève, far from rejecting Hegel in light of the turbulent events of the next century and a half, insisted that the latter had been essentially correct.[2] The Battle of Jena marked the end of history because it was at that point that the *vanguard* of humanity (a term quite familiar to Marxists) actualized the principles of the French Revolution. While there was considerable work to be done after 1806—abolishing slavery and the slave trade, extending the franchise to workers, women, blacks, and other racial minorities, etc.—the basic *principles* of the liberal democratic state could not be improved upon. The two world wars in this century and their attendant revolutions and upheavals simply had the effect of extending those principles spatially, such that the various provinces of human civilization were brought up to the level of its most advanced outposts, and of forcing those societies in Europe and North America at the vanguard of civilization to implement their liberalism more fully.

The state that emerges at the end of history is liberal insofar as it recognizes and protects through a system of law man's universal right to freedom, and democratic insofar as it exists only with the consent of the governed. For Kojève, this so-called "universal homogenous state" found real-life embodiment in the countries of postwar Western Europe—precisely those flabby, prosperous, self-satisfied, inward-looking, weak-willed states whose grandest project was nothing more heroic than the creation of the Common Market.[3] But this was only to be expected. For human history and the conflict that characterized it was based on the existence of "contradictions": primitive man's quest for mutual recognition, the dialectic of the master and slave, the transformation and mastery of nature, the struggle for the universal recognition of rights, and the dichotomy between proletarian and capitalist. But in the universal homogenous state, all prior contradictions are resolved and all human needs are satisfied. There is no struggle or conflict over "large" issues, and consequently no need for generals or statesmen; what remains is primarily economic activity. And indeed, Kojève's life was consistent with his teaching. Believing that there was no more work for philosophers as well, since Hegel (correctly understood) had already achieved absolute knowledge, Kojève left teaching after the war and spent the remainder of his life working as a bureaucrat in the European Economic Community, until his death in 1968.

To his contemporaries at mid-century, Kojève's proclamation of the end of history must have seemed like the typical eccentric solipsism of a French intellectual, coming as it did on the heels of World War II and at the very height of the Cold War. To comprehend how Kojève could have been so audacious as to assert that history has ended, we must first of all understand the meaning of Hegelian idealism.

II

FOR HEGEL, the contradictions that drive history exist first of all in the realm of human consciousness, i.e. on the level of ideas[4]—not the trivial election year proposals of American politicians, but ideas in the sense of large unifying world views that might best be understood under the rubric of ideology. Ideology in this sense is not restricted to the secular and explicit political doctrines we usually associate with the term, but can include religion, culture, and the complex

[2] In this respect Kojève stands in sharp contrast to contemporary German interpreters of Hegel like Herbert Marcuse who, being more sympathetic to Marx, regarded Hegel ultimately as an historically bound and incomplete philosopher.

[3] Kojève alternatively identified the end of history with the postwar "American way of life," toward which he thought the Soviet Union was moving as well.

[4] This notion was expressed in the famous aphorism from the preface to the *Philosophy of History* to the effect that "everything that is rational is real, and everything that is real is rational."

go to 25

change was in no way made inevitable by the material conditions in which either country found itself on the eve of the reform, but instead came about as the result of the victory of one idea over another.[9]

For Kojève, as for all good Hegelians, understanding the underlying processes of history requires understanding developments in the realm of consciousness or ideas, since consciousness will ultimately remake the material world in its own image. To say that history ended in 1806 meant that mankind's ideological evolution ended in the ideals of the French or American Revolutions: while particular regimes in the real world might not implement these ideals fully, their theoretical truth is absolute and could not be improved upon. Hence it did not matter to Kojève that the consciousness of the postwar generation of Europeans had not been universalized throughout the world; if ideological development had in fact ended, the homogenous state would eventually become victorious throughout the material world.

I have neither the space nor, frankly, the ability to defend in depth Hegel's radical idealist perspective. The issue is not whether Hegel's system was right, but whether his perspective might uncover the problematic nature of many materialist explanations we often take for granted. This is not to deny the role of material factors as such. To a literal-minded idealist, human society can be built around any arbitrary set of principles regardless of their relationship to the material world. And in fact men have proven themselves able to endure the most extreme material hardships in the name of ideas that exist in the realm of the spirit alone, be it the divinity of cows or the nature of the Holy Trinity.[10]

But while man's very perception of the material world is shaped by his historical consciousness of it, the material world can clearly affect in return the viability of a particular state of consciousness. In particular, the spectacular abundance of advanced liberal economies and the infinitely diverse consumer culture made possible by them seem to both foster and preserve liberalism in the political sphere. I want to avoid the materialist determinism that says that liberal economics inevitably produces liberal politics, because I believe that both economics and politics presuppose an autonomous prior state of consciousness that makes them possible. But that state of consciousness that permits the growth of liberalism seems to stabilize in the way one would expect at the end of history if it is underwritten by the abundance of a modern free market economy. We might summarize the content of the universal homogenous state as liberal democracy in the political sphere combined with easy access to VCRs and stereos in the economic.

III

HAVE WE in fact reached the end of history? Are there, in other words, any fundamental "contradictions" in human life that cannot be resolved in the context of modern liberalism, that would be resolvable by an alternative political-economic structure? If we accept the idealist premises

nological-military realm. Nonetheless, neither country on the eve of its reforms was in such a state of *material* crisis that one could have predicted the surprising reform paths ultimately taken.

[9] It is still not clear whether the Soviet peoples are as "Protestant" as Gorbachev and will follow him down that path.

[10] The internal politics of the Byzantine Empire at the time of Justinian revolved around a conflict between the so-called monophysites and monothelites, who believed that the unity of the Holy Trinity was alternatively one of nature or of will. This conflict corresponded to some extent to one between proponents of different racing teams in the Hippodrome in Byzantium and led to a not insignificant level of political violence. Modern historians would tend to seek the roots of such conflicts in antagonisms between social classes or some other modern economic category, being unwilling to believe that men would kill each other over the nature of the Trinity.

go to 29

Protestant and Catholic communities throughout Europe and America, summed up in the proverb that Protestants eat well while Catholics sleep well. Weber notes that according to any economic theory that posited man as a rational profit-maximizer, raising the piece-work rate should increase labor productivity. But in fact, in many traditional peasant communities, raising the piece-work rate actually had the opposite effect of *lowering* labor productivity: at the higher rate, a peasant accustomed to earning two and one-half marks per day found he could earn the same amount by working less, and did so because he valued leisure more than income. The choices of leisure over income, or of the militaristic life of the Spartan hoplite over the wealth of the Athenian trader, or even the ascetic life of the early capitalist entrepreneur over that of a traditional leisured aristocrat, cannot possibly be explained by the impersonal working of material forces, but come preeminently out of the sphere of consciousness—what we have labeled here broadly as ideology. And indeed, a central theme of Weber's work was to prove that contrary to Marx, the material mode of production, far from being the "base," was itself a "superstructure" with roots in religion and culture, and that to understand the emergence of modern capitalism and the profit motive one had to study their antecedents in the realm of the spirit.

As we look around the contemporary world, the poverty of materialist theories of economic development is all too apparent. The *Wall Street Journal* school of deterministic materialism habitually points to the stunning economic success of Asia in the past few decades as evidence of the viability of free market economics, with the implication that all societies would see similar development were they simply to allow their populations to pursue their material self-interest freely. Surely free markets and stable political systems are a necessary precondition to capitalist economic growth. But just as surely the cultural heritage of those Far Eastern societies, the ethic of work and saving and family, a religious heritage that does not, like Islam, place restrictions on certain forms of economic behavior, and other deeply ingrained moral qualities, are equally important in explaining their economic performance.[7] And yet the intellectual weight of materialism is such that not a single respectable contemporary theory of economic development addresses consciousness and culture seriously as the matrix within which economic behavior is formed.

FAILURE to understand that the roots of economic behavior lie in the realm of consciousness and culture leads to the common mistake of attributing material causes to phenomena that are essentially ideal in nature. For example, it is commonplace in the West to interpret the reform movements first in China and most recently in the Soviet Union as the victory of the material over the ideal—that is, a recognition that ideological incentives could not replace material ones in stimulating a highly productive modern economy, and that if one wanted to prosper one had to appeal to baser forms of self-interest. But the deep defects of socialist economies were evident thirty or forty years ago to anyone who chose to look. Why was it that these countries moved away from central planning only in the 1980s? The answer must be found in the consciousness of the elites and leaders ruling them, who decided to opt for the "Protestant" life of wealth and risk over the "Catholic" path of poverty and security.[8] That

[7]One need look no further than the recent performance of Vietnamese immigrants in the U.S. school system when compared to their black or Hispanic classmates to realize that culture and consciousness are absolutely crucial to explain not only economic behavior but virtually every other important aspect of life as well.

[8]I understand that a full explanation of the origins of the reform movements in China and Russia is a good deal more complicated than this simple formula would suggest. The Soviet reform, for example, was motivated in good measure by Moscow's sense of *insecurity* in the tech-

go to 27

laid out above, we must seek an answer to this question in the realm of ideology and consciousness. Our task is not to answer exhaustively the challenges to liberalism promoted by every crackpot messiah around the world, but only those that are embodied in important social or political forces and movements, and which are therefore part of world history. For our purposes, it matters very little what strange thoughts occur to people in Albania or Burkina Faso, for we are interested in what one could in some sense call the common ideological heritage of mankind.

In the past century, there have been two major challenges to liberalism, those of fascism and of communism. The former[11] saw the political weakness, materialism, anomie, and lack of community of the West as fundamental contradictions in liberal societies that could only be resolved by a strong state that forged a new "people" on the basis of national exclusiveness. Fascism was destroyed as a living ideology by World War II. This was a defeat, of course, on a very material level, but it amounted to a defeat of the idea as well. What destroyed fascism as an idea was not universal moral revulsion against it, since plenty of people were willing to endorse the idea as long as it seemed the wave of the future, but its lack of success. After the war, it seemed to most people that German fascism as well as its other European and Asian variants were bound to self-destruct. There was no material reason why new fascist movements could not have sprung up again after the war in other locales, but for the fact that expansionist ultranationalism, with its promise of unending conflict leading to disastrous military defeat, had completely lost its appeal. The ruins of the Reich chancellory as well as the atomic bombs dropped on Hiroshima and Nagasaki killed this ideology on the level of consciousness as well as materially, and all of the proto-fascist movements spawned by the German and Japanese examples like the Peronist movement in Argentina or Subhas Chandra Bose's Indian National Army withered after the war.

The ideological challenge mounted by the other great alternative to liberalism, communism, was far more serious. Marx, speaking Hegel's language, asserted that liberal society contained a fundamental contradiction that could not be resolved within its context, that between capital and labor, and this contradiction has constituted the chief accusation against liberalism ever since. But surely, the class issue has actually been successfully resolved in the West. As Kojève (among others) noted, the egalitarianism of modern America represents the essential achievement of the classless society envisioned by Marx. This is not to say that there are not rich people and poor people in the United States, or that the gap between them has not grown in recent years. But the root causes of economic inequality do not have to do with the underlying legal and social structure of our society, which remains fundamentally egalitarian and moderately redistributionist, so much as with the cultural and social characteristics of the groups that make it up, which are in turn the historical legacy of premodern conditions. Thus black poverty in the United States is not the inherent product of liberalism, but is rather the "legacy of slavery and racism" which persisted long after the formal abolition of slavery.

As a result of the receding of the class issue, the appeal of communism in the developed Western world, it is safe to say, is lower

[11]I am not using the term "fascism" here in its most precise sense, fully aware of the frequent misuse of this term to denounce anyone to the right of the user. "Fascism" here denotes any organized ultra-nationalist movement with universalistic pretensions—not universalistic with regard to its nationalism, of course, since the latter is exclusive by definition, but with regard to the movement's belief in its right to rule other people. Hence Imperial Japan would qualify as fascist while former strongman Stoessner's Paraguay or Pinochet's Chile would not. Obviously fascist ideologies cannot be universalistic in the sense of Marxism or liberalism, but the structure of the doctrine can be transferred from country to country.

today than any time since the end of the First World War. This can be measured in any number of ways: in the declining membership and electoral pull of the major European communist parties, and their overtly revisionist programs; in the corresponding electoral success of conservative parties from Britain and Germany to the United States and Japan, which are unabashedly pro-market and anti-statist; and in an intellectual climate whose most "advanced" members no longer believe that bourgeois society is something that ultimately needs to be overcome. This is not to say that the opinions of progressive intellectuals in Western countries are not deeply pathological in any number of ways. But those who believe that the future must inevitably be socialist tend to be very old, or very marginal to the real political discourse of their societies.

ONE MAY argue that the socialist alternative was never terribly plausible for the North Atlantic world, and was sustained for the last several decades primarily by its success outside of this region. But it is precisely in the non-European world that one is most struck by the occurrence of major ideological transformations. Surely the most remarkable changes have occurred in Asia. Due to the strength and adaptability of the indigenous cultures there, Asia became a battleground for a variety of imported Western ideologies early in this century. Liberalism in Asia was a very weak reed in the period after World War I; it is easy today to forget how gloomy Asia's political future looked as recently as ten or fifteen years ago. It is easy to forget as well how momentous the outcome of Asian ideological struggles seemed for world political development as a whole.

The first Asian alternative to liberalism to be decisively defeated was the fascist one represented by Imperial Japan. Japanese fascism (like its German version) was defeated by the force of American arms in the Pacific war, and liberal democracy was imposed on Japan by a victorious United States. Western capitalism and political liberalism when transplanted to Japan were adapted and transformed by the Japanese in such a way as to be scarcely recognizable.[12] Many Americans are now aware that Japanese industrial organization is very different from that prevailing in the United States or Europe, and it is questionable what relationship the factional maneuvering that takes place with the governing Liberal Democratic Party bears to democracy. Nonetheless, the very fact that the essential elements of economic and political liberalism have been so successfully grafted onto uniquely Japanese traditions and institutions guarantees their survival in the long run. More important is the contribution that Japan has made in turn to world history by following in the footsteps of the United States to create a truly universal consumer culture that has become both a symbol and an underpinning of the universal homogenous state. V.S. Naipaul travelling in Khomeini's Iran shortly after the revolution noted the omnipresent signs advertising the products of Sony, Hitachi, and JVC, whose appeal remained virtually irresistible and gave the lie to the regime's pretensions of restoring a state based on the rule of the *Shariah.* Desire for access to the consumer culture, created in large measure by Japan, has played a crucial role in fostering the spread of economic liberalism throughout Asia, and hence in promoting political liberalism as well.

The economic success of the other newly industrializing countries (NICs) in Asia following on the example of Japan is by now a familiar story. What is important from a Hegelian standpoint is that political liberalism has been following economic liberalism, more slowly than many had hoped but with seeming inevitability. Here again we see the vic-

[12]I use the example of Japan with some caution, since Kojève late in his life came to conclude that Japan, with its culture based on purely formal arts, proved that the universal homogenous state was not victorious and that history had perhaps not ended. See the long note at the end of the second edition of *Introduction à la Lecture de Hegel*, 462–3.

tory of the idea of the universal homogenous state. South Korea had developed into a modern, urbanized society with an increasingly large and well-educated middle class that could not possibly be isolated from the larger democratic trends around them. Under these circumstances it seemed intolerable to a large part of this population that it should be ruled by an anachronistic military regime while Japan, only a decade or so ahead in economic terms, had parliamentary institutions for over forty years. Even the former socialist regime in Burma, which for so many decades existed in dismal isolation from the larger trends dominating Asia, was buffeted in the past year by pressures to liberalize both its economy and political system. It is said that unhappiness with strongman Ne Win began when a senior Burmese officer went to Singapore for medical treatment and broke down crying when he saw how far socialist Burma had been left behind by its ASEAN neighbors.

BUT THE power of the liberal idea would seem much less impressive if it had not infected the largest and oldest culture in Asia, China. The simple existence of communist China created an alternative pole of ideological attraction, and as such constituted a threat to liberalism. But the past fifteen years have seen an almost total discrediting of Marxism-Leninism as an economic system. Beginning with the famous third plenum of the Tenth Central Committee in 1978, the Chinese Communist party set about decollectivizing agriculture for the 800 million Chinese who still lived in the countryside. The role of the state in agriculture was reduced to that of a tax collector, while production of consumer goods was sharply increased in order to give peasants a taste of the universal homogenous state and thereby an incentive to work. The reform doubled Chinese grain output in only five years, and in the process created for Deng Xiao-ping a solid political base from which he was able to extend the reform to other parts of the economy. Economic statistics do not begin to describe the dynamism, initiative, and openness evident in China since the reform began.

China could not now be described in any way as a liberal democracy. At present, no more than 20 percent of its economy has been marketized, and most importantly it continues to be ruled by a self-appointed Communist party which has given no hint of wanting to devolve power. Deng has made none of Gorbachev's promises regarding democratization of the political system and there is no Chinese equivalent of *glasnost.* The Chinese leadership has in fact been much more circumspect in criticizing Mao and Maoism than Gorbachev with respect to Brezhnev and Stalin, and the regime continues to pay lip service to Marxism-Leninism as its ideological underpinning. But anyone familiar with the outlook and behavior of the new technocratic elite now governing China knows that Marxism and ideological principle have become virtually irrelevant as guides to policy, and that bourgeois consumerism has a real meaning in that country for the first time since the revolution. The various slowdowns in the pace of reform, the campaigns against "spiritual pollution" and crackdowns on political dissent are more properly seen as tactical adjustments made in the process of managing what is an extraordinarily difficult political transition. By ducking the question of political reform while putting the economy on a new footing, Deng has managed to avoid the breakdown of authority that has accompanied Gorbachev's *perestroika.* Yet the pull of the liberal idea continues to be very strong as economic power devolves and the economy becomes more open to the outside world. There are currently over 20,000 Chinese students studying in the U.S. and other Western countries, almost all of them the children of the Chinese elite. It is hard to believe that when they return home to run the country they will be content for China to be the only country in Asia unaffected by the larger democratizing trend. The student demonstrations in Beijing that broke out first in December 1986 and recurred recently on the occasion of Hu Yao-bang's death were only the beginning of what will inevitably be mounting pressure for change in the political system as well.

What is important about China from the standpoint of world history is not the present state of the reform or even its future prospects. The central issue is the fact that the People's Republic of China can no longer act as a beacon for illiberal forces around the world, whether they be guerrillas in some Asian jungle or middle class students in Paris. Maoism, rather than being the pattern for Asia's future, became an anachronism, and it was the mainland Chinese who in fact were decisively influenced by the prosperity and dynamism of their overseas co-ethnics—the ironic ultimate victory of Taiwan.

Important as these changes in China have been, however, it is developments in the Soviet Union—the original "homeland of the world proletariat"—that have put the final nail in the coffin of the Marxist-Leninist alternative to liberal democracy. It should be clear that in terms of formal institutions, not much has changed in the four years since Gorbachev has come to power: free markets and the cooperative movement represent only a small part of the Soviet economy, which remains centrally planned; the political system is still dominated by the Communist party, which has only begun to democratize internally and to share power with other groups; the regime continues to assert that it is seeking only to modernize socialism and that its ideological basis remains Marxism-Leninism; and, finally, Gorbachev faces a potentially powerful conservative opposition that could undo many of the changes that have taken place to date. Moreover, it is hard to be too sanguine about the chances for success of Gorbachev's proposed reforms, either in the sphere of economics or politics. But my purpose here is not to analyze events in the short-term, or to make predictions for policy purposes, but to look at underlying trends in the sphere of ideology and consciousness. And in that respect, it is clear that an astounding transformation has occurred.

Emigres from the Soviet Union have been reporting for at least the last generation now that virtually nobody in that country truly believed in Marxism-Leninism any longer, and that this was nowhere more true than in the Soviet elite, which continued to mouth Marxist slogans out of sheer cynicism. The corruption and decadence of the late Brezhnev-era Soviet state seemed to matter little, however, for as long as the state itself refused to throw into question any of the fundamental principles underlying Soviet society, the system was capable of functioning adequately out of sheer inertia and could even muster some dynamism in the realm of foreign and defense policy. Marxism-Leninism was like a magical incantation which, however absurd and devoid of meaning, was the only common basis on which the elite could agree to rule Soviet society.

WHAT HAS happened in the four years since Gorbachev's coming to power is a revolutionary assault on the most fundamental institutions and principles of Stalinism, and their replacement by other principles which do not amount to liberalism *per se* but whose only connecting thread is liberalism. This is most evident in the economic sphere, where the reform economists around Gorbachev have become steadily more radical in their support for free markets, to the point where some like Nikolai Shmelev do not mind being compared in public to Milton Friedman. There is a virtual consensus among the currently dominant school of Soviet economists now that central planning and the command system of allocation are the root cause of economic inefficiency, and that if the Soviet system is ever to heal itself, it must permit free and decentralized decision-making with respect to investment, labor, and prices. After a couple of initial years of ideological confusion, these principles have finally been incorporated into policy with the promulgation of new laws on enterprise autonomy, cooperatives, and finally in 1988 on lease arrangements and family farming. There are, of course, a number of fatal flaws in the current implementation of the reform, most notably the absence of a thoroughgoing price reform. But the problem is no longer a *conceptual* one: Gorbachev and his lieutenants seem to understand the economic logic of marketization well enough, but like the leaders of a Third World country facing the IMF, are afraid of the social consequences of ending consumer subsidies and other forms of dependence on the state sector.

In the political sphere, the proposed changes to the Soviet constitution, legal system, and party rules amount to much less than the establishment of a liberal state. Gorbachev has spoken of democratization primarily in the sphere of internal party affairs, and has shown little intention of ending the Communist party's monopoly of power; indeed, the political reform seeks to legitimize and therefore strengthen the CPSU's rule.[13] Nonetheless, the general principles underlying many of the reforms—that the "people" should be truly responsible for their own affairs, that higher political bodies should be answerable to lower ones, and not vice versa, that the rule of law should prevail over arbitrary police actions, with separation of powers and an independent judiciary, that there should be legal protection for property rights, the need for open discussion of public issues and the right of public dissent, the empowering of the Soviets as a forum in which the whole Soviet people can participate, and of a political culture that is more tolerant and pluralistic—come from a source fundamentally alien to the USSR's Marxist-Leninist tradition, even if they are incompletely articulated and poorly implemented in practice.

Gorbachev's repeated assertions that he is doing no more than trying to restore the original meaning of Leninism are themselves a kind of Orwellian doublespeak. Gorbachev and his allies have consistently maintained that intraparty democracy was somehow the essence of Leninism, and that the various liberal practices of open debate, secret ballot elections, and rule of law were all part of the Leninist heritage, corrupted only later by Stalin. While almost anyone would look good compared to Stalin, drawing so sharp a line between Lenin and his successor is questionable. The essence of Lenin's democratic centralism was centralism, not democracy; that is, the absolutely rigid, monolithic, and disciplined dictatorship of a hierarchically organized vanguard Communist party, speaking in the name of the *demos*. All of Lenin's vicious polemics against Karl Kautsky, Rosa Luxemburg, and various other Menshevik and Social Democratic rivals, not to mention his contempt for "bourgeois legality" and freedoms, centered around his profound conviction that a revolution could not be successfully made by a democratically run organization.

Gorbachev's claim that he is seeking to return to the true Lenin is perfectly easy to understand: having fostered a thorough denunciation of Stalinism and Brezhnevism as the root of the USSR's present predicament, he needs some point in Soviet history on which to anchor the legitimacy of the CPSU's continued rule. But Gorbachev's tactical requirements should not blind us to the fact that the democratizing and decentralizing principles which he has enunciated in both the economic and political spheres are highly subversive of some of the most fundamental precepts of both Marxism and Leninism. Indeed, if the bulk of the present economic reform proposals were put into effect, it is hard to know how the Soviet economy would be more socialist than those of other Western countries with large public sectors.

The Soviet Union could in no way be described as a liberal or democratic country now, nor do I think that it is terribly likely that *perestroika* will succeed such that the label will be thinkable any time in the near future. But at the end of history it is not necessary that all societies become successful liberal societies, merely that they end their ideological pretensions of representing different and higher forms of human society. And in this respect I believe that something very important has happened in the Soviet Union in the past few years: the criticisms of the Soviet

[13]This is not true in Poland and Hungary, however, whose Communist parties have taken moves toward true power-sharing and pluralism.

system sanctioned by Gorbachev have been so thorough and devastating that there is very little chance of going back to either Stalinism or Brezhnevism in any simple way. Gorbachev has finally permitted people to say what they had privately understood for many years, namely, that the magical incantations of Marxism-Leninism were nonsense, that Soviet socialism was not superior to the West in any respect but was in fact a monumental failure. The conservative opposition in the USSR, consisting both of simple workers afraid of unemployment and inflation and of party officials fearful of losing their jobs and privileges, is outspoken and may be strong enough to force Gorbachev's ouster in the next few years. But what both groups desire is tradition, order, and authority; they manifest no deep commitment to Marxism-Leninism, except insofar as they have invested much of their own lives in it.[14] For authority to be restored in the Soviet Union after Gorbachev's demolition work, it must be on the basis of some new and vigorous ideology which has not yet appeared on the horizon.

IF WE ADMIT for the moment that the fascist and communist challenges to liberalism are dead, are there any other ideological competitors left? Or put another way, are there contradictions in liberal society beyond that of class that are not resolvable? Two possibilities suggest themselves, those of religion and nationalism.

The rise of religious fundamentalism in recent years within the Christian, Jewish, and Muslim traditions has been widely noted. One is inclined to say that the revival of religion in some way attests to a broad unhappiness with the impersonality and spiritual vacuity of liberal consumerist societies. Yet while the emptiness at the core of liberalism is most certainly a defect in the ideology—indeed, a flaw that one does not need the perspective of religion to recognize[15]—it is not at all clear that it is remediable through politics. Modern liberalism itself was historically a consequence of the weakness of religiously-based societies which, failing to agree on the nature of the good life, could not provide even the minimal preconditions of peace and stability. In the contemporary world only Islam has offered a theocratic state as a political alternative to both liberalism and communism. But the doctrine has little appeal for non-Muslims, and it is hard to believe that the movement will take on any universal significance. Other less organized religious impulses have been successfully satisfied within the sphere of personal life that is permitted in liberal societies.

The other major "contradiction" potentially unresolvable by liberalism is the one posed by nationalism and other forms of racial and ethnic consciousness. It is certainly true that a very large degree of conflict since the Battle of Jena has had its roots in nationalism. Two cataclysmic world wars in this century have been spawned by the nationalism of the developed world in various guises, and if those passions have been muted to a certain extent in postwar Europe, they are still extremely powerful in the Third World. Nationalism has been a threat to liberalism historically in Germany, and continues to be one in isolated parts of "post-historical" Europe like Northern Ireland.

But it is not clear that nationalism represents an irreconcilable contradiction in the heart of liberalism. In the first place, nationalism is not one single phenomenon but several, ranging from mild cultural nostalgia to the highly organized and elaborately articulated doctrine of National Socialism. Only systematic nationalisms of the latter sort can qualify as a formal ideology on the level of liberalism or communism. The vast majority

[14] This is particularly true of the leading Soviet conservative, former Second Secretary Yegor Ligachev, who has publicly recognized many of the deep defects of the Brezhnev period.

[15] I am thinking particularly of Rousseau and the Western philosophical tradition that flows from him that was highly critical of Lockean or Hobbesian liberalism, though one could criticize liberalism from the standpoint of classical political philosophy as well.

of the world's nationalist movements do not have a political program beyond the negative desire of independence *from* some other group or people, and do not offer anything like a comprehensive agenda for socio-economic organization. As such, they are compatible with doctrines and ideologies that do offer such agendas. While they may constitute a source of conflict for liberal societies, this conflict does not arise from liberalism itself so much as from the fact that the liberalism in question is incomplete. Certainly a great deal of the world's ethnic and nationalist tension can be explained in terms of peoples who are forced to live in unrepresentative political systems that they have not chosen.

While it is impossible to rule out the sudden appearance of new ideologies or previously unrecognized contradictions in liberal societies, then, the present world seems to confirm that the fundamental principles of socio-political organization have not advanced terribly far since 1806. Many of the wars and revolutions fought since that time have been undertaken in the name of ideologies which claimed to be more advanced than liberalism, but whose pretensions were ultimately unmasked by history. In the meantime, they have helped to spread the universal homogenous state to the point where it could have a significant effect on the overall character of international relations.

IV

WHAT ARE the implications of the end of history for international relations? Clearly, the vast bulk of the Third World remains very much mired in history, and will be a terrain of conflict for many years to come. But let us focus for the time being on the larger and more developed states of the world who after all account for the greater part of world politics. Russia and China are not likely to join the developed nations of the West as liberal societies any time in the foreseeable future, but suppose for a moment that Marxism-Leninism ceases to be a factor driving the foreign policies of these states—a prospect which, if not yet here, the last few years have made a real possibility. How will the overall characteristics of a de-ideologized world differ from those of the one with which we are familiar at such a hypothetical juncture?

The most common answer is—not very much. For there is a very widespread belief among many observers of international relations that underneath the skin of ideology is a hard core of great power national interest that guarantees a fairly high level of competition and conflict between nations. Indeed, according to one academically popular school of international relations theory, conflict inheres in the international system as such, and to understand the prospects for conflict one must look at the shape of the system—for example, whether it is bipolar or multipolar—rather than at the specific character of the nations and regimes that constitute it. This school in effect applies a Hobbesian view of politics to international relations, and assumes that aggression and insecurity are universal characteristics of human societies rather than the product of specific historical circumstances.

Believers in this line of thought take the relations that existed between the participants in the classical nineteenth century European balance of power as a model for what a de-ideologized contemporary world would look like. Charles Krauthammer, for example, recently explained that if as a result of Gorbachev's reforms the USSR is shorn of Marxist-Leninist ideology, its behavior will revert to that of nineteenth century imperial Russia.[16] While he finds this more reassuring than the threat posed by a communist Russia, he implies that there will still be a substantial degree of competition and conflict in the international system, just as there was say between Russia and Britain or Wilhelmine Germany in the last century. This is, of course, a convenient point of view for people who want to admit that something major is chang-

[16]See his article, "Beyond the Cold War," *New Republic,* December 19, 1988.

ing in the Soviet Union, but do not want to accept responsibility for recommending the radical policy redirection implicit in such a view. But is it true?

In fact, the notion that ideology is a superstructure imposed on a substratum of permanent great power interest is a highly questionable proposition. For the way in which any state defines its national interest is not universal but rests on some kind of prior ideological basis, just as we saw that economic behavior is determined by a prior state of consciousness. In this century, states have adopted highly articulated doctrines with explicit foreign policy agendas legitimizing expansionism, like Marxism-Leninism or National Socialism.

THE EXPANSIONIST and competitive behavior of nineteenth-century European states rested on no less ideal a basis; it just so happened that the ideology driving it was less explicit than the doctrines of the twentieth century. For one thing, most "liberal" European societies were illiberal insofar as they believed in the legitimacy of imperialism, that is, the right of one nation to rule over other nations without regard for the wishes of the ruled. The justifications for imperialism varied from nation to nation, from a crude belief in the legitimacy of force, particularly when applied to non-Europeans, to the White Man's Burden and Europe's Christianizing mission, to the desire to give people of color access to the culture of Rabelais and Molière. But whatever the particular ideological basis, every "developed" country believed in the acceptability of higher civilizations ruling lower ones—including, incidentally, the United States with regard to the Philippines. This led to a drive for pure territorial aggrandizement in the latter half of the century and played no small role in causing the Great War.

The radical and deformed outgrowth of nineteenth-century imperialism was German fascism, an ideology which justified Germany's right not only to rule over non-European peoples, but over *all* non-German ones. But in retrospect it seems that Hitler represented a diseased bypath in the general course of European development, and since his fiery defeat, the legitimacy of any kind of territorial aggrandizement has been thoroughly discredited.[17] Since the Second World War, European nationalism has been defanged and shorn of any real relevance to foreign policy, with the consequence that the nineteenth-century model of great power behavior has become a serious anachronism. The most extreme form of nationalism that any Western European state has mustered since 1945 has been Gaullism, whose self-assertion has been confined largely to the realm of nuisance politics and culture. International life for the part of the world that has reached the end of history is far more preoccupied with economics than with politics or strategy.

The developed states of the West do maintain defense establishments and in the postwar period have competed vigorously for influence to meet a worldwide communist threat. This behavior has been driven, however, by an external threat from states that possess overtly expansionist ideologies, and would not exist in their absence. To take the "neo-realist" theory seriously, one would have to believe that "natural" competitive behavior would reassert itself among the OECD states were Russia and China to disappear from the face of the earth. That is, West Germany and France would arm themselves against each other as they did in the 1930s, Australia and New Zealand would send military advisers to block each others' advances in Africa, and the U.S.-Canadian border would become fortified. Such a prospect is, of course, ludicrous: minus Marxist-Leninist ideology, we are far more likely to see the "Common Marketization" of world politics than the disintegration of the EEC into nineteenth-century competitiveness.

[17] It took European colonial powers like France several years after the war to admit the illegitimacy of their empires, but decolonialization was an inevitable consequence of the Allied victory which had been based on the promise of a restoration of democratic freedoms.

Indeed, as our experience in dealing with Europe on matters such as terrorism or Libya prove, they are much further gone than we down the road that denies the legitimacy of the use of force in international politics, even in self-defense.

The automatic assumption that Russia shorn of its expansionist communist ideology should pick up where the czars left off just prior to the Bolshevik Revolution is therefore a curious one. It assumes that the evolution of human consciousness has stood still in the meantime, and that the Soviets, while picking up currently fashionable ideas in the realm of economics, will return to foreign policy views a century out of date in the rest of Europe. This is certainly not what happened to China after it began its reform process. Chinese competitiveness and expansionism on the world scene have virtually disappeared: Beijing no longer sponsors Maoist insurgencies or tries to cultivate influence in distant African countries as it did in the 1960s. This is not to say that there are not troublesome aspects to contemporary Chinese foreign policy, such as the reckless sale of ballistic missile technology in the Middle East; and the PRC continues to manifest traditional great power behavior in its sponsorship of the Khmer Rouge against Vietnam. But the former is explained by commercial motives and the latter is a vestige of earlier ideologically-based rivalries. The new China far more resembles Gaullist France than pre-World War I Germany.

The real question for the future, however, is the degree to which Soviet elites have assimilated the consciousness of the universal homogenous state that is post-Hitler Europe. From their writings and from my own personal contacts with them, there is no question in my mind that the liberal Soviet intelligentsia rallying around Gorbachev has arrived at the end-of-history view in a remarkably short time, due in no small measure to the contacts they have had since the Brezhnev era with the larger European civilization around them. "New political thinking," the general rubric for their views, describes a world dominated by economic concerns, in which there are no ideological grounds for major conflict between nations, and in which, consequently, the use of military force becomes less legitimate. As Foreign Minister Shevardnadze put it in mid-1988:

> The struggle between two opposing systems is no longer a determining tendency of the present-day era. At the modern stage, the ability to build up material wealth at an accelerated rate on the basis of front-ranking science and high-level techniques and technology, and to distribute it fairly, and through joint efforts to restore and protect the resources necessary for mankind's survival acquires decisive importance.[18]

The post-historical consciousness represented by "new thinking" is only one possible future for the Soviet Union, however. There has always been a very strong current of great Russian chauvinism in the Soviet Union, which has found freer expression since the advent of *glasnost*. It may be possible to return to traditional Marxism-Leninism for a while as a simple rallying point for those who want to restore the authority that Gorbachev has dissipated. But as in Poland, Marxism-Leninism is dead as a mobilizing ideology: under its banner people cannot be made to work harder, and its adherents have lost confidence in themselves. Unlike the propagators of traditional Marxism-Leninism, however, ultranationalists in the USSR believe in their Slavophile cause passionately, and one gets the sense that the fascist alternative is not one that has played itself out entirely there.

The Soviet Union, then, is at a fork in the road: it can start down the path that was staked out by Western Europe forty-five years ago, a path that most of Asia has followed, or it can realize its own uniqueness and remain stuck in history. The choice it makes will be highly important for us, given the Soviet

[18] *Vestnik Ministerstva Inostrannikh Del SSSR* no. 15 (August 1988), 27–46. "New thinking" does of course serve a propagandistic purpose in persuading Western audiences of Soviet good intentions. But the fact that it is good propaganda does not mean that its formulators do not take many of its ideas seriously.

Union's size and military strength, for that power will continue to preoccupy us and slow our realization that we have already emerged on the other side of history.

V

THE PASSING of Marxism-Leninism first from China and then from the Soviet Union will mean its death as a living ideology of world historical significance. For while there may be some isolated true believers left in places like Managua, Pyongyang, or Cambridge, Massachusetts, the fact that there is not a single large state in which it is a going concern undermines completely its pretensions to being in the vanguard of human history. And the death of this ideology means the growing "Common Marketization" of international relations, and the diminution of the likelihood of large-scale conflict between states.

This does not by any means imply the end of international conflict *per se.* For the world at that point would be divided between a part that was historical and a part that was post-historical. Conflict between states still in history, and between those states and those at the end of history, would still be possible. There would still be a high and perhaps rising level of ethnic and nationalist violence, since those are impulses incompletely played out, even in parts of the post-historical world. Palestinians and Kurds, Sikhs and Tamils, Irish Catholics and Walloons, Armenians and Azeris, will continue to have their unresolved grievances. This implies that terrorism and wars of national liberation will continue to be an important item on the international agenda. But large-scale conflict must involve large states still caught in the grip of history, and they are what appear to be passing from the scene.

The end of history will be a very sad time. The struggle for recognition, the willingness to risk one's life for a purely abstract goal, the worldwide ideological struggle that called forth daring, courage, imagination, and idealism, will be replaced by economic calculation, the endless solving of technical problems, environmental concerns, and the satisfaction of sophisticated consumer demands. In the post-historical period there will be neither art nor philosophy, just the perpetual caretaking of the museum of human history. I can feel in myself, and see in others around me, a powerful nostalgia for the time when history existed. Such nostalgia, in fact, will continue to fuel competition and conflict even in the post-historical world for some time to come. Even though I recognize its inevitability, I have the most ambivalent feelings for the civilization that has been created in Europe since 1945, with its north Atlantic and Asian offshoots. Perhaps this very prospect of centuries of boredom at the end of history will serve to get history started once again.

The Clash of Civilizations?

Samuel P. Huntington

THE NEXT PATTERN OF CONFLICT

WORLD POLITICS IS entering a new phase, and intellectuals have not hesitated to proliferate visions of what it will be—the end of history, the return of traditional rivalries between nation states, and the decline of the nation state from the conflicting pulls of tribalism and globalism, among others. Each of these visions catches aspects of the emerging reality. Yet they all miss a crucial, indeed a central, aspect of what global politics is likely to be in the coming years.

It is my hypothesis that the fundamental source of conflict in this new world will not be primarily ideological or primarily economic. The great divisions among humankind and the dominating source of conflict will be cultural. Nation states will remain the most powerful actors in world affairs, but the principal conflicts of global politics will occur between nations and groups of different civilizations. The clash of civilizations will dominate global politics. The fault lines between civilizations will be the battle lines of the future.

Conflict between civilizations will be the latest phase in the evolution of conflict in the modern world. For a century and a half after the emergence of the modern international system with the Peace of Westphalia, the conflicts of the Western world were largely among

---

SAMUEL P. HUNTINGTON is the Eaton Professor of the Science of Government and Director of the John M. Olin Institute for Strategic Studies at Harvard University. This article is the product of the Olin Institute's project on "The Changing Security Environment and American National Interests."

princes—emperors, absolute monarchs and constitutional monarchs attempting to expand their bureaucracies, their armies, their mercantilist economic strength and, most important, the territory they ruled. In the process they created nation states, and beginning with the French Revolution the principal lines of conflict were between nations rather than princes. In 1793, as R. R. Palmer put it, "The wars of kings were over; the wars of peoples had begun." This nineteenth-century pattern lasted until the end of World War I. Then, as a result of the Russian Revolution and the reaction against it, the conflict of nations yielded to the conflict of ideologies, first among communism, fascism-Nazism and liberal democracy, and then between communism and liberal democracy. During the Cold War, this latter conflict became embodied in the struggle between the two superpowers, neither of which was a nation state in the classical European sense and each of which defined its identity in terms of its ideology.

These conflicts between princes, nation states and ideologies were primarily conflicts within Western civilization, "Western civil wars," as William Lind has labeled them. This was as true of the Cold War as it was of the world wars and the earlier wars of the seventeenth, eighteenth and nineteenth centuries. With the end of the Cold War, international politics moves out of its Western phase, and its centerpiece becomes the interaction between the West and non-Western civilizations and among non-Western civilizations. In the politics of civilizations, the peoples and governments of non-Western civilizations no longer remain the objects of history as targets of Western colonialism but join the West as movers and shapers of history.

THE NATURE OF CIVILIZATIONS

DURING THE COLD WAR the world was divided into the First, Second and Third Worlds. Those divisions are no longer relevant. It is far more meaningful now to group countries not in terms of their political or economic systems or in terms of their level of economic development but rather in terms of their culture and civilization.

What do we mean when we talk of a civilization? A civilization is a cultural entity. Villages, regions, ethnic groups, nationalities, religious groups, all have distinct cultures at different levels of cultural heterogeneity. The culture of a village in southern Italy may be different from that of a village in northern Italy, but both will share in a common Italian culture that distinguishes them from German villages. European communities, in turn, will share cultural features that distinguish them from Arab or Chinese communities. Arabs, Chinese and Westerners, however, are not part of any broader cultural entity. They constitute civilizations. A civilization is thus the highest cultural grouping of people and the broadest level of cultural identity people have short of that which distinguishes humans from other species. It is defined both by common objective elements, such as language, history, religion, customs, institutions, and by the subjective self-identification of people. People have levels of identity: a resident of Rome may define himself with varying degrees of intensity as a Roman, an Italian, a Catholic, a Christian, a European, a Westerner. The civilization to which he belongs is the broadest level of identification with which he intensely identifies. People can and do redefine their identities and, as a result, the composition and boundaries of civilizations change.

Civilizations may involve a large number of people, as with China ("a civilization pretending to be a state," as Lucian Pye put it), or a very small number of people, such as the Anglophone Caribbean. A civilization may include several nation states, as is the case with Western, Latin American and Arab civilizations, or only one, as is the case with Japanese civilization. Civilizations obviously blend and overlap, and may include subcivilizations. Western civilization has two major variants, European and North American, and Islam has its Arab, Turkic and Malay subdivisions. Civilizations are nonetheless meaningful entities, and while the lines between them are seldom sharp, they are real. Civilizations are dynamic; they rise and fall; they divide and merge. And, as any student of history knows, civilizations disappear and are buried in the sands of time.

Westerners tend to think of nation states as the principal actors in global affairs. They have been that, however, for only a few centuries. The broader reaches of human history have been the history of civilizations. In *A Study of History*, Arnold Toynbee identified 21 major civilizations; only six of them exist in the contemporary world.

WHY CIVILIZATIONS WILL CLASH

CIVILIZATION IDENTITY will be increasingly important in the future, and the world will be shaped in large measure by the interactions among seven or eight major civilizations. These include Western, Confucian, Japanese, Islamic, Hindu, Slavic-Orthodox, Latin American and possibly African civilization. The most important conflicts of the future will occur along the cultural fault lines separating these civilizations from one another.

Why will this be the case?

First, differences among civilizations are not only real; they are basic. Civilizations are differentiated from each other by history, language, culture, tradition and, most important, religion. The people of different civilizations have different views on the relations between God and man, the individual and the group, the citizen and the state, parents and children, husband and wife, as well as differing views of the relative importance of rights and responsibilities, liberty and authority, equality and hierarchy. These differences are the product of centuries. They will not soon disappear. They are far more fundamental than differences among political ideologies and political regimes. Differences do not necessarily mean conflict, and conflict does not necessarily mean violence. Over the centuries, however, differences among civilizations have generated the most prolonged and the most violent conflicts.

The conflicts of the future will occur along the cultural fault lines separating civilizations.

Second, the world is becoming a smaller place. The interactions between peoples of different civilizations are increasing; these increasing interactions intensify civilization consciousness and awareness of differences between civilizations and commonalities within civilizations. North African immigration to France generates hostility among Frenchmen and at the same time increased receptivity to immigration by "good" European Catholic Poles. Americans react far more negatively to Japanese investment than to larger investments from Canada and European countries. Similarly, as Donald Horowitz has pointed out, "An Ibo may be ... an Owerri Ibo or an Onitsha Ibo in what was the Eastern region of Nigeria. In Lagos, he is simply an Ibo. In London, he is a Nigerian. In New York, he is an African." The interactions among peoples of different civilizations enhance the civilization-consciousness of people that, in turn, invigorates differences and animosities stretching or thought to stretch back deep into history.

Third, the processes of economic modernization and social change throughout the world are separating people from longstanding local identities. They also weaken the nation state as a source of identity. In much of the world religion has moved in to fill this gap, often in the form of movements that are labeled "fundamentalist." Such movements are found in Western Christianity, Judaism, Buddhism and Hinduism, as well as in Islam. In most countries and most religions the people active in fundamentalist movements are young, college-educated, middle-class technicians, professionals and business persons. The "unsecularization of the world," George Weigel has remarked, "is one of the dominant social facts of life in the late twentieth century." The revival of religion, "la revanche de Dieu," as Gilles Kepel labeled it, provides a basis for identity and commitment that transcends national boundaries and unites civilizations.

Fourth, the growth of civilization-consciousness is enhanced by the dual role of the West. On the one hand, the West is at a peak of power. At the same time, however, and perhaps as a result, a return to the roots phenomenon is occurring among non-Western civilizations. Increasingly one hears references to trends toward a turning inward and "Asianization" in Japan, the end of the Nehru legacy and the "Hinduization" of India, the failure of Western ideas of socialism and nationalism and hence "re-Islamization" of the Middle East, and now a debate over Westernization versus Russianization in Boris Yeltsin's country. A West at the peak of its power confronts non-Wests that increasingly have the desire, the will and the resources to shape the world in non-Western ways.

In the past, the elites of non-Western societies were usually the people who were most involved with the West, had been educated at Oxford, the Sorbonne or Sandhurst, and had absorbed Western attitudes and values. At the same time, the populace in non-Western countries often remained deeply imbued with the indigenous culture. Now, however, these relationships are being reversed. A de-Westernization and indigenization of elites is occurring in many non-Western countries at the same time that Western, usually American, cultures, styles and habits become more popular among the mass of the people.

Fifth, cultural characteristics and differences are less mutable and hence less easily compromised and resolved than political and economic ones. In the former Soviet Union, communists can become democrats, the rich can become poor and the poor rich, but Russians cannot become Estonians and Azeris cannot become Armenians. In class and ideological conflicts, the key question was "Which side are you on?" and people could and did choose sides and change sides. In conflicts between civilizations, the question is "What are you?" That is a given that cannot be changed. And as we know, from Bosnia to the Caucasus to the Sudan, the wrong answer to that question can mean a bullet in the head. Even more than ethnicity, religion discriminates sharply and exclusively among people. A person can be half-French and half-Arab and simultaneously even a citizen of two countries. It is more difficult to be half-Catholic and half-Muslim.

Finally, economic regionalism is increasing. The proportions of total trade that were intraregional rose between 1980 and 1989 from 51 percent to 59 percent in Europe, 33 percent to 37 percent in East Asia, and 32 percent to 36 percent in North America. The importance of regional economic blocs is likely to continue to increase in the future. On the one hand, successful economic regionalism will reinforce civilization-consciousness. On the other hand, economic regionalism may succeed only when it is rooted in a common civilization. The European Community rests on the shared foundation of European culture and Western Christianity. The success of the North American Free Trade Area depends on the convergence now underway of Mexican, Canadian and American cultures. Japan, in contrast, faces difficulties in creating a comparable economic entity in East Asia because Japan is a society and civilization unique to itself. However strong the trade and investment links Japan may develop with other East Asian countries, its cultural differences with those countries inhibit and perhaps preclude its promoting regional economic integration like that in Europe and North America.

Common culture, in contrast, is clearly facilitating the rapid expansion of the economic relations between the People's Republic of China and Hong Kong, Taiwan, Singapore and the overseas Chinese communities in other Asian countries. With the Cold War over, cultural commonalities increasingly overcome ideological differences, and mainland China and Taiwan move closer together. If cultural commonality is a prerequisite for economic integration, the principal East Asian economic bloc of the future is likely to be centered on China. This bloc is, in fact, already coming into existence. As Murray Weidenbaum has observed,

> Despite the current Japanese dominance of the region, the Chinese-based economy of Asia is rapidly emerging as a new epicenter for industry, commerce and finance. This strategic area contains substantial amounts of technology and manufacturing capability (Taiwan), outstanding entrepreneurial, marketing and services acumen (Hong Kong), a fine communications network (Singapore), a tremendous pool of financial capital (all three), and very large endowments of land, resources and labor (mainland China).... From Guangzhou to Singapore, from Kuala Lumpur to Manila, this influential network—often based on extensions of the traditional clans—has been described as the backbone of the East Asian economy.[1]

Culture and religion also form the basis of the Economic Cooperation Organization, which brings together ten non-Arab Muslim countries: Iran, Pakistan, Turkey, Azerbaijan, Kazakhstan, Kyrgyzstan, Turkmenistan, Tadjikistan, Uzbekistan and Afghanistan. One impetus to the revival and expansion of this organization, founded originally in the 1960s by Turkey, Pakistan and Iran, is the realization by the leaders of several of these countries that they had no chance of admission to the European Community. Similarly, Caricom, the Central American Common Market and Mercosur rest

[1]Murray Weidenbaum, *Greater China: The Next Economic Superpower?*, St. Louis: Washington University Center for the Study of American Business, Contemporary Issues, Series 57, February 1993, pp. 2-3.

on common cultural foundations. Efforts to build a broader Caribbean-Central American economic entity bridging the Anglo-Latin divide, however, have to date failed.

As people define their identity in ethnic and religious terms, they are likely to see an "us" versus "them" relation existing between themselves and people of different ethnicity or religion. The end of ideologically defined states in Eastern Europe and the former Soviet Union permits traditional ethnic identities and animosities to come to the fore. Differences in culture and religion create differences over policy issues, ranging from human rights to immigration to trade and commerce to the environment. Geographical propinquity gives rise to conflicting territorial claims from Bosnia to Mindanao. Most important, the efforts of the West to promote its values of democracy and liberalism as universal values, to maintain its military predominance and to advance its economic interests engender countering responses from other civilizations. Decreasingly able to mobilize support and form coalitions on the basis of ideology, governments and groups will increasingly attempt to mobilize support by appealing to common religion and civilization identity.

The clash of civilizations thus occurs at two levels. At the micro-level, adjacent groups along the fault lines between civilizations struggle, often violently, over the control of territory and each other. At the macro-level, states from different civilizations compete for relative military and economic power, struggle over the control of international institutions and third parties, and competitively promote their particular political and religious values.

THE FAULT LINES BETWEEN CIVILIZATIONS

THE FAULT LINES between civilizations are replacing the political and ideological boundaries of the Cold War as the flash points for crisis and bloodshed. The Cold War began when the Iron Curtain divided Europe politically and ideologically. The Cold War ended with the end of the Iron Curtain. As the ideological division of Europe has disappeared, the cultural division of Europe between Western Christianity, on the one hand, and Orthodox Christianity

Source: W. Wallace, THE TRANSFORMATION OF WESTERN EUROPE. London: Pinter, 1990. Map by Ib Ohlsson for FOREIGN AFFAIRS.

and Islam, on the other, has reemerged. The most significant dividing line in Europe, as William Wallace has suggested, may well be the eastern boundary of Western Christianity in the year 1500. This line runs along what are now the boundaries between Finland and Russia and between the Baltic states and Russia, cuts through Belarus and Ukraine separating the more Catholic western Ukraine from Orthodox eastern Ukraine, swings westward separating Transylvania from the rest of Romania, and then goes through Yugoslavia almost exactly along the line now separating Croatia and Slovenia from the rest of Yugoslavia. In the Balkans this line, of course, coincides with the historic boundary between the Hapsburg and Ottoman empires. The peoples to the north and west of this line are Protestant or Catholic; they shared the common experiences of European history—feudalism, the Renaissance, the Reformation, the Enlightenment, the French Revolution, the Industrial Revolution; they are generally economically better off than the peoples to the east; and they may now look forward to increasing involvement in a common European economy and to the consolidation of democratic political systems. The peoples to the east and south of this line are Orthodox or Muslim; they historically belonged to the Ottoman or Tsarist empires and were only lightly touched by the shaping events in the rest of Europe; they are generally less advanced economically; they seem much less likely to develop stable democratic political systems. The Velvet Curtain of culture has replaced the Iron Curtain of ideology as the most significant dividing line in Europe. As the events in Yugoslavia show, it is not only a line of difference; it is also at times a line of bloody conflict.

Conflict along the fault line between Western and Islamic civilizations has been going on for 1,300 years. After the founding of Islam, the Arab and Moorish surge west and north only ended at Tours in 732. From the eleventh to the thirteenth century the Crusaders attempted with temporary success to bring Christianity and Christian rule to the Holy Land. From the fourteenth to the seventeenth century, the Ottoman Turks reversed the balance, extended their sway over the Middle East and the Balkans, captured Constantinople, and twice laid siege to Vienna. In the nineteenth and early twentieth centuries as Ottoman power declined Britain, France, and Italy established Western control over most of North Africa and the Middle East.

After World War II, the West, in turn, began to retreat; the colonial empires disappeared; first Arab nationalism and then Islamic fundamentalism manifested themselves; the West became heavily dependent on the Persian Gulf countries for its energy; the oil-rich Muslim countries became money-rich and, when they wished to, weapons-rich. Several wars occurred between Arabs and Israel (created by the West). France fought a bloody and ruthless war in Algeria for most of the 1950s; British and French forces invaded Egypt in 1956; American forces went into Lebanon in 1958; subsequently American forces returned to Lebanon, attacked Libya, and engaged in various military encounters with Iran; Arab and Islamic terrorists, supported by at least three Middle Eastern governments, employed the weapon of the weak and bombed Western planes and installations and seized Western hostages. This warfare between Arabs and the West culminated in 1990, when the United States sent a massive army to the Persian Gulf to defend some Arab countries against aggression by another. In its aftermath NATO planning is increasingly directed to potential threats and instability along its "southern tier."

This centuries-old military interaction between the West and

Islam is unlikely to decline. It could become more virulent. The Gulf War left some Arabs feeling proud that Saddam Hussein had attacked Israel and stood up to the West. It also left many feeling humiliated and resentful of the West's military presence in the Persian Gulf, the West's overwhelming military dominance, and their apparent inability to shape their own destiny. Many Arab countries, in addition to the oil exporters, are reaching levels of economic and social development where autocratic forms of government become inappropriate and efforts to introduce democracy become stronger. Some openings in Arab political systems have already occurred. The principal beneficiaries of these openings have been Islamist movements. In the Arab world, in short, Western democracy strengthens anti-Western political forces. This may be a passing phenomenon, but it surely complicates relations between Islamic countries and the West.

Those relations are also complicated by demography. The spectacular population growth in Arab countries, particularly in North Africa, has led to increased migration to Western Europe. The movement within Western Europe toward minimizing internal boundaries has sharpened political sensitivities with respect to this development. In Italy, France and Germany, racism is increasingly open, and political reactions and violence against Arab and Turkish migrants have become more intense and more widespread since 1990.

On both sides the interaction between Islam and the West is seen as a clash of civilizations. The West's "next confrontation," observes M. J. Akbar, an Indian Muslim author, "is definitely going to come from the Muslim world. It is in the sweep of the Islamic nations from the Maghreb to Pakistan that the struggle for a new world order will begin." Bernard Lewis comes to a similar conclusion:

> We are facing a mood and a movement far transcending the level of issues and policies and the governments that pursue them. This is no less than a clash of civilizations—the perhaps irrational but surely historic reaction of an ancient rival against our Judeo-Christian heritage, our secular present, and the worldwide expansion of both.[2]

---

[2]Bernard Lewis, "The Roots of Muslim Rage," *The Atlantic Monthly*, vol. 266, September 1990, p. 60; *Time*, June 15, 1992, pp. 24–28.

Historically, the other great antagonistic interaction of Arab Islamic civilization has been with the pagan, animist, and now increasingly Christian black peoples to the south. In the past, this antagonism was epitomized in the image of Arab slave dealers and black slaves. It has been reflected in the on-going civil war in the Sudan between Arabs and blacks, the fighting in Chad between Libyan-supported insurgents and the government, the tensions between Orthodox Christians and Muslims in the Horn of Africa, and the political conflicts, recurring riots and communal violence between Muslims and Christians in Nigeria. The modernization of Africa and the spread of Christianity are likely to enhance the probability of violence along this fault line. Symptomatic of the intensification of this conflict was the Pope John Paul II's speech in Khartoum in February 1993 attacking the actions of the Sudan's Islamist government against the Christian minority there.

On the northern border of Islam, conflict has increasingly erupted between Orthodox and Muslim peoples, including the carnage of Bosnia and Sarajevo, the simmering violence between Serb and Albanian, the tenuous relations between Bulgarians and their Turkish minority, the violence between Ossetians and Ingush, the unremitting slaughter of each other by Armenians and Azeris, the tense relations between Russians and Muslims in Central Asia, and the deployment of Russian troops to protect Russian interests in the Caucasus and Central Asia. Religion reinforces the revival of ethnic identities and restimulates Russian fears about the security of their southern borders. This concern is well captured by Archie Roosevelt:

> Much of Russian history concerns the struggle between the Slavs and the Turkic peoples on their borders, which dates back to the foundation of the Russian state more than a thousand years ago. In the Slavs' millennium-long confrontation with their eastern neighbors lies the key to an understanding not only of Russian history, but Russian character. To understand Russian realities today one has to have a concept of the great Turkic ethnic group that has preoccupied Russians through the centuries.[3]

The conflict of civilizations is deeply rooted elsewhere in Asia. The historic clash between Muslim and Hindu in the subcontinent

---

[3]Archie Roosevelt, *For Lust of Knowing*, Boston: Little, Brown, 1988, pp. 332-333.

manifests itself now not only in the rivalry between Pakistan and India but also in intensifying religious strife within India between increasingly militant Hindu groups and India's substantial Muslim minority. The destruction of the Ayodhya mosque in December 1992 brought to the fore the issue of whether India will remain a secular democratic state or become a Hindu one. In East Asia, China has outstanding territorial disputes with most of its neighbors. It has pursued a ruthless policy toward the Buddhist people of Tibet, and it is pursuing an increasingly ruthless policy toward its Turkic-Muslim minority. With the Cold War over, the underlying differences between China and the United States have reasserted themselves in areas such as human rights, trade and weapons proliferation. These differences are unlikely to moderate. A "new cold war," Deng Xaioping reportedly asserted in 1991, is under way between China and America.

The crescent-shaped Islamic bloc, from the bulge of Africa to central Asia, has bloody borders.

The same phrase has been applied to the increasingly difficult relations between Japan and the United States. Here cultural difference exacerbates economic conflict. People on each side allege racism on the other, but at least on the American side the antipathies are not racial but cultural. The basic values, attitudes, behavioral patterns of the two societies could hardly be more different. The economic issues between the United States and Europe are no less serious than those between the United States and Japan, but they do not have the same political salience and emotional intensity because the differences between American culture and European culture are so much less than those between American civilization and Japanese civilization.

The interactions between civilizations vary greatly in the extent to which they are likely to be characterized by violence. Economic competition clearly predominates between the American and European subcivilizations of the West and between both of them and Japan. On the Eurasian continent, however, the proliferation of ethnic conflict, epitomized at the extreme in "ethnic cleansing," has not been totally random. It has been most frequent and most violent between groups belonging to different civilizations. In Eurasia the great historic fault lines between civilizations are once more aflame. This is particularly true along the boundaries of the crescent-shaped Islamic bloc of nations from the bulge of Africa to central Asia. Violence also occurs between Muslims, on the one hand, and Orthodox Serbs in the Balkans, Jews in Israel, Hindus in India, Buddhists in Burma and Catholics in the Philippines. Islam has bloody borders.

CIVILIZATION RALLYING: THE KIN-COUNTRY SYNDROME

GROUPS OR STATES belonging to one civilization that become involved in war with people from a different civilization naturally try to rally support from other members of their own civilization. As the post-Cold War world evolves, civilization commonality, what H. D. S. Greenway has termed the "kin-country" syndrome, is replacing political ideology and traditional balance of power considerations as the principal basis for cooperation and coalitions. It can be seen gradually emerging in the post-Cold War conflicts in the Persian Gulf, the Caucasus and Bosnia. None of these was a full-scale war between civilizations, but each involved some elements of civilizational rallying, which seemed to become more important as the conflict continued and which may provide a foretaste of the future.

First, in the Gulf War one Arab state invaded another and then fought a coalition of Arab, Western and other states. While only a few Muslim governments overtly supported Saddam Hussein, many Arab elites privately cheered him on, and he was highly popular among large sections of the Arab publics. Islamic fundamentalist movements universally supported Iraq rather than the Western-backed governments of Kuwait and Saudi Arabia. Forswearing Arab nationalism, Saddam Hussein explicitly invoked an Islamic appeal. He and his supporters attempted to define the war as a war between civilizations. "It is not the world against Iraq," as Safar Al-Hawali, dean of Islamic Studies at the Umm Al-Qura University in Mecca, put it in a widely circulated tape. "It is the West against Islam." Ignoring the rivalry between Iran and Iraq, the chief Iranian religious leader, Ayatollah Ali Khamenei, called for a holy war against the West: "The struggle against American aggression, greed, plans and policies will be counted as a jihad, and anybody who is killed on that path is a martyr." "This is a war," King Hussein of Jordan argued, "against all Arabs and all Muslims and not against Iraq alone."

The rallying of substantial sections of Arab elites and publics behind Saddam Hussein caused those Arab governments in the anti-Iraq coalition to moderate their activities and temper their public statements. Arab governments opposed or distanced themselves from subsequent Western efforts to apply pressure on Iraq, including enforcement of a no-fly zone in the summer of 1992 and the bombing of Iraq in January 1993. The Western-Soviet-Turkish-Arab anti-Iraq coalition of 1990 had by 1993 become a coalition of almost only the West and Kuwait against Iraq.

Muslims contrasted Western actions against Iraq with the West's failure to protect Bosnians against Serbs and to impose sanctions on Israel for violating U.N. resolutions. The West, they alleged, was using a double standard. A world of clashing civilizations, however, is inevitably a world of double standards: people apply one standard to their kin-countries and a different standard to others.

Second, the kin-country syndrome also appeared in conflicts in the former Soviet Union. Armenian military successes in 1992 and 1993 stimulated Turkey to become increasingly supportive of its religious, ethnic and linguistic brethren in Azerbaijan. "We have a Turkish nation feeling the same sentiments as the Azerbaijanis," said one Turkish official in 1992. "We are under pressure. Our newspapers are full of the photos of atrocities and are asking us if we are still serious about pursuing our neutral policy. Maybe we should show Armenia that there's a big Turkey in the region." President Turgut Özal agreed, remarking that Turkey should at least "scare the Armenians a little bit." Turkey, Özal threatened again in 1993, would "show its fangs." Turkish Air Force jets flew reconnaissance flights along the Armenian border; Turkey suspended food shipments and air flights to Armenia; and Turkey and Iran announced they would not accept dismemberment of Azerbaijan. In the last years of its existence, the Soviet government supported Azerbaijan because its government was dominated by former communists. With the end of the Soviet Union, however, political considerations gave way to religious ones. Russian troops fought on the side of the Armenians, and Azerbaijan accused the "Russian government of turning 180 degrees" toward support for Christian Armenia.

Third, with respect to the fighting in the former Yugoslavia, Western publics manifested sympathy and support for the Bosnian Muslims and the horrors they suffered at the hands of the Serbs. Relatively little concern was expressed, however, over Croatian attacks on Muslims and participation in the dismemberment of Bosnia-Herzegovina. In the early stages of the Yugoslav breakup, Germany, in an unusual display of diplomatic initiative and muscle, induced the other 11 members of the European Community to follow its lead in recognizing Slovenia and Croatia. As a result of the pope's determination to provide strong backing to the two Catholic countries, the Vatican extended recognition even before the Community did. The United States followed the European lead. Thus the leading actors in Western civilization rallied behind their coreligionists. Subsequently Croatia was reported to be receiving substantial quantities of arms from Central European and other Western countries. Boris Yeltsin's government, on the other hand, attempted to pursue a middle course that would be sympathetic to the Orthodox Serbs but not alienate Russia from the West. Russian conservative and nationalist groups, however, including many legislators, attacked the government for not being more forthcoming in its support for the Serbs. By early 1993 several hundred Russians apparently were serving with the Serbian forces, and reports circulated of Russian arms being supplied to Serbia.

Islamic governments and groups, on the other hand, castigated the West for not coming to the defense of the Bosnians. Iranian leaders urged Muslims from all countries to provide help to Bosnia; in violation of the U.N. arms embargo, Iran supplied weapons and men for the Bosnians; Iranian-supported Lebanese groups sent guerrillas to train and organize the Bosnian forces. In 1993 up to 4,000 Muslims from over two dozen Islamic countries were reported to be fighting in Bosnia. The governments of Saudi Arabia and other countries felt under increasing pressure from fundamentalist groups in their own societies to provide more vigorous support for the Bosnians. By the end of 1992, Saudi Arabia had reportedly supplied substantial funding for weapons and supplies for the Bosnians, which significantly increased their military capabilities vis-à-vis the Serbs.

In the 1930s the Spanish Civil War provoked intervention from countries that politically were fascist, communist and democratic. In the 1990s the Yugoslav conflict is provoking intervention from countries that are Muslim, Orthodox and Western Christian. The parallel has not gone unnoticed. "The war in Bosnia-Herzegovina has become the emotional equivalent of the fight against fascism in the Spanish Civil War," one Saudi editor observed. "Those who died there are regarded as martyrs who tried to save their fellow Muslims."

Conflicts and violence will also occur between states and groups within the same civilization. Such conflicts, however, are likely to be less intense and less likely to expand than conflicts between civilizations. Common membership in a civilization reduces the probability of violence in situations where it might otherwise occur. In 1991 and 1992 many people were alarmed by the possibility of violent conflict between Russia and Ukraine over territory, particularly Crimea, the Black Sea fleet, nuclear weapons and economic issues. If civilization is what counts, however, the likelihood of violence between Ukrainians and Russians should be low. They are two Slavic, primarily Orthodox peoples who have had close relationships with each other for centuries. As of early 1993, despite all the reasons for conflict, the leaders of the two countries were effectively negotiating and defusing the issues between the two countries. While there has been serious fighting between Muslims and Christians elsewhere in the former Soviet Union and much tension and some fighting between Western and Orthodox Christians in the Baltic states, there has been virtually no violence between Russians and Ukrainians.

Civilization rallying to date has been limited, but it has been growing, and it clearly has the potential to spread much further. As the conflicts in the Persian Gulf, the Caucasus and Bosnia continued, the positions of nations and the cleavages between them increasingly were along civilizational lines. Populist politicians, religious leaders and the media have found it a potent means of arousing mass support and of pressuring hesitant governments. In the coming years, the local conflicts most likely to escalate into major wars will be those, as in Bosnia and the Caucasus, along the fault lines between civilizations. The next world war, if there is one, will be a war between civilizations.

THE WEST VERSUS THE REST

THE WEST IS NOW at an extraordinary peak of power in relation to other civilizations. Its superpower opponent has disappeared from the map. Military conflict among Western states is unthinkable, and Western military power is unrivaled. Apart from Japan, the West faces no economic challenge. It dominates international political and security institutions and with Japan international economic institutions. Global political and security issues are effectively settled by a directorate of the United States, Britain and France, world economic issues by a directorate of the United States, Germany and Japan, all of which maintain extraordinarily close relations with each other to the exclusion of lesser and largely non-Western countries. Decisions made at the U.N. Security Council or in the International Monetary Fund that reflect the interests of the West are presented to the world as reflecting the desires of the world community. The very phrase "the world community" has become the euphemistic collective noun (replacing "the Free World") to give global legitimacy to actions reflecting the interests of the United States and other Western powers.[4] Through the IMF and other international economic institutions, the West promotes its economic interests and imposes on other nations the economic policies it thinks appropriate. In any poll of non-Western peoples, the IMF undoubtedly would win the support of finance ministers and a few others, but get an overwhelmingly unfavorable rating from just about everyone else, who would agree

[4]Almost invariably Western leaders claim they are acting on behalf of "the world community." One minor lapse occurred during the run-up to the Gulf War. In an interview on "Good Morning America," Dec. 21, 1990, British Prime Minister John Major referred to the actions "the West" was taking against Saddam Hussein. He quickly corrected himself and subsequently referred to "the world community." He was, however, right when he erred.

with Georgy Arbatov's characterization of IMF officials as "neo-Bolsheviks who love expropriating other people's money, imposing undemocratic and alien rules of economic and political conduct and stifling economic freedom."

Western domination of the U.N. Security Council and its decisions, tempered only by occasional abstention by China, produced U.N. legitimation of the West's use of force to drive Iraq out of Kuwait and its elimination of Iraq's sophisticated weapons and capacity to produce such weapons. It also produced the quite unprecedented action by the United States, Britain and France in getting the Security Council to demand that Libya hand over the Pan Am 103 bombing suspects and then to impose sanctions when Libya refused. After defeating the largest Arab army, the West did not hesitate to throw its weight around in the Arab world. The West in effect is using international institutions, military power and economic resources to run the world in ways that will maintain Western predominance, protect Western interests and promote Western political and economic values.

The very phrase "world community" has become a euphemism to give legitimacy to the actions of the West.

That at least is the way in which non-Westerners see the new world, and there is a significant element of truth in their view. Differences in power and struggles for military, economic and institutional power are thus one source of conflict between the West and other civilizations. Differences in culture, that is basic values and beliefs, are a second source of conflict. V. S. Naipaul has argued that Western civilization is the "universal civilization" that "fits all men." At a superficial level much of Western culture has indeed permeated the rest of the world. At a more basic level, however, Western concepts differ fundamentally from those prevalent in other civilizations. Western ideas of individualism, liberalism, constitutionalism, human rights, equality, liberty, the rule of law, democracy, free markets, the separation of church and state, often have little resonance in Islamic, Confucian, Japanese, Hindu, Buddhist or Orthodox cultures. Western efforts to propagate such ideas produce instead a reaction against "human rights imperialism" and a reaffirmation of indigenous values, as can be seen in the support for religious fundamentalism by the younger generation in non-Western cultures. The very notion that there could be a "universal civilization" is a Western idea, directly at odds with the particularism of most Asian societies and their emphasis on what distinguishes one people from another. Indeed, the author of a review of 100 comparative studies of values in different societies concluded that "the values that are most important in the West are least important worldwide."[5] In the political realm, of course, these differences are most manifest in the efforts of the United States and other Western powers to induce other peoples to adopt Western ideas concerning democracy and human rights. Modern democratic government originated in the West. When it has developed in non-Western societies it has usually been the product of Western colonialism or imposition.

The central axis of world politics in the future is likely to be, in Kishore Mahbubani's phrase, the conflict between "the West and the Rest" and the responses of non-Western civilizations to Western power and values.[6] Those responses generally take one or a combination of three forms. At one extreme, non-Western states can, like Burma and North Korea, attempt to pursue a course of isolation, to insulate their societies from penetration or "corruption" by the West, and, in effect, to opt out of participation in the Western-dominated global community. The costs of this course, however, are high, and few states have pursued it exclusively. A second alternative, the equivalent of "band-wagoning" in international relations theory, is to attempt to join the West and accept its values and institutions. The third alternative is to attempt to "balance" the West by developing economic and military power and cooperating with other non-Western societies against the West, while preserving indigenous values and institutions; in short, to modernize but not to Westernize.

---

[5]Harry C. Triandis, *The New York Times*, Dec. 25, 1990, p. 41, and "Cross-Cultural Studies of Individualism and Collectivism," Nebraska Symposium on Motivation, vol. 37, 1989, pp. 41-133.

[6]Kishore Mahbubani, "The West and the Rest," *The National Interest*, Summer 1992, pp. 3-13.

THE TORN COUNTRIES

IN THE FUTURE, as people differentiate themselves by civilization, countries with large numbers of peoples of different civilizations, such as the Soviet Union and Yugoslavia, are candidates for dismemberment. Some other countries have a fair degree of cultural homogeneity but are divided over whether their society belongs to one civilization or another. These are torn countries. Their leaders typically wish to pursue a bandwagoning strategy and to make their countries members of the West, but the history, culture and traditions of their countries are non-Western. The most obvious and prototypical torn country is Turkey. The late twentieth-century leaders of Turkey have followed in the Attatürk tradition and defined Turkey as a modern, secular, Western nation state. They allied Turkey with the West in NATO and in the Gulf War; they applied for membership in the European Community. At the same time, however, elements in Turkish society have supported an Islamic revival and have argued that Turkey is basically a Middle Eastern Muslim society. In addition, while the elite of Turkey has defined Turkey as a Western society, the elite of the West refuses to accept Turkey as such. Turkey will not become a member of the European Community, and the real reason, as President Özal said, "is that we are Muslim and they are Christian and they don't say that." Having rejected Mecca, and then being rejected by Brussels, where does Turkey look? Tashkent may be the answer. The end of the Soviet Union gives Turkey the opportunity to become the leader of a revived Turkic civilization involving seven countries from the borders of Greece to those of China. Encouraged by the West, Turkey is making strenuous efforts to carve out this new identity for itself.

During the past decade Mexico has assumed a position somewhat similar to that of Turkey. Just as Turkey abandoned its historic opposition to Europe and attempted to join Europe, Mexico has stopped defining itself by its opposition to the United States and is instead attempting to imitate the United States and to join it in the North American Free Trade Area. Mexican leaders are engaged in the great task of redefining Mexican identity and have introduced fundamental economic reforms that eventually will lead to fundamental political change. In 1991 a top adviser to President Carlos Salinas de Gortari described at length to me all the changes the Salinas government was making. When he finished, I remarked: "That's most impressive. It seems to me that basically you want to change Mexico from a Latin American country into a North American country." He looked at me with surprise and exclaimed: "Exactly! That's precisely what we are trying to do, but of course we could never say so publicly." As his remark indicates, in Mexico as in Turkey, significant elements in society resist the redefinition of their country's identity. In Turkey, European-oriented leaders have to make gestures to Islam (Özal's pilgrimage to Mecca); so also Mexico's North American-oriented leaders have to make gestures to those who hold Mexico to be a Latin American country (Salinas' Ibero-American Guadalajara summit).

Historically Turkey has been the most profoundly torn country. For the United States, Mexico is the most immediate torn country. Globally the most important torn country is Russia. The question of whether Russia is part of the West or the leader of a distinct Slavic-Orthodox civilization has been a recurring one in Russian history. That issue was obscured by the communist victory in Russia, which imported a Western ideology, adapted it to Russian conditions and then challenged the West in the name of that ideology. The dominance of communism shut off the historic debate over Westernization versus Russification. With communism discredited Russians once again face that question.

President Yeltsin is adopting Western principles and goals and seeking to make Russia a "normal" country and a part of the West. Yet both the Russian elite and the Russian public are divided on this issue. Among the more moderate dissenters, Sergei Stankevich argues that Russia should reject the "Atlanticist" course, which would lead it "to become European, to become a part of the world economy in rapid and organized fashion, to become the eighth member of the Seven, and to put particular emphasis on Germany and the United States as the two dominant members of the Atlantic alliance." While also rejecting an exclusively Eurasian policy, Stankevich nonetheless argues that Russia should give priority to the protection of Russians in other countries, emphasize its Turkic and Muslim connections, and promote "an appreciable redistribution of our resources, our options, our ties, and our interests in favor of Asia, of the eastern direction." People of this persuasion criticize Yeltsin for subordinating Russia's interests to those of the West, for reducing Russian military strength, for failing to support traditional friends such as Serbia, and for pushing economic and political reform in ways injurious to the Russian people. Indicative of this trend is the new popularity of the ideas of Petr Savitsky, who in the 1920s argued that Russia was a unique Eurasian civilization.[7] More extreme dissidents voice much more blatantly nationalist, anti-Western and anti-Semitic views, and urge Russia to redevelop its military strength and to establish closer ties with China and Muslim countries. The people of Russia are as divided as the elite. An opinion survey in European Russia in the spring of 1992 revealed that 40 percent of the public had positive attitudes toward the West and 36 percent had negative attitudes. As it has been for much of its history, Russia in the early 1990s is truly a torn country.

To redefine its civilization identity, a torn country must meet three requirements. First, its political and economic elite has to be generally supportive of and enthusiastic about this move. Second, its public has to be willing to acquiesce in the redefinition. Third, the dominant groups in the recipient civilization have to be willing to embrace the convert. All three requirements in large part exist with respect to Mexico. The first two in large part exist with respect to Turkey. It is not clear that any of them exist with respect to Russia's joining the West. The conflict between liberal democracy and Marxism-Leninism was between ideologies which, despite their major differences, ostensibly shared ultimate goals of freedom, equality and prosperity. A traditional, authoritarian, nationalist Russia could have quite different goals. A Western democrat could carry on an intellectual debate with a Soviet Marxist. It would be virtually

[7]Sergei Stankevich, "Russia in Search of Itself," *The National Interest*, Summer 1992, pp. 47-51; Daniel Schneider, "A Russian Movement Rejects Western Tilt," *Christian Science Monitor*, Feb. 5, 1993, pp. 5-7.

impossible for him to do that with a Russian traditionalist. If, as the Russians stop behaving like Marxists, they reject liberal democracy and begin behaving like Russians but not like Westerners, the relations between Russia and the West could again become distant and conflictual.[8]

THE CONFUCIAN-ISLAMIC CONNECTION

THE OBSTACLES TO non-Western countries joining the West vary considerably. They are least for Latin American and East European countries. They are greater for the Orthodox countries of the former Soviet Union. They are still greater for Muslim, Confucian, Hindu and Buddhist societies. Japan has established a unique position for itself as an associate member of the West: it is in the West in some respects but clearly not of the West in important dimensions. Those countries that for reason of culture and power do not wish to, or cannot, join the West compete with the West by developing their own economic, military and political power. They do this by promoting their internal development and by cooperating with other non-Western countries. The most prominent form of this cooperation is the Confucian-Islamic connection that has emerged to challenge Western interests, values and power.

Almost without exception, Western countries are reducing their military power; under Yeltsin's leadership so also is Russia. China, North Korea and several Middle Eastern states, however, are significantly expanding their military capabilities. They are doing this by the import of arms from Western and non-Western sources and by the development of indigenous arms industries. One result is the emergence of what Charles Krauthammer has called "Weapon

---

[8]Owen Harries has pointed out that Australia is trying (unwisely in his view) to become a torn country in reverse. Although it has been a full member not only of the West but also of the ABCA military and intelligence core of the West, its current leaders are in effect proposing that it defect from the West, redefine itself as an Asian country and cultivate close ties with its neighbors. Australia's future, they argue, is with the dynamic economies of East Asia. But, as I have suggested, close economic cooperation normally requires a common cultural base. In addition, none of the three conditions necessary for a torn country to join another civilization is likely to exist in Australia's case.

States," and the Weapon States are not Western states. Another result is the redefinition of arms control, which is a Western concept and a Western goal. During the Cold War the primary purpose of arms control was to establish a stable military balance between the United States and its allies and the Soviet Union and its allies. In the post-Cold War world the primary objective of arms control is to prevent the development by non-Western societies of military capabilities that could threaten Western interests. The West attempts to do this through international agreements, economic pressure and controls on the transfer of arms and weapons technologies.

The conflict between the West and the Confucian-Islamic states focuses largely, although not exclusively, on nuclear, chemical and biological weapons, ballistic missiles and other sophisticated means for delivering them, and the guidance, intelligence and other electronic capabilities for achieving that goal. The West promotes nonproliferation as a universal norm and nonproliferation treaties and inspections as means of realizing that norm. It also threatens a variety of sanctions against those who promote the spread of sophisticated weapons and proposes some benefits for those who do not. The attention of the West focuses, naturally, on nations that are actually or potentially hostile to the West.

A Confucian-Islamic connection has emerged to challenge Western interests, values and power.

The non-Western nations, on the other hand, assert their right to acquire and to deploy whatever weapons they think necessary for their security. They also have absorbed, to the full, the truth of the response of the Indian defense minister when asked what lesson he learned from the Gulf War: "Don't fight the United States unless you have nuclear weapons." Nuclear weapons, chemical weapons and missiles are viewed, probably erroneously, as the potential equalizer of superior Western conventional power. China, of course, already has nuclear weapons; Pakistan and India have the capability to deploy them. North Korea, Iran, Iraq, Libya and Algeria appear to be attempting to acquire them. A top Iranian official has declared that all Muslim states should acquire nuclear weapons, and in 1988 the president of

Iran reportedly issued a directive calling for development of "offensive and defensive chemical, biological and radiological weapons."

Centrally important to the development of counter-West military capabilities is the sustained expansion of China's military power and its means to create military power. Buoyed by spectacular economic development, China is rapidly increasing its military spending and vigorously moving forward with the modernization of its armed forces. It is purchasing weapons from the former Soviet states; it is developing long-range missiles; in 1992 it tested a one-megaton nuclear device. It is developing power-projection capabilities, acquiring aerial refueling technology, and trying to purchase an aircraft carrier. Its military buildup and assertion of sovereignty over the South China Sea are provoking a multilateral regional arms race in East Asia. China is also a major exporter of arms and weapons technology. It has exported materials to Libya and Iraq that could be used to manufacture nuclear weapons and nerve gas. It has helped Algeria build a reactor suitable for nuclear weapons research and production. China has sold to Iran nuclear technology that American officials believe could only be used to create weapons and apparently has shipped components of 300-mile-range missiles to Pakistan. North Korea has had a nuclear weapons program under way for some while and has sold advanced missiles and missile technology to Syria and Iran. The flow of weapons and weapons technology is generally from East Asia to the Middle East. There is, however, some movement in the reverse direction; China has received Stinger missiles from Pakistan.

A Confucian-Islamic military connection has thus come into being, designed to promote acquisition by its members of the weapons and weapons technologies needed to counter the military power of the West. It may or may not last. At present, however, it is, as Dave McCurdy has said, "a renegades' mutual support pact, run by the proliferators and their backers." A new form of arms competition is thus occurring between Islamic-Confucian states and the West. In an old-fashioned arms race, each side developed its own arms to balance or to achieve superiority against the other side. In this new form of arms competition, one side is developing its arms and the other side is attempting not to balance but to limit and prevent that arms build-up while at the same time reducing its own military capabilities.

IMPLICATIONS FOR THE WEST

THIS ARTICLE DOES not argue that civilization identities will replace all other identities, that nation states will disappear, that each civilization will become a single coherent political entity, that groups within a civilization will not conflict with and even fight each other. This paper does set forth the hypotheses that differences between civilizations are real and important; civilization-consciousness is increasing; conflict between civilizations will supplant ideological and other forms of conflict as the dominant global form of conflict; international relations, historically a game played out within Western civilization, will increasingly be de-Westernized and become a game in which non-Western civilizations are actors and not simply objects; successful political, security and economic international institutions are more likely to develop within civilizations than across civilizations; conflicts between groups in different civilizations will be more frequent, more sustained and more violent than conflicts between groups in the same civilization; violent conflicts between groups in different civilizations are the most likely and most dangerous source of escalation that could lead to global wars; the paramount axis of world politics will be the relations between "the West and the Rest"; the elites in some torn non-Western countries will try to make their countries part of the West, but in most cases face major obstacles to accomplishing this; a central focus of conflict for the immediate future will be between the West and several Islamic-Confucian states.

This is not to advocate the desirability of conflicts between civilizations. It is to set forth descriptive hypotheses as to what the future may be like. If these are plausible hypotheses, however, it is necessary to consider their implications for Western policy. These implications should be divided between short-term advantage and long-term accommodation. In the short term it is clearly in the interest of the West to promote greater cooperation and unity within its own civilization, particularly between its European and North American components; to incorporate into the West societies in Eastern Europe and Latin America whose cultures are close to those of the West; to promote and maintain cooperative relations with Russia and Japan; to prevent escalation of local inter-civilization conflicts into major inter-civilization wars; to limit the expansion of the military strength of Confucian and Islamic states; to moderate the reduction of Western military capabilities and maintain military superiority in East and Southwest Asia; to exploit differences and conflicts among Confucian and Islamic states; to support in other civilizations groups sympathetic to Western values and interests; to strengthen international institutions that reflect and legitimate Western interests and values and to promote the involvement of non-Western states in those institutions.

In the longer term other measures would be called for. Western civilization is both Western and modern. Non-Western civilizations have attempted to become modern without becoming Western. To date only Japan has fully succeeded in this quest. Non-Western civilizations will continue to attempt to acquire the wealth, technology, skills, machines and weapons that are part of being modern. They will also attempt to reconcile this modernity with their traditional culture and values. Their economic and military strength relative to the West will increase. Hence the West will increasingly have to accommodate these non-Western modern civilizations whose power approaches that of the West but whose values and interests differ significantly from those of the West. This will require the West to maintain the economic and military power necessary to protect its interests in relation to these civilizations. It will also, however, require the West to develop a more profound understanding of the basic religious and philosophical assumptions underlying other civilizations and the ways in which people in those civilizations see their interests. It will require an effort to identify elements of commonality between Western and other civilizations. For the relevant future, there will be no universal civilization, but instead a world of different civilizations, each of which will have to learn to coexist with the others.

The Summoning

'But They Said, We Will Not Hearken.'

JEREMIAH 6: 17

Fouad Ajami

In Joseph Conrad's *Youth*, a novella published at the turn of the century, Marlowe, the narrator, remembers when he first encountered "the East":

> And then, before I could open my lips, the East spoke to me, but it was in a Western voice. A torrent of words was poured into the enigmatical, the fateful silence; outlandish, angry words mixed with words and even whole sentences of good English, less strange but even more surprising. The voice swore and cursed violently; it riddled the solemn peace of the bay by a volley of abuse. It began by calling me Pig, and from that went crescendo into unmentionable adjectives —in English.

The young Marlowe knew that even the most remote civilization had been made and remade by the West, and taught new ways.

Not so Samuel P. Huntington. In a curious essay, "The Clash of Civilizations," Huntington has found his civilizations whole and intact, watertight under an eternal sky. Buried alive, as it were, during the years of the Cold War, these civilizations (Islamic, Slavic-Orthodox, Western, Confucian, Japanese, Hindu, etc.) rose as soon as the stone was rolled off, dusted themselves off, and proceeded to claim the loyalty of their adherents. For this student of history and culture, civilizations have always seemed messy creatures. Furrows run across whole civilizations, across individuals themselves—that was modernity's verdict. But Huntington looks past all that. The crooked and meandering alleyways of the world are straightened out. With a sharp pencil and a steady hand Huntington marks out where one civilization ends and the wilderness of "the other" begins.

More surprising still is Huntington's attitude toward states, and their place in his scheme of things. From one of the most influential and brilliant students of the state and its national interest there now comes an essay that misses the slyness of states, the unsentimental and cold-blooded nature of so much of what they do as they pick their way through

---

FOUAD AJAMI is Majid Khadduri Professor of Middle Eastern Studies at the School of Advanced International Studies, The Johns Hopkins University.

chaos. Despite the obligatory passage that states will remain "the most powerful actors in world affairs," states are written off, their place given over to clashing civilizations. In Huntington's words, "The next world war, if there is one, will be a war between civilizations."

THE POWER OF MODERNITY

Huntington's meditation is occasioned by his concern about the state of the West, its power and the terms of its engagement with "the rest."[1] "He who gives, dominates," the great historian Fernand Braudel observed of the traffic of civilizations. In making itself over the centuries, the West helped make the others as well. We have come to the end of this trail, Huntington is sure. He is impressed by the "de-Westernization" of societies, their "indigenization" and apparent willingness to go their own way. In his view of things such phenomena as the "Hinduization" of India and Islamic fundamentalism are ascendant. To these detours into "tradition" Huntington has assigned great force and power.

But Huntington is wrong. He has underestimated the tenacity of modernity and secularism in places that acquired these ways against great odds, always perilously close to the abyss, the darkness never far. India will not become a Hindu state. The inheritance of Indian secularism will hold. The vast middle class will defend it, keep the order intact to maintain India's—and its own—place in the modern world of nations. There exists in that anarchic polity an instinctive dread of playing with fires that might consume it. Hindu chauvinism may coarsen the public life of the country, but the state and the middle class that sustains it know that a detour into religious fanaticism is a fling with ruin. A resourceful middle class partakes of global culture and norms. A century has passed since the Indian bourgeoisie, through its political vehicle the Indian National Congress, set out to claim for itself and India a place among nations. Out of that long struggle to overturn British rule and the parallel struggle against "communalism," the advocates of the national idea built a large and durable state. They will not cede all this for a political kingdom of Hindu purity.

We have been hearing from the traditionalists, but we should not exaggerate their power, for traditions are often most insistent and loud when they rupture, when people no longer really believe and when age-old customs lose their ability to keep men and women at home. The phenomenon we have dubbed as Islamic fundamentalism is less a sign of resurgence than of panic and bewilderment and guilt that the border with "the other" has been crossed. Those young urban poor, half-educated in the cities of the Arab world, and their Sorbonne-educated lay preachers, can they be evidence of a genuine return to tradition? They crash Europe's and America's gates in search of liberty and work, and they rail against the

---

[1]The West itself is unexamined in Huntington's essay. No fissures run through it. No multiculturalists are heard from. It is orderly within its ramparts. What doubts Huntington has about the will within the walls, he has kept within himself. He has assumed that his call to unity will be answered, for outside flutter the banners of the Saracens and the Confucians.

THE BETTMANN ARCHIVE

Ayatollah, airborne.

sins of the West. It is easy to understand Huntington's frustration with this kind of complexity, with the strange mixture of attraction and repulsion that the West breeds, and his need to simplify matters, to mark out the borders of civilizations.

Tradition-mongering is no proof, though, that these civilizations outside the West are intact, or that their thrashing about is an indication of their vitality, or that they present a conventional threat of arms. Even so thorough and far-reaching an attack against Western hegemony as Iran's theocratic revolution could yet fail to wean that society from the culture of the West. That country's cruel revolution was born of the realization of the "armed Imam" that his people were being seduced by America's ways. The gates had been thrown wide open in the 1970s, and the high walls Ayatollah Khomeini built around his polity were a response to that cultural seduction. Swamped, Iran was "rescued" by men claiming authenticity as their banner. One extreme led to another.

"We prayed for the rain of mercy and received floods," was the way Mehdi Bazargan, the decent modernist who was Khomeini's first prime minister, put it. But the millennium has been brought down to earth, and the dream of a pan-Islamic revolt in Iran's image has vanished into the wind. The terror and the shabbiness have caught up with the utopia. Sudan could emulate the Iranian "revolutionary example." But this will only mean the further pauperization and ruin of a desperate land. There is no rehabilitation of the Iranian example.

A battle rages in Algeria, a society of the Mediterranean, close to Europe—a wine-producing country for that matter—and in Egypt between the secular powers that be and an Islamic alternative. But we should not rush to print with obituaries of these states. In Algeria the nomenklatura of the National Liberation Front failed and triggered a revolt of the young, the underclass and the excluded. The revolt raised an Islamic banner. Caught between a regime they despised and a reign of virtue they feared, the professionals and the women and the modernists of the middle class threw their support to the forces of "order." They hailed the army's crackdown on the Islamicists; they allowed the interruption of a democratic process sure to bring the Islamicists to power; they accepted the "liberties" protected by the repression, the devil you know rather than the one you don't.

The Algerian themes repeat in the Egyptian case, although Egypt's dilemma over its Islamicist opposition is not as acute. The Islamicists continue to hound the state, but they cannot bring it down. There is no likelihood that the Egyptian state—now riddled with enough complacency and corruption to try the celebrated patience and good humor of the Egyptians—will go under. This is an old and skeptical country. It knows better than to trust its fate to enforcers of radical religious dogma. These are not deep and secure structures of order that the national middle classes have put in place. But they will not be blown away overnight.

Nor will Turkey lose its way, turn its back on Europe and chase after some imperial temptation in the scorched domains of Central Asia. Huntington sells that country's modernity and secularism short when he writes that the Turks—rejecting Mecca and rejected by Brussels—are likely to head to Tashkent in search of a Pan-Turkic role. There is no journey to that imperial past. Ataturk severed that link with fury, pointed his country westward, embraced the civilization of Europe and did it without qualms or second thoughts. It is on Frankfurt and Bonn—and Washington—not on Baku and Tashkent that the attention of the Turks is fixed. The inheritors of Ataturk's legacy are too shrewd to go chasing after imperial glory, gathering about them the scattered domains of the Turkish peoples. After their European possessions were lost, the Turks clung to Thrace and to all that this link to Europe represents.

Huntington would have nations battle for civilizational ties and fidelities when they would rather scramble for their market shares, learn how to compete in a merciless world economy, provide jobs, move out of poverty. For their part, the "management gurus" and those who believe that the interests have vanquished the passions in today's world tell us that men want Sony, not soil.[2] There is a good deal of truth in what they say, a terrible exhaustion with utopias, a reluctance to set out on expeditions of principle or

[2]Kenichi Ohmae, "Global Consumers Want Sony, Not Soil," *New Perspectives Quarterly*, Fall 1991.

belief. It is hard to think of Russia, ravaged as it is by inflation, taking up the grand cause of a "second Byzantium," the bearer of the orthodox-Slavic torch.

And where is the Confucian world Huntington speaks of? In the busy and booming lands of the Pacific Rim, so much of politics and ideology has been sublimated into finance that the nations of East Asia have turned into veritable workshops. The civilization of Cathay is dead; the Indonesian archipelago is deaf to the call of the religious radicals in Tehran as it tries to catch up with Malaysia and Singapore. A different wind blows in the lands of the Pacific. In that world economics, not politics, is in command. The world is far less antiseptic than Lee Kuan Yew, the sage of Singapore, would want it to be. A nemesis could lie in wait for all the prosperity that the 1980s brought to the Pacific. But the lands of the Pacific Rim—protected, to be sure, by an American security umbrella—are not ready for a great falling out among the nations. And were troubles to visit that world they would erupt within its boundaries, not across civilizational lines.

The things and ways that the West took to "the rest"—those whole sentences of good English that Marlowe heard a century ago—have become the ways of the world. The secular idea, the state system and the balance of power, pop culture jumping tariff walls and barriers, the state as an instrument of welfare, all these have been internalized in the remotest places. We have stirred up the very storms into which we now ride.

THE WEAKNESS OF TRADITION

Nations "cheat": they juggle identities and interests. Their ways meander. One would think that the traffic of arms from North Korea and China to Libya and Iran and Syria shows this—that states will consort with any civilization, however alien, as long as the price is right and the goods are ready. Huntington turns this routine act of selfishness into a sinister "Confucian-Islamic connection." There are better explanations: the commerce of renegades, plain piracy, an "underground economy" that picks up the slack left by the great arms suppliers (the United States, Russia, Britain and France).

Contrast the way Huntington sees things with Braudel's depiction of the traffic between Christendom and Islam across the Mediterranean in the sixteenth century—and this was in a religious age, after the fall of Constantinople to the Turks and of Granada to the Spanish: "Men passed to and fro, indifferent to frontiers, states and creeds. They were more aware of the necessities for shipping and trade, the hazards of war and piracy, the opportunities for complicity or betrayal provided by circumstances."[3]

Those kinds of "complicities" and ambiguities are missing in Huntington's analysis. Civilizations are crammed into the nooks and crannies—and checkpoints—of the Balkans. Huntington goes where only the brave would venture, into that belt of mixed populations stretching from the Adriatic to the Baltic. Countless nationalisms make their home there, all aggrieved, all possessed of memories of a

[3]Ferdinand Braudel, *The Mediterranean and the Mediterranean World in the Age of Philip II*, Vol. II, New York: Harper & Row, 1976, p. 759.

fabled past and equally ready for the demagogues vowing to straighten a messy map. In the thicket of these pan-movements he finds the line that marked "the eastern boundary of Western Christianity in the year 1500." The scramble for turf between Croatian nationalism and its Serbian counterpart, their "joint venture" in carving up Bosnia, are made into a fight of the inheritors of Rome, Byzantium and Islam.

But why should we fall for this kind of determinism? "An outsider who travels the highway between Zagreb and Belgrade is struck not by the decisive historical fault line which falls across the lush Slavonian plain but by the opposite. Serbs and Croats speak the same language, give or take a few hundred words, have shared the same village way of life for centuries."[4] The cruel genius of Slobodan Milosevic and Franjo Tudjman, men on horseback familiar in lands and situations of distress, was to make their bids for power into grand civilizational undertakings—the ramparts of the Enlightenment defended against Islam or, in Tudjman's case, against the heirs of the Slavic-Orthodox faith. Differences had to be magnified. Once Tito, an equal opportunity oppressor, had passed from the scene, the balancing act among the nationalities was bound to come apart. Serbia had had a measure of hegemony in the old system. But of the world that loomed over the horizon—privatization and economic reform—the Serbs were less confident. The citizens of Sarajevo and the Croats and the Slovenes had a head start on the rural Serbs. And so the Serbs hacked at the new order of things with desperate abandon.

Some Muslim volunteers came to Bosnia, driven by faith and zeal. Huntington sees in these few stragglers the sweeping power of "civilizational rallying," proof of the hold of what he calls the "kin-country syndrome." This is delusion. No Muslim cavalry was ever going to ride to the rescue. The Iranians may have railed about holy warfare, but the Chetniks went on with their work. The work of order and mercy would have had to be done by the United States if the cruel utopia of the Serbs was to be contested.

It should have taken no powers of prophecy to foretell where the fight in the Balkans would end. The abandonment of Bosnia was of a piece with the ways of the world. No one wanted to die for Srebrenica. The Europeans averted their gaze, as has been their habit. The Americans hesitated for a moment as the urge to stay out of the Balkans did battle with the scenes of horror. Then "prudence" won out. Milosevic and Tudjman may need civilizational legends, but there is no need to invest their projects of conquest with this kind of meaning.

In his urge to find that relentless war across Islam's "bloody borders," Huntington buys Saddam Hussein's interpretation of the Gulf War. It was, for Saddam and Huntington, a civilizational battle. But the Gulf War's verdict was entirely different. For if there was a campaign that laid bare the interests of states, the lengths to which they will go to restore a tolerable balance of power in a place that matters, this was it. A local despot had

[4] Michael Ignatieff, "The Balkan Tragedy," *New York Review of Books*, May 13, 1993.

belief. It is hard to think of Russia, ravaged as it is by inflation, taking up the grand cause of a "second Byzantium," the bearer of the orthodox-Slavic torch.

And where is the Confucian world Huntington speaks of? In the busy and booming lands of the Pacific Rim, so much of politics and ideology has been sublimated into finance that the nations of East Asia have turned into veritable workshops. The civilization of Cathay is dead; the Indonesian archipelago is deaf to the call of the religious radicals in Tehran as it tries to catch up with Malaysia and Singapore. A different wind blows in the lands of the Pacific. In that world economics, not politics, is in command. The world is far less antiseptic than Lee Kuan Yew, the sage of Singapore, would want it to be. A nemesis could lie in wait for all the prosperity that the 1980s brought to the Pacific. But the lands of the Pacific Rim—protected, to be sure, by an American security umbrella—are not ready for a great falling out among the nations. And were troubles to visit that world they would erupt within its boundaries, not across civilizational lines.

The things and ways that the West took to "the rest"—those whole sentences of good English that Marlowe heard a century ago—have become the ways of the world. The secular idea, the state system and the balance of power, pop culture jumping tariff walls and barriers, the state as an instrument of welfare, all these have been internalized in the remotest places. We have stirred up the very storms into which we now ride.

THE WEAKNESS OF TRADITION

Nations "cheat": they juggle identities and interests. Their ways meander. One would think that the traffic of arms from North Korea and China to Libya and Iran and Syria shows this—that states will consort with any civilization, however alien, as long as the price is right and the goods are ready. Huntington turns this routine act of selfishness into a sinister "Confucian-Islamic connection." There are better explanations: the commerce of renegades, plain piracy, an "underground economy" that picks up the slack left by the great arms suppliers (the United States, Russia, Britain and France).

Contrast the way Huntington sees things with Braudel's depiction of the traffic between Christendom and Islam across the Mediterranean in the sixteenth century—and this was in a religious age, after the fall of Constantinople to the Turks and of Granada to the Spanish: "Men passed to and fro, indifferent to frontiers, states and creeds. They were more aware of the necessities for shipping and trade, the hazards of war and piracy, the opportunities for complicity or betrayal provided by circumstances."[3]

Those kinds of "complicities" and ambiguities are missing in Huntington's analysis. Civilizations are crammed into the nooks and crannies—and checkpoints—of the Balkans. Huntington goes where only the brave would venture, into that belt of mixed populations stretching from the Adriatic to the Baltic. Countless nationalisms make their home there, all aggrieved, all possessed of memories of a

[3]Ferdinand Braudel, *The Mediterranean and the Mediterranean World in the Age of Philip II*, Vol. II, New York: Harper & Row, 1976, p. 759.

risen close to the wealth of the Persian Gulf, and a Great Power from afar had come to the rescue. The posse assembled by the Americans had Saudi, Turkish, Egyptian, Syrian, French, British and other riders.

True enough, when Saddam Hussein's dream of hegemony was shattered, the avowed secularist who had devastated the *ulama*, the men of religion in his country, fell back on Ayatollah Khomeini's language of fire and brimstone and borrowed the symbolism and battle cry of his old Iranian nemesis. But few, if any, were fooled by this sudden conversion to the faith. They knew the predator for what he was: he had a Christian foreign minister (Tariq Aziz); he had warred against the Iranian revolution for nearly a decade and had prided himself on the secularism of his regime. Prudent men of the social and political order, the *ulama* got out of the way and gave their state the room it needed to check the predator at the Saudi/Kuwaiti border.[5] They knew this was one of those moments when purity bows to necessity. Ten days after Saddam swept into Kuwait, Saudi Arabia's most authoritative religious body, the Council of Higher Ulama, issued a *fatwa*, or a ruling opinion, supporting the presence of Arab and Islamic and "other friendly forces." All means of defense, the ulama ruled, were legitimate to guarantee the people "the safety of their religion, their wealth, and their honor and their blood, to protect what they enjoy of safety and stability." At some remove, in Egypt, that country's leading religious figure, the Shaykh of Al Ashar, Shaykh Jadd al Haqq, denounced Saddam as a tyrant and brushed aside his Islamic pretensions as a cover for tyranny.

Nor can the chief Iranian religious leader Ayatollah Ali Khamenei's rhetoric against the Americans during the Gulf War be taken as evidence of Iran's disposition toward that campaign. Crafty men, Iran's rulers sat out that war. They stood to emerge as the principal beneficiaries of Iraq's defeat. The American-led campaign against Iraq held out the promise of tilting the regional balance in their favor. No tears were shed in Iran for what befell Saddam Hussein's regime.

It is the mixed gift of living in hard places that men and women know how to distinguish between what they hear and what there is: no illusions were thus entertained in vast stretches of the Arab Muslim world about Saddam, or about the campaign to thwart him for that matter. The fight in the gulf was seen for what it was: a bid for primacy met by an imperial expedition that laid it to waste. A circle was closed in the gulf: where once the order in the region "east of Suez" had been the work of the British, it was now provided by Pax Americana. The new power standing sentry in the gulf belonged to the civilization of the West, as did the prior one. But the American presence had the anxious con-

[5]Huntington quotes one Safar al Hawali, a religious radical at Umm al Qura Univeristy in Mecca, to the effect that the campaign against Iraq was another Western campaign against Islam. But this can't do as evidence. Safar al Hawali was a crank. Among the *ulama* class and the religious scholars in Saudi Arabia he was, for all practical purposes, a loner.

sent of the Arab lands of the Persian Gulf. The stranger coming in to check the kinsmen.

The world of Islam divides and subdivides. The battle lines in the Caucasus, too, are not coextensive with civilizational fault lines. The lines follow the interests of states. Where Huntington sees a civilizational duel between Armenia and Azerbaijan, the Iranian state has cast religious zeal and fidelity to the wind. Indeed, in that battle the Iranians have tilted toward Christian Armenia.

THE WRIT OF STATES

We have been delivered into a new world, to be sure. But it is not a world where the writ of civilizations runs. Civilizations and civilizational fidelities remain. There is to them an astonishing measure of permanence. But let us be clear: civilizations do not control states, states control civilizations. States avert their gaze from blood ties when they need to; they see brotherhood and faith and kin when it is in their interest to do so.

We remain in a world of self-help. The solitude of states continues; the disorder in the contemporary world has rendered that solitude more pronounced. No way has yet been found to reconcile France to Pax Americana's hegemony, or to convince it to trust its security or cede its judgment to the preeminent Western power. And no Azeri has come up with a way the lands of Islam could be rallied to the fight over Nagorno Karabakh. The sky has not fallen in Kuala Lumpur or in Tunis over the setbacks of Azerbaijan in its fight with Armenia.

The lesson bequeathed us by Thucydides in his celebrated dialogue between the Melians and the Athenians remains. The Melians, it will be recalled, were a colony of the Lacedaemonians. Besieged by Athens, they held out and were sure that the Lacedaemonians were "bound, if only for very shame, to come to the aid of their kindred." The Melians never wavered in their confidence in their "civilizational" allies: "Our common blood insures our fidelity."[6] We know what became of the Melians. Their allies did not turn up, their island was sacked, their world laid to waste.

---

[6]Thucydides, *The Peloponnesian War*, New York: The Modern American Library, 1951, pp. 334-335.

risen close to the wealth of the Persian Gulf, and a Great Power from afar had come to the rescue. The posse assembled by the Americans had Saudi, Turkish, Egyptian, Syrian, French, British and other riders.

True enough, when Saddam Hussein's dream of hegemony was shattered, the avowed secularist who had devastated the *ulama*, the men of religion in his country, fell back on Ayatollah Khomeini's language of fire and brimstone and borrowed the symbolism and battle cry of his old Iranian nemesis. But few, if any, were fooled by this sudden conversion to the faith. They knew the predator for what he was: he had a Christian foreign minister (Tariq Aziz); he had warred against the Iranian revolution for nearly a decade and had prided himself on the secularism of his regime. Prudent men of the social and political order, the *ulama* got out of the way and gave their state the room it needed to check the predator at the Saudi/Kuwaiti border.[5] They knew this was one of those moments when purity bows to necessity. Ten days after Saddam swept into Kuwait, Saudi Arabia's most authoritative religious body, the Council of Higher Ulama, issued a *fatwa*, or a ruling opinion, supporting the presence of Arab and Islamic and "other friendly forces." All means of defense, the ulama ruled, were legitimate to guarantee the people "the safety of their religion, their wealth, and their honor and their blood, to protect what they enjoy of safety and stability." At some remove, in Egypt, that country's leading religious figure, the Shaykh of Al Ashar, Shaykh Jadd al Haqq, denounced Saddam as a tyrant and brushed aside his Islamic pretensions as a cover for tyranny.

Nor can the chief Iranian religious leader Ayatollah Ali Khamenei's rhetoric against the Americans during the Gulf War be taken as evidence of Iran's disposition toward that campaign. Crafty men, Iran's rulers sat out that war. They stood to emerge as the principal beneficiaries of Iraq's defeat. The American-led campaign against Iraq held out the promise of tilting the regional balance in their favor. No tears were shed in Iran for what befell Saddam Hussein's regime.

It is the mixed gift of living in hard places that men and women know how to distinguish between what they hear and what there is: no illusions were thus entertained in vast stretches of the Arab Muslim world about Saddam, or about the campaign to thwart him for that matter. The fight in the gulf was seen for what it was: a bid for primacy met by an imperial expedition that laid it to waste. A circle was closed in the gulf: where once the order in the region "east of Suez" had been the work of the British, it was now provided by Pax Americana. The new power standing sentry in the gulf belonged to the civilization of the West, as did the prior one. But the American presence had the anxious con-

[5]Huntington quotes one Safar al Hawali, a religious radical at Umm al Qura Univeristy in Mecca, to the effect that the campaign against Iraq was another Western campaign against Islam. But this can't do as evidence. Safar al Hawali was a crank. Among the *ulama* class and the religious scholars in Saudi Arabia he was, for all practical purposes, a loner.

Where Are the Great Powers?

At Home with the Kids

Edward N. Luttwak

During the Cold War as before it, local and regional conflicts were often instigated or at least encouraged and materially supported by rival great powers. Now, by contrast, the absence of functioning great powers is the cause of the world's inability to cope with all manner of violent disorders. The result is that not only groups of secessionists and aggressive small powers, such as Serbia, but even mere armed bands can now impose their will or simply rampage, unchecked by any greater force from without. Today there is neither the danger of great power wars nor the relative tranquillity once imposed by each great power within its own sphere of influence.

By the traditional definition, great powers were states strong enough to successfully wage war without calling on allies. But that distinction is now outdated, because the issue today is not whether war can be made with or without allies, but whether war can be made at all. Historically, there have been tacit preconditions to great power status: a readiness to use force whenever it was advantageous to do so and an acceptance of the resulting combat casualties with equanimity, as long as the number was not disproportionate.

In the past, those preconditions were too blatantly obvious and too easily satisfied to deserve a mention by either practitioners or theoreticians. Great powers normally relied on intimidation rather than combat, but only because a willingness to use force was assumed. Moreover, they would use force undeterred by the prospect of the ensuing casualties, within limits of course.

NOT-SO-GREAT BEHAVIOR

The Somalia debacle, precipitated by the loss of 18 U.S. soldiers, and the Haiti fiasco, caused by the fear that a handful of U.S. troops might be killed while defeating that country's military dictatorship, sufficiently exposed the current unreality of the great power concept. In

Edward N. Luttwak is a Senior Fellow at the Center for Strategic and International Studies in Washington, D.C. He is the author of *The Endangered American Dream*.

pride or shame, Americans might dispute any wider conclusion from those events. They would like to reserve for themselves the special sensitivity that forces policy to change completely because 18 professional soldiers are killed (soldiers, one might add, who come from a country in which gun-related deaths were last clocked at one every 14 minutes). But in fact the virtue or malady, as the case may be, is far from exclusively American.

Most recently, Britain and France (not to mention that other putative great power, Germany) flatly refused to risk their ground troops in combat to resist aggression in the former Yugoslavia. Overcoming the fear of reprisals against their own troops, it was only with great reluctance, after almost two years of horrific outrages, that the two countries finally consented to the carefully circumscribed threat of NATO air strikes issued in February 1994. To be sure, neither Britain nor France nor any other European power has any vital interests at stake in the former Yugoslavia. But that is the very essence of the matter: the great powers of history would have viewed the disintegration of Yugoslavia not as a noxious problem to be avoided but as an opportunity to be exploited. Using the need to protect populations under attack as their propaganda excuse and with the restoration of law and order as their ostensible motive, they would have intervened to establish zones of influence for themselves, just as the genuine great powers did in their time (even distant Russia disputed the Austro-Hungarian annexation of Bosnia-Herzegovina in 1908). Thus the power vacuum would have been filled, to the disappointment of local small power ambitions, and to the great advantage of local populations and peace.

As for why nothing of the kind happened in the former Yugoslavia in the face of atrocities not seen since the Second World War, the reason is not in dispute: no European government was any more willing than the U.S. government to risk its soldiers in combat. Of Japan, literally nothing need be said on this score.

The refusal to tolerate combat casualties is not confined to democracies. The Soviet Union was still an intact totalitarian dictatorship when it engaged in the classic great power venture of Afghanistan, only to find that even its tightly regimented society would not tolerate the resulting casualties. At the time, outside observers were distinctly puzzled by the minimal Soviet theater strategy in Afghanistan. After an abortive effort to establish territorial control, the Soviet strategy defended only the largest towns and the ring road that connected them, otherwise conceding almost the entire country to guerrillas. Likewise, knowledgeable observers were astonished by the inordinately prudent tactics of Soviet ground forces. Except for a few commando units, they mostly remained confined inside their fortified garrisons, often failing to sally out even when guerrillas were known to be nearby. At the time, the explanation most commonly offered was the reluctance of Soviet commanders to rely on their poorly trained conscript troops. But there is a better explanation: the Soviet headquarters was under constant and intense pressure from Moscow to avoid casualties at all costs because of the outraged reactions of families and friends.

This example also allows us to eliminate another superficial explanation for the novel refusal to accept even modest numbers of combat casualties: the impact of television coverage. The Soviet Union never allowed its population to see any television images of war like those shown in the United States, and still the reaction of Soviet society to the casualties of the Afghan war was essentially identical to the American reaction to the Vietnam War. Although in both cases cumulative casualties over the span of many years did not reach the casualty figures of one day of battle in past wars, they were nevertheless deeply traumatic.

THE WAR OF ALL MOTHERS

There is a more fundamental explanation that remains valid in cases with or without democratic governance, with or without uncontrolled war reportage by television: the demographic character of modern, postindustrial societies. The populations of the great powers of history were commonly comprised of families of four, five or six children; families of one, two or three were rarer than families of seven, eight or nine. On the other hand, infant mortality rates were also high. When it was normal to lose one or more children to disease, the loss of one more youngster in war had a different meaning than it has for today's families, which have two or three children, all of whom are expected to survive, and each of whom represents a larger share of the family's emotional economy.

As any number of historical studies have shown, death itself was a much more normal part of the familial experience when it was not confined mostly to the very old. To lose a young family member for any reason was no doubt always tragic, yet a death in combat was not the extraordinary and fundamentally unacceptable event that it has now become. Parents who commonly approved of their sons' and daughters' decisions to join the armed forces, thereby choosing a career dedicated to combat and its preparation just as a fireman's career is dedicated to the fighting of fires, now often react with astonishment and anger when their children are actually sent into potential combat situations. And they are apt to view their wounding or death as an outrageous scandal, rather than as an occupational hazard.

The Italians, perhaps more postindustrial than most in this sense, with Europe's lowest birthrate, have a word for these reactions: *mammismo*, which might be translated as "motherism." These attitudes have great political resonance nowadays, powerfully constraining the use of force. The Soviet experience in Afghanistan proves that the constraint can become operative even without a mass media eager to publicize private grief, members of Congress ready to complain at the instance of relatives, or pointed questions being asked in a parliament.

Present attitudes toward combat losses that derive from the new family demography are powerful because they are not confined to the relatives and friends of servicemen on active duty. They are shared throughout society—and were shared even within the Soviet elite, it turns out—generating an extreme reluctance to impose a possible sacrifice that has become so much greater than it was when national populations were perhaps much smaller but families were much larger.

What of the Gulf War, then, or for that matter Britain's war to reconquer the Falklands? Do they not suggest a much simpler explanation: that attitudes depend on the perceived importance of the undertaking, the objective value of what is at stake, or—more realistically—the sheer ability of political leaders to justify the necessity of combat? After all, even during World War II, soldiers greatly resented assignments to what were described as secondary fronts, quickly dubbing any theater that was less than highly publicized as "forgotten." The less immediately compelling the justification, the more likely combat and its casualties are to be opposed. It might therefore seem that the new 2.2-children-per-family demographics and the resulting *mammismo* are irrelevant, that what counts is only what has always counted, namely the importance of the interests at stake, the political orchestration of the event and plain leadership.

Those contentions undoubtedly have some merit, but much less than meets the eye. In the first place, if lives can only be placed at risk in situations already dramatically prominent on the national scene, hence on a larger rather than a smaller scale, and only in final extremities, that in itself already rules out the most efficient use of force—early and on a small scale to prevent escalation.

CONSTRICTED VISIONS

In the past, there was no question of limiting the use of force to situations in which genuinely vital interests, that is, survival interests, were at stake. To struggle for mere survival was the unhappy predicament of threatened small powers, which had to fight purely to defend themselves and could not hope to achieve anything more with their modest strength. Great powers were different; they could only remain great if they were seen as willing and able to use force to acquire and protect even non-vital interests, including distant possessions or minor additions to their spheres of influence. To lose a few hundred soldiers in some minor probing operation or a few thousand in a small war or expeditionary venture were routine events for the great powers of history.

Great powers are in the business of threatening, rather than being threatened. A great power cannot be that unless it asserts all sorts of claims that far exceed the needs of its own immediate security, including the protection of allies and clients as well as other less-than-vital interests. It must therefore risk combat for purposes that may be fairly recondite, perhaps in little-known distant lands, but definitely in situations in which it is not compelled to fight but rather deliberately chooses to do so. And that is the choice now denied by the fear of casualties.

Even now, exceptional strivings by exceptionally determined leaders skilled in the art of political leadership can widen a great power's freedom of action, overcoming at least in part the effects of the new family demographics. That was obviously the case in the Persian Gulf intervention and the Falklands reconquest; both would have been impossible undertakings had it not been for the exceptional leadership of President George Bush and Prime Minister Margaret Thatcher, respectively. Their leadership was the decisive factor, not the undoubted significance of keeping Iraq from controlling Saudi and Kuwaiti oil, or the equally undoubted insignificance of the Falklands for any practical purpose whatsoever (another illustration of the irrelevance of the "objective" value of whatever is at stake).

Leadership is important, but that consideration cuts both ways, because the routine functioning of a great power cannot depend on the fortuitous presence of exceptional leadership. It will be recalled, moreover, that a very low opinion of Argentine military strength (indeed, a gross underestimate of Argentine air power) and the resulting belief that casualties would be very low were crucial to Britain's commitment to war in the Falklands. Likewise, the imperative of minimizing casualties was the leitmotiv of the entire Persian Gulf intervention, from the initial deployment, which was originally presented as purely defensive, to the sudden decision to call off the ground war. (To be sure, there were other considerations as well, notably the fear that Iran would become the next threat if Iraq's army were utterly destroyed.) In any case, it seems clear that the freedom of action gained by successful leadership was still very narrow; it is not hard to guess what would have happened to President Bush and his administration if the casualties of the Persian Gulf venture had reached the levels of any one day of serious fighting in either world war.

NATIONS OF FAMILIES

If the significance of the new family demographics is accepted, it follows that no advanced low-birth-rate countries can play the role of a classic great power anymore, not the United States or Russia, not Britain, France or, least of all, Germany or Japan. They may still possess the physical attributes of military strength or the economic base to develop such strength even on a great scale, but their societies are so allergic to casualties that they are effectively debellicized, or nearly so.

Aside from self-defense and exceptional cases à la the Persian Gulf War, only such conflict as can take place without soldiers is likely to be tolerated. Much can be done by air power, with few lives at risk, especially if bureaucratic resistance to the use of air power alone can be overcome. Sea power too can be useful at times, and robotic weapons will be used increasingly. But Bosnia, Somalia and Haiti remind us that the typical great power business of restoring order still requires ground forces. In the end, the infantry, albeit mechanized, is still indispensable, although now mostly withheld by the fear of casualties. It is true of course that high-birth-rate countries can still fight wars by choice, and several have in recent years. But even those very few among them that have competent armed forces lack other key great power attributes, including any significant strategic reach.

In the absence of functioning great powers, the entire character of world politics has changed. Under the old *machtpolitik* rules, for example, the United States should have been eager to extend its military influence to the Russian border by granting full NATO membership to Poland and other former Warsaw Pact countries. Instead the United States opposed NATO's expansion. In the central arena of world affairs, only the commercial and industrial policies that I have elsewhere labeled "geo-economic" still have a recognizably conflictual flavor.

Unless the world is content to cohabit with chronic disorder and widespread violence, a synthetic version of law-and-order interventionism by great powers will have to be invented. The remedies we already have are certainly inadequate. To keep the armed forces of the United States as powerful as possible—the preferred military option, of course—is ineffectual when intimidation will not do it, yet the United States refuses to fight. And U.S. ability to intimidate cannot but decline as the word spreads.

IMPROBABLE STAND-INS

Two rather improbable schemes are therefore left. Both satisfy the essential requirement of circumventing the intolerance of casualties. Both could be organized quite efficiently, given the will to do so. Yet both would be furiously opposed by the military establishment, and both undeniably have unpleasant moral connotations.

One scheme would be to copy the Ghurka model, recruiting troops in some suitable region abroad, if not in Nepal itself. They would be mercenaries, of course, but they would be of high quality, and a common ethnic origin would assure their basic cohesion. In practice, U.S. Ghurkas would provide the infantry units, with native U.S. forces providing the more technical forms of combat support involving smaller risks and fewer casualties.

The alternative is to copy the foreign legion model, with units that combine U.S. officers and nonnative volunteers who have renounced their national allegiance, perhaps attracted by the offer of U.S. citizenship after a given term of service. Under both schemes, political responsibility for any casualties would be much reduced, even if not eliminated. The United States, by the way, raised ethnic mercenary units in Indochina with rather good results, and it recruited individual foreign volunteers for Europe-based special forces. So neither scheme is as outlandish or unprecedented as it may seem. Still, one would not want to bet that they would be seriously considered, let alone adopted.

If no remedy can be found for the passing of the great powers and the conspicuous inability of the United States itself to play that role, both the United States and the world had better become habituated to the consequences. Violent disorders unchecked by effective great power interventions have both immediate and delayed effects, including disrupted export markets, refugees and new sources of international crime and terrorism. But Americans will also have to learn not to see, hear or feel much that would otherwise offend their moral sensitivities. Richer inhabitants of the poorest countries learn from childhood how to step politely over the quadruple-amputee beggar in their path without ever actually looking at him, and how not to see the starving mother and child, the waif and the abandoned elderly who try to beg from them as they walk into a restaurant or bank. Blindness can be learned, and Americans will have to learn how to passively ignore avoidable tragedies and horrific atrocities. The experience of Bosnia-Herzegovina shows that Americans have already made much progress in that direction.

A Post-Heroic Military Policy

Edward N. Luttwak

THE NEW SEASON OF BELLICOSITY

THE STRATEGIC culture of the Cold War combined great eagerness to accumulate weapons with great caution in their use. Fearing that any act of war might start a progression of moves and countermoves leading to catastrophe, the nuclear powers strenuously avoided any direct combat with each other. There were many wars, but the remarkably deliberate and controlled behavior that became a new norm for nations around the world deterred the thoughtless escalation of confrontation and the eruption of war through sheer miscalculation. With the end of the Cold War, the size of armed forces, military expenditures, fear of nuclear attack, and learned habits of restraint are all much diminished. Today, disputes over minor diplomatic aims or mere posturing for domestic constituencies are enough to provoke reckless displays of bellicosity or imprudence. Thus China advanced its claim of sovereignty over Taiwan in March with military exercises that were clearly meant to be as alarming as possible. For their part, Taiwan's leaders, in their futile pursuit of U.N. membership, had earlier seen fit to score largely symbolic diplomatic points in defiance of emphatic Chinese warnings—as if there were no danger of war, and the balance of power were nothing more than an academic construct.

Likewise, a long-standing territorial dispute between Greece and Turkey over an islet in the Aegean Sea inhabited only by about a dozen goats quickly escalated in January to a confrontation. Naval forces were deployed in dangerous proximity to each other, accompanied by much nationalist bombast from politicians on both sides

EDWARD N. LUTTWAK is a Senior Fellow at the Center for Strategic and International Studies.

and frenzied media coverage. A group of Turkish journalists deliberately exacerbated tensions by planting a flag on the ten acres of rock. When a mutual withdrawal of forces was eventually negotiated with U.S. help, Greek editorialists accused newly installed Prime Minister Costas Simitis of treason. The episode was reminiscent of the warmongering press campaigns of the last fin-de-siècle, being not merely prenuclear but pre-1914 in its raw truculence.

The Republic of Korea also asserted a claim earlier this year over small uninhabited islands, in the Sea of Japan. President Kim Young Sam, beleaguered by accusations of corruption, sent warships to the scene against a backdrop of foolhardy taunts and idle threats against Japan in the South Korean media. Pakistan, too, has of late seemed bent on starting a war with India over Kashmir by smuggling in weapons and making inflammatory declarations.

As in prenuclear times, when fighting breaks out there is no great concern by either protagonists or outside powers to limit its scope. Consequently, infantry clashes can escalate directly to aerial bombing, as in the border fighting last year between Ecuador and Peru, or to artillery barrages against cities, as in the diverse struggles within the former Yugoslavia and the former Soviet Union.

None of these quarrels is new. But while the Cold War induced caution, present circumstances evidently do not. A new season of bellicosity is upon us, and it is unlikely to long endure without consequences. Because wars have become less dangerous to fight, the danger that wars will be fought has increased.

When national leaders manufacture or amplify external crises for internal political purposes, as noted above, they rarely intend to start a war. But as each side's gesticulations turn into the other side's perceived threats, confrontations can easily get out of hand. That happened often enough before the Cold War and is now likely to happen again. Indeed, in the case of Ecuador and Peru it has already occurred, not coincidentally when each was in the midst of a presidential campaign.

COLD WAR MINDS

A STRATEGIC environment so greatly transformed calls for an equally transformed U.S. military policy. Certainly there have already been important changes. The stock of long-range nuclear weapons has been greatly reduced, and both the defense budget and the number of personnel in the armed forces are considerably smaller than a decade ago. But at a more fundamental level, much remains unchanged and is therefore outdated.

That the end of the Cold War should leave disorientation in its wake was inevitable. Previous great wars entailed strenuous mobilizations, so that in 1918 and 1945 rapid demobilizations naturally ensued once hostilities ended. On both occasions the U.S. military went beyond the steep reduction or outright disbanding of war-inflated forces. It tried to resuscitate prewar routines and customs while attempting to recast doctrines and force structures in light of the presumed lessons of the last war. Thus battleships gave way to aircraft carriers, armored formations became the standard for ground forces, and jet aviation became the norm.

Military forces were thought to be most useful when they were not used.

The Cold War required a vast effort, but well short of an all-out mobilization. When it ended, therefore, there was no overwhelming pressure to drastically demobilize. Nor was there any urge to abandon its peculiar habits and institutions. On the contrary, the U.S. military has striven to preserve continuity in all things and has resisted as much as possible the effects of declining budgets.

Cold War military practices and priorities persist in all sorts of subtle ways because they are embodied in the millions of people who make up the armed forces, the Pentagon's civilian bureaucracies, intelligence organizations, defense laboratories, research centers, and military industries large and small, but mainly because they are simply not recognized as products of that era. The Cold War lasted so long that nobody remembers any prewar normality to which the military should revert. Nor are there are any sharply defined threats to which the military can adjust. A deliberate refusal to break with the past is not the issue, nor is the habitual conservatism of military institutions; the issue is the persistence of unquestioned premises. Because all but the youngest officers and virtually all defense officials were educated throughout their professional lives in the strategic culture of the Cold War, its axioms remain embedded in their mentality.

Of these axioms, by far the most significant is the paradox of deterrence: military forces are most useful when they are not used at all. Despite this, the U.S. military constantly struggled throughout the Cold War to maintain high standards of combat readiness, essentially as a matter of principle. But this axiom had a powerful effect on all other core policy decisions—on the sizes, roles, and budgets of the branches of the armed forces. The risk of combat casualties faced by different categories of the armed forces varies dramatically. The prospect of high casualties, which can rapidly undermine domestic support for any military operation, is the key political constraint when decisions must be made on which forces to deploy in a crisis, and at what levels. Yet the distinction between forces that are only theoretically available and those that are in fact politically usable in real-life confrontations is still largely disregarded. The composition of U.S. military forces reflects the lingering priorities of the Cold War, when U.S. forces served primarily for deterrence display and self-reassurance. Today, however, the former is largely ineffectual and the latter unnecessary. Calculations of the cost-effectiveness of conventional forces should therefore be governed by their usability. That is far from being the case at present, and the result is a contradictory military policy.

SEND MISSILES

WHEN SENIOR Pentagon officials and military officers discuss how the United States might intervene in this or that outbreak of violence somewhere in the world, the likelihood of combat and the probable magnitude of U.S. casualties are invariably dominant in their deliberations. Hence the usual recommendation of such conclaves is to avoid armed intervention altogether, except for bloodless visits by American naval forces to nearby waters or perhaps reconnaissance flights, if possible by remotely piloted aircraft. If the situation is seen as requiring more forceful action, a strike by cruise missiles launched by ships or submarines from a safe distance might be suggested. Because of the considerable cost and limited supply of cruise missiles, however, only manned aircraft are suitable if more persistent bombardment is required. Yet the Pentagon is extremely reluctant to allow their use. The difficulty of finding and hitting specific targets, the possibility that stray bombs will kill innocent civilians, and the strength of enemy antiaircraft defenses are the standard objections, invariably coupled with pessimistic assessments of the likely impact on the enemy and his decisions.

In spite of the Pentagon's huge annual expenditure on airpower, many officers and officials endorse the most critical estimates of its worth and discount claims of its efficacy as "the airpower myth." That was certainly the case during the prolonged controversy from 1992 to 1994 over the use of tactical bombing against Bosnian Serb forces. When the strikes were finally carried out last year, their swift technical and political success surprised the Pentagon, for the accomplishments of airpower in the 1991 Persian Gulf War had been attributed to uniquely favorable circumstances.

Pentagon decision-makers rarely propose the use of ground forces, for which the risk of casualties is inherently high because of their proximity to enemy fire. If the introduction of ground forces is nevertheless advocated by State Department or White House officials, military leaders almost always strongly resist it, arguing for demanding preconditions, beginning with the insistence that "vital" U.S. interests be at stake. With the United States now as secure as it can be in a nuclear world, and with its closest allies largely unthreatened, such a precondition is a virtual prohibition. The United States has all sorts of interests that are or might be threatened, but few can accurately be said to be vital—that is, encompassing the country's very survival.

Should that most stringent prerequisite not suffice, however, the military has others. One is that the goal of any military action be precisely and permanently defined in advance, with no "mission creep" allowed—a demand almost impossible to satisfy in this world of human ambiguities and inconstancies. Another is that a swift and decisive resolution to the conflict be assured, a highly desirable aim to be sure, but one that will always depend on what both sides do and how well they do it. Nor can any results be truly decisive for long. With Iraqi President Saddam Hussein still in power and recurrently threatening Kuwait, was the Persian Gulf War truly decisive?

PLANNING FOR THE WRONG WARS

YET WHEN SENIOR Pentagon officials and military officers convene to discuss the overall composition of the armed forces rather than their use in combat, the wide variance in the risk of casualties of the different kinds of military forces does not seem to matter very much. To cite the largest differential, Army and Marine Corps troops are the most likely to suffer combat casualties, while long-range missiles are of course immune, and so-called "strategic" bombers expose very few people to enemy attack. If the entire B-2 force now planned were to be deployed in a conflict, the operation would risk the lives of only 32 crew members. Yet under current plans, in 2000 the United States would have the equivalent of 29 divisions of ground forces but only modest numbers of cruise missiles, very few standoff missiles for tactical aircraft, and only six wings of long-range bombers, with 130 aircraft in all.[1] Compare the long-term prorated costs: the annual bill for an active-duty armored or mechanized division is almost $3 billion, and a much smaller light-infantry division requires almost $2 billion, while the average annual cost of the costliest bomber wings, comprised of 16 B-2 bombers, is less than $1 billion. Likewise, for the annual cost of one armored division, the United States could buy more than 2,000 cruise missiles—a truly formidable force, seven times larger than the number launched during the Persian Gulf War.

Ground forces are undoubtedly more versatile than bombers or cruise missiles. Through well-publicized redeployments, bombers can be used as diplomatic instruments during crises, as well as weapons against valuable targets. And cruise missiles have the virtue of being usable in isolation, for one-time strikes. However, none of that compares with the versatility of ground troops across the entire spectrum of conflict, from mere observation for peacekeeping to high-intensity warfare.

Versatility, however, presumes that the ground forces be usable in combat. In reality, political constraints greatly restrict their availability. The best evidence of that, paradoxically, is last year's decision to

[1]"Standoff" missiles are air-to-surface missiles capable of attacking enemy targets from beyond the reach of local air defenses and counterattacks, or from friendly airspace behind a battlefield area.

send 16,000 troops to Bosnia to oversee the Dayton peace accords. Only after five years of intense national debate, amid countless reports of widespread atrocities and exceptionally destructive warfare, was the Pentagon's opposition to the deployment overcome. Even then, very restrictive conditions were imposed: a rigid one-year time limit and an equally rigid troop limit.

No adversary, should any emerge, need fear that attacking U.S. troops would only provoke the arrival of more U.S. troops. Thus the deterrent effect normally inherent in a great power expedition—the high risk that attacks against it may well backfire by provoking an expansion of the force and its role—was renounced at the start. With that risk removed, the danger to the troops in Bosnia would be correspondingly increased were it not for the time limit, which invites prospective troublemakers to wait a while before acting. That constraint makes it more likely that the expedition will have a violent aftermath, and will thus be seen as futile. Both restrictions may yet prove unfortunate, but under the circumstances they were politically inevitable. They accurately reflect the current underlying reality that U.S. ground forces are not available as instruments of U.S. foreign policy, except under very unusual conditions.

Political constraints make ground forces effectively unavailable.

In theory, the lack of obvious "vital" U.S. interests in Bosnia's vicissitudes conditioned the debate and resulted in the ambivalent decision, although the advocates of intervention did make a rather strong case for a wider U.S. interest in world order. In practice, however, the decisive consideration for opponents of intervention was not the presence or absence of U.S. interests but the fear that too many U.S. troops would be killed. The most senior U.S. military officers stated that explicitly in 1992. Remarkably, General Colin Powell, then chairman of the Joint Chiefs of Staff, not only gave background press briefings to that effect, but even published an article in the daily press to argue against any form of U.S. military intervention in Bosnia.[2]

There is clear evidence that the much-cited calculus of U.S. interests was in fact irrelevant to the Bosnia debate. At the very time the

[2]Colin L. Powell, "Why Generals Get Nervous," *The New York Times*, October 8, 1992.

Pentagon was successfully resisting any use of force in the former Yugoslavia in the closing months of 1992, it proffered a U.S. expedition to Somalia. Senior military officers were willing to send U.S. troops there because they mistakenly believed that no casualties would ensue in a mission labeled as humanitarian. They were unwilling to send troops or even use tactical airpower in the former Yugoslavia because they feared there would be fighting and casualties. As always, talk of U.S. interests, present or absent, vital or not, was merely part of the rhetorical carapace of policy decisions driven by more compelling motives.

WAR FROM AFAR

IN A WORLD of wars that are less dangerous but much less likely to be prevented, U.S. military forces must once again be kept primarily for combat rather than for deterrent display. Thus the current composition of U.S. forces as a whole, however versatile in theory, is no longer appropriate. What this or that type of force could do in combat—if only the United States had high birthrates, large families, and a hypernationalistic population that sanctioned with equanimity thousands of casualties in any minor military affray—is or should be irrelevant when deciding the composition of the armed forces. What counts is not cost-effectiveness in general, but the cost-effectiveness of the military forces and materiel that can actually be used during a conflict. The two criteria yield widely divergent results because it is invariably expensive to reduce casualties by developing and deploying ways to move personnel and materiel farther from harm's way on the battlefield while maintaining their effectiveness.

U.S. military policy must also prepare for possible drastic changes in the strategic environment, including the emergence of situations that would require the large-scale use of ground forces and the toleration of high casualties. A full range of military capabilities is needed, but that can be assured by preserving capacity for remobilization and by maintaining lower-cost reserve forces. Once the necessary precautions against sudden and powerful new threats are in place, the United States should acquire the military forces it can actually use as instruments of policy. That would be a prosaic prescription— indeed a mere banality—were it not for America's half-century of immersion in Cold War deterrence, during which weapons and forces were most useful precisely insofar as they were not used.

A wholesale recalibration of U.S. military policy is needed to shift money and resources to the forces actually usable, at the expense of the less usable. There is no way of measuring how usable different kinds of military forces are, even in theory. Such a quality is not fixed and inherent, but depends on the perceived political importance of the task at hand, which can change very quickly indeed. On August 3, 1990, President George Bush evoked scarcely any criticism when he ruled out the use of American military strength to expel Iraqi invasion forces from Kuwait. Yet that became the imperative of his administration very soon thereafter. No U.S. forces were usable under the first decision; all nonnuclear forces were equally usable under the second.

Money should be shifted to the forces that are actually usable.

What *can* be measured as a surrogate for political usability is the inherent exposure to casualties of different categories of forces. As a first approximation of what might be called a casualty exposure index, it would be enough to count the personnel in the close-combat echelons of each kind of force. By that measure, for example, armored brigades with their 400 or so tank crewmen and 300 or so riflemen would have a significantly lower exposure index than light infantry or Marine brigades, which have several times as many riflemen and few heavy weapons. Therefore, under current strategic conditions, the use of armored forces would be advantageous, even in terrain and for tasks that would call for infantry forces according to traditional tactical criteria. One lesson of the Somalia debacle is that armored forces nowadays are preferable to light infantry forces in almost any environment, in spite of their tactical limitations. Inserting forces that are theoretically more suitable only to have to withdraw them abruptly because of politically intolerable casualties accomplishes nothing.

Such rudimentary casualty exposure indexes could be made somewhat more realistic by taking into account the proximity of U.S. combat echelons, broadly defined to include the crews of ships and aircraft, to a combat locale, under the reasonable assumption that the closer the proximity, the greater the likelihood of casualties. With that adjustment, for example, the Navy's amphibian and gunfire-support warships, which must come fairly close to shore, would be assigned higher casualty exposure indexes than Navy ships used primarily to launch cruise missiles. Admittedly, complications intrude when a given type of force can be employed for different purposes; most combat aircraft, for example, can carry out both close-support missions against antiaircraft fire and remote attacks with standoff missiles.

U.S. funding decisions should incorporate a casualty exposure index.

Whether adjusted for proximity or not, meaningful casualty exposure indexes could readily be calculated for each type of force. As proxies for political usability, they would define which forces are most suited for current post–Cold War and "post-heroic" conditions, in which the invariable limiting factor for U.S. military operations is Americans' low tolerance of casualties.

In descending order, a rough ranking of usability would begin with unmanned, long-range weapons (notably ballistic and cruise missiles) and proceed through remote forces with small combat echelons, such as air crews that launch standoff weapons, to the least usable forces, the Army and Marine infantry forces whose combat echelons are useful only in close proximity to the fighting. Such a ranking system should become a central criterion of U.S. military policy, as it would further the acquisition of the forces that are less exposed to casualties and therefore more usable in present conditions.

The United States requires reasonably substantial forces in all categories, from aircraft carriers to infantry divisions. But the current inventory of combat forces contains too many manpower-intensive ground units that are highly exposed to casualties and simply unavailable as instruments of foreign policy.

The overall effect of spending too much money on the upkeep of unusable forces instead of merely maintaining a remobilization capacity for them is that Congress now deems an exceptionally rich menu of important technological innovations unaffordable. The list includes the first practical directed-energy, or laser, weapons capable of intercepting rockets and ballistic missiles, which are a scourge from Sarajevo to Israel; stealth aircraft, which are substantially immune to radar detection in most situations and therefore capable of doing much with few fliers exposed to enemy attack and even fewer losses; remotely piloted aerial vehicles, now available only in sample numbers and not yet for strike roles; more and better cruise and standoff missiles; versatile advanced munitions; and all the diverse applications of information technology that only await funding to be implemented, not to mention those that could be developed with more money.

The promise of these innovations is not a stronger United States—it is strong enough—but rather a greater ability to use force remotely, yet accurately and with discrimination. Tactical bombing, guided and protected by a host of electronic ancillaries and aimed with now-routine precision, proved very effective in Bosnia notwithstanding the seemingly decisive reasons why it should have failed. So far, however, only fixed or large, easily recognizable targets are vulnerable to remote attack. That may be good enough in classic war situations, as in the Persian Gulf War, but the lower the intensity of conflict, the less can be achieved by attacking airfields, depots, headquarters, or other major targets. The promise of the potential innovations is a greater ability to contend with more elusive enemies in more ambiguous situations.

Spending on unusable forces has crowded out important military technology.

It is unwise to retard these innovations in the armed forces, but not because dangerous threats to vital U.S. interests are imminent. On the contrary, capital-intensive forces that have the lowest possible exposure to casualties are needed precisely because at present there are no threats that might justify substantial American casualties. The use of military forces will likely continue to be discretionary, as it has been in Bosnia, Haiti, and Somalia, rather than imperative. Some continue to argue against all such discretionary interventions, not coincidentally with the vehement support of senior officers who represent the most manpower-intensive forces. Abstention from all interventions would certainly allow an indefinite delay in the refocusing of U.S. military policy at the expense of those very forces.

There are always strong arguments against any particular U.S. military intervention, and all discretionary interventions can be dismissed as "social work," i.e., feel-good endeavors disconnected from core U.S. interests. But what may be true of any single intervention—

and was certainly true of the Somalia expedition—is not true of all. If the possessor of much of the world's military power refuses to use it, greater world disorder is only the most immediate consequence. At a time when Cold War restraint has given way to adventurism, if U.S. military power is withheld in one crisis after another, it is bound to stimulate the growth of other military powers. A vacuum will have been created that other countries will fill.

A policy of nonintervention would yield a world not only less stable, but also more militarized. That would certainly affect core U.S. interests, at the very least by damaging economic development and undermining civilian rule, even if no direct threats were to emerge or increase. Hence the urgency of redefining the priorities of U.S. military policy, to yield forces that can more readily be deployed for discretionary interventions. To fight only when necessity compels is the attribute of small powers. The United States fortunately lacks the classic expansionist proclivities of the great powers of history, but it does have widespread responsibilities that call for appropriate military means.

Give War a Chance

Edward N. Luttwak

PREMATURE PEACEMAKING

AN UNPLEASANT truth often overlooked is that although war is a great evil, it does have a great virtue: it can resolve political conflicts and lead to peace. This can happen when all belligerents become exhausted or when one wins decisively. Either way the key is that the fighting must continue until a resolution is reached. War brings peace only after passing a culminating phase of violence. Hopes of military success must fade for accommodation to become more attractive than further combat.

Since the establishment of the United Nations and the enshrinement of great-power politics in its Security Council, however, wars among lesser powers have rarely been allowed to run their natural course. Instead, they have typically been interrupted early on, before they could burn themselves out and establish the preconditions for a lasting settlement. Cease-fires and armistices have frequently been imposed under the aegis of the Security Council in order to halt fighting. NATO's intervention in the Kosovo crisis follows this pattern.

But a cease-fire tends to arrest war-induced exhaustion and lets belligerents reconstitute and rearm their forces. It intensifies and prolongs the struggle once the cease-fire ends—and it does usually end. This was true of the Arab-Israeli war of 1948–49, which might have come to closure in a matter of weeks if two cease-fires ordained by the Security Council had not let the combatants recuperate. It has recently been true in the Balkans. Imposed cease-fires frequently interrupted the fighting between Serbs and Croats in Krajina, between

---

EDWARD N. LUTTWAK is Senior Fellow at the Center for Strategic and International Studies.

the forces of the rump Yugoslav federation and the Croat army, and between the Serbs, Croats, and Muslims in Bosnia. Each time, the opponents used the pause to recruit, train, and equip additional forces for further combat, prolonging the war and widening the scope of its killing and destruction. Imposed armistices, meanwhile—again, unless followed by negotiated peace accords—artificially freeze conflict and perpetuate a state of war indefinitely by shielding the weaker side from the consequences of refusing to make concessions for peace.

The Cold War provided compelling justification for such behavior by the two superpowers, which sometimes collaborated in coercing less-powerful belligerents to avoid being drawn into their conflicts and clashing directly. Although imposed cease-fires ultimately did increase the total quantity of warfare among the lesser powers, and armistices did perpetuate states of war, both outcomes were clearly lesser evils (from a global point of view) than the possibility of nuclear war. But today, neither Americans nor Russians are inclined to intervene *competitively* in the wars of lesser powers, so the unfortunate consequences of interrupting war persist while no greater danger is averted. It might be best for all parties to let minor wars burn themselves out.

THE PROBLEMS OF PEACEKEEPERS

TODAY CEASE-FIRES and armistices are imposed on lesser powers by multilateral agreement—not to avoid great-power competition but for essentially disinterested and indeed frivolous motives, such as television audiences' revulsion at harrowing scenes of war. But this, perversely, can *systematically* prevent the transformation of war into peace. The Dayton accords are typical of the genre: they have condemned Bosnia to remain divided into three rival armed camps, with combat suspended momentarily but a state of hostility prolonged indefinitely. Since no side is threatened by defeat and loss, none has a sufficient incentive to negotiate a lasting settlement; because no path to peace is even visible, the dominant priority is to prepare for future war rather than to reconstruct devastated economies and ravaged societies. Uninterrupted war would certainly have caused further suffering and led to an unjust outcome from one perspective or another, but it would also have led to a more stable situation that would have let the postwar era truly begin. Peace takes hold only when war is truly over.

A variety of multilateral organizations now make it their business to intervene in other peoples' wars. The defining characteristic of these entities is that they insert themselves in war situations while refusing to engage in combat. In the long run this only adds to the damage. If the United Nations helped the strong defeat the weak faster and more decisively, it would actually enhance the peacemaking potential of war. But the first priority of U.N. peacekeeping contingents is to avoid casualties among their own personnel. Unit commanders therefore habitually appease the *locally* stronger force, accepting its dictates and tolerating its abuses. This appeasement is not strategically purposeful, as siding with the stronger power overall would be; rather, it merely reflects the determination of each U.N. unit to avoid confrontation. The final result is to prevent the emergence of a coherent outcome, which requires an imbalance of strength sufficient to end the fighting.

Peacekeepers chary of violence are also unable to effectively protect civilians who are caught up in the fighting or deliberately attacked. At best, U.N. peacekeeping forces have been passive spectators to outrages and massacres, as in Bosnia and Rwanda; at worst, they collaborate with it, as Dutch U.N. troops did in the fall of Srebenica by helping the Bosnian Serbs separate the men of military age from the rest of the population.

The very presence of U.N. forces, meanwhile, inhibits the normal remedy of endangered civilians, which is to escape from the combat zone. Deluded into thinking that they will be protected, civilians in danger remain in place until it is too late to flee. During the 1992–94 siege of Sarajevo, appeasement interacted with the pretense of protection in an especially perverse manner: U.N. personnel inspected outgoing flights to prevent the escape of Sarajevo civilians in obedience to a cease-fire agreement negotiated with the locally dominant Bosnian Serbs—who habitually violated that deal. The more sensible, realistic response to a raging war would have been for the Muslims to either flee the city or drive the Serbs out.

Institutions such as the European Union, the Western European Union, and the Organization for Security and Cooperation in Europe lack even the U.N.'s rudimentary command structure and personnel,

AP/WIDE WORLD PHOTOS

Playing games: U.N. peacekeepers with refugees, Tyre, Lebanon, 1996

yet they too now seek to intervene in warlike situations, with predictable consequences. Bereft of forces even theoretically capable of combat, they satisfy the interventionist urges of member states (or their own institutional ambitions) by sending unarmed or lightly armed "observer" missions, which have the same problems as U.N. peacekeeping missions, only more so.

Military organizations such as NATO or the West African Peacekeeping Force (ECOMOG, recently at work in Sierra Leone) are capable of stopping warfare. Their interventions still have the destructive consequence of prolonging the state of war, but they can at least protect civilians from its consequences. Even that often fails to happen, however, because multinational military commands engaged in disinterested interventions tend to avoid any risk of combat, thereby limiting their effectiveness. U.S. troops in Bosnia, for example, repeatedly failed to arrest known war criminals passing through their checkpoints lest this provoke confrontation.

Multinational commands, moreover, find it difficult to control the quality and conduct of member states' troops, which can reduce the performance of all forces involved to the lowest common denominator. This was true of otherwise fine British troops in Bosnia and of the Nigerian marines in Sierra Leone. The phenomenon of troop degradation can rarely be detected by external observers, although its consequences are abundantly visible in the litter of dead, mutilated, raped, and tortured victims that attends such interventions. The true state of affairs is illuminated by the rare exception, such as the vigorous Danish tank battalion in Bosnia that replied to any attack on it by firing back in full force, quickly stopping the fighting.

THE FIRST "POST-HEROIC" WAR

ALL PRIOR examples of disinterested warfare and its crippling limitations, however, have been cast into shadow by NATO's current intervention against Serbia for the sake of Kosovo. The alliance has relied on airpower alone to minimize the risk of NATO casualties, bombing targets in Serbia, Montenegro, and Kosovo for weeks without losing a single pilot. This seemingly miraculous immunity from Yugoslav anti-aircraft guns and missiles was achieved by multiple layers of precautions. First, for all the noise and imagery suggestive of a massive operation, very few strike sorties were actually flown during the first few weeks. That reduced the risks to pilots and aircraft but of course also limited the scope of the bombing to a mere fraction of NATO's potential. Second, the air campaign targeted air-defense systems first and foremost, minimizing present and future allied casualties, though at the price of very limited destruction and the loss of any shock effect. Third, NATO avoided most anti-aircraft weapons by releasing munitions not from optimal altitudes but from an ultra-safe 15,000 feet or more. Fourth, the alliance greatly restricted its operations in less-than-perfect weather conditions. NATO officials complained that dense clouds were impeding the bombing campaign, often limiting nightly operations to a few cruise-missile strikes against fixed targets of known location. In truth, what the cloud ceiling prohibited was not all bombing—low-altitude attacks could easily have taken place—but rather perfectly safe bombing.

On the ground far beneath the high-flying planes, small groups of Serb soldiers and police in armored vehicles were terrorizing hundreds of thousands of Albanian Kosovars. NATO has a panoply of aircraft designed for finding and destroying such vehicles. All its major powers have anti-tank helicopters, some equipped to operate without base support. But no country offered to send them into Kosovo when the ethnic cleansing began—after all, they might have been shot down. When U.S. Apache helicopters based in Germany were finally ordered to Albania, in spite of the vast expenditure devoted to their instantaneous "readiness" over the years, they required more than three weeks of "predeployment preparations" to make the journey. Six weeks into the war, the Apaches had yet to fly their first mission, although two had already crashed during training. More than mere bureaucratic foot-dragging was responsible for this inordinate delay: the U.S. Army insisted that the Apaches could not operate on their own, but would need the support of heavy rocket barrages to suppress Serb anti-aircraft weapons. This created a much larger logistical load than the Apaches alone, and an additional, evidently welcome delay.

Even before the Apache saga began, NATO already had aircraft deployed on Italian bases that could have done the job just as well: U.S. A-10 "Warthogs" built around their powerful 30 mm antitank guns and British Royal Air Force Harriers ideal for low-altitude bombing at close range. Neither was employed, again because it could not be done in perfect safety. In the calculus of the NATO democracies, the immediate possibility of saving thousands of Albanians from massacre and hundreds of thousands from deportation was obviously not worth the lives of a few pilots. That may reflect unavoidable political reality, but it demonstrates how even a large-scale disinterested intervention can fail to achieve its ostensibly humanitarian aim. It is worth wondering whether the Kosovars would have been better off had NATO simply done nothing.

REFUGEE NATIONS

THE MOST disinterested of all interventions in war—and the most destructive—are humanitarian relief activities. The largest and most protracted is the United Nations Relief and Works Agency (UNRWA). It was built on the model of its predecessor, the United Nations Relief and Rehabilitation Agency (UNRRA), which operated displaced-persons' camps in Europe immediately after World War II. The UNRWA was established immediately after the 1948–49 Arab-Israeli war to feed, shelter, educate, and provide health services for Arab refugees who had fled Israeli zones in the former territory of Palestine.

By keeping refugees alive in spartan conditions that encouraged their rapid emigration or local resettlement, the UNRRA's camps in Europe had assuaged postwar resentments and helped disperse revanchist concentrations of national groups. But UNRWA camps in Lebanon, Syria, Jordan, the West Bank, and the Gaza Strip provided on the whole a higher standard of living than most Arab villagers had previously enjoyed, with a more varied diet, organized schooling, superior medical care, and no backbreaking labor in stony fields. They had, therefore, the opposite effect, becoming desirable homes rather than eagerly abandoned transit camps. With the encouragement of several Arab countries, the UNRWA turned escaping civilians into lifelong refugees who gave birth to refugee children, who have in turn had refugee children of their own.

Refugee camps prevent integration, inhibit emigration, and keep resentments aflame.

During its half-century of operation, the UNRWA has thus perpetuated a Palestinian refugee nation, preserving its resentments in as fresh a condition as they were in 1948 and keeping the first bloom of revanchist emotion intact. By its very existence, the UNRWA dissuades integration into local society and inhibits emigration. The concentration of Palestinians in the camps, moreover, has facilitated the voluntary or forced enlistment of refugee youths by armed organizations that fight both Israel and each other. The UNRWA has contributed to a half-century of Arab-Israeli violence and still retards the advent of peace.

If each European war had been attended by its own postwar UNRWA, today's Europe would be filled with giant camps for millions of descendants of uprooted Gallo-Romans, abandoned Vandals, defeated Burgundians, and misplaced Visigoths—not to speak of more recent refugee nations such as post-1945 Sudeten Germans (three million of whom were expelled from Czechoslovakia in 1945). Such a Europe would have remained a mosaic of warring tribes, undigested and unreconciled in their separate feeding camps. It might have assuaged consciences to help each one at each remove, but it would have led to permanent instability and violence.

The UNRWA has counterparts elsewhere, such as the Cambodian camps along the Thai border, which incidentally provided safe havens for the mass-murdering Khmer Rouge. But because the United Nations is limited by stingy national contributions, these camps' sabotage of peace is at least localized.

That is not true of the proliferating, feverishly competitive non-governmental organizations (NGOs) that now aid war refugees. Like any other institution, these NGOs are interested in perpetuating themselves, which means that their first priority is to attract charitable contributions by being seen to be active in high-visibility situations. Only the most dramatic natural disasters attract any significant mass-media attention, and then only briefly; soon after an earthquake or flood, the cameras depart. War refugees, by contrast, can win sustained press coverage if kept concentrated in reasonably accessible camps. Regular warfare among well-developed countries is rare and offers few opportunities for such NGOs, so they focus their efforts on aiding refugees in the poorest parts of the world. This ensures that the food, shelter, and health care offered—although abysmal by Western standards—exceeds what is locally available to non-refugees. The consequences are entirely predictable. Among many examples, the huge refugee camps along the Democratic Republic of Congo's border with Rwanda stand out. They sustain a Hutu nation that would otherwise have been dispersed, making the consolidation of Rwanda impossible and providing a base for radicals to launch more Tutsi-killing raids across the border. Humanitarian intervention has worsened the chances of a stable, long-term resolution of the tensions in Rwanda.

To keep refugee nations intact and preserve their resentments forever is bad enough, but inserting material aid into ongoing conflicts is even worse. Many NGOs that operate in an odor of sanctity routinely supply active combatants. Defenseless, they cannot exclude armed warriors from their feeding stations, clinics, and shelters. Since refugees are presumptively on the losing side, the warriors among them are usually in retreat. By intervening to help, NGOs systematically impede the progress of their enemies toward a decisive victory that could end the war. Sometimes NGOs, impartial to a fault, even help both sides, thus preventing mutual exhaustion and a resulting settlement. And in some extreme cases, such as Somalia, NGOs even pay protection money to local war bands, which use those funds to buy arms. Those NGOs are therefore helping prolong the warfare whose consequences they ostensibly seek to mitigate.

MAKE WAR TO MAKE PEACE

TOO MANY wars nowadays become endemic conflicts that never end because the transformative effects of both decisive victory and exhaustion are blocked by outside intervention. Unlike the ancient problem of war, however, the compounding of its evils by disinterested interventions is a new malpractice that could be curtailed. Policy elites should actively resist the emotional impulse to intervene in other peoples' wars—not because they are indifferent to human suffering but precisely because they care about it and want to facilitate the advent of peace. The United States should dissuade multilateral interventions instead of leading them. New rules should be established for U.N. refugee relief activities to ensure that immediate succor is swiftly followed by repatriation, local absorption, or emigration, ruling out the establishment of permanent refugee camps. And although it may not be possible to constrain interventionist NGOs, they should at least be neither officially encouraged nor funded. Underlying these seemingly perverse measures would be a true appreciation of war's paradoxical logic and a commitment to let it serve its sole useful function: to bring peace.

Relearning Intervention

by Charles William Maynes

One of the most difficult questions in American foreign policy is the use of force—its legitimacy, its utility, its desirability. A run for the White House requires that a candidate address it, and a successful candidate is often not considered a successful president until he actually employs it.

But it may be that the nature of the political debate on the use of force will soon change. It may be that the very purpose for which American leaders threaten the use of force has shifted without many people paying much attention.

The combination of the Persian Gulf war and the demise of Soviet communism had a profound impact on U.S. discussions of the use of force. For a while it seemed as though the U.S. military had been liberated—or at least many observers implied that it had. The United States, it was suggested, was the world's sole remaining superpower. It could intervene wherever it wished without worrying that global rivals would back the other side and risk escalation into a global conflagration.

The Gulf war's demonstration of astounding new technology contributed to the view that the use of force for policy goals was now far more feasible. Soon-to-be secretary of defense Les Aspin noted in a September 21, 1992, speech that in the Gulf war it often took only a few bombs to destroy a target, whereas in Vietnam it required an

---

CHARLES WILLIAM MAYNES *is the editor of* FOREIGN POLICY. *He presented an earlier version of this paper to the Aspen Strategy Group.*

average of 175 and in World War II, 9,000. A former Defense Department official who calculated casualties after the Gulf war wrote that the experience in Kuwait suggested the possibility of "war without excessive brutality." (See John Heidenrich, "The Gulf War: How Many Iraqis Died?" in FOREIGN POLICY 90.)

For many, the vision was intoxicating. America had arrived at its "unipolar moment," according to conservative columnist Charles Krauthammer. Aspin predicted that the United States could now develop a military force "flexible enough to do a number of simultaneous, smaller contingencies."

As the Clinton administration approached its third year, such widely shared optimism seemed badly misplaced. It is important to understand the reasons: The demise of the Soviet Union did not give the United States the clear international field that was earlier predicted; the new consensus failed to take into account whether the gains derived from the use of force had remained constant—in fact, they have gone down; and it failed to acknowledge that the reasons for using force had changed. Earlier, the purpose was deterrence and ensuring acceptable external behavior. Now, it is increasingly becoming compellence and appropriate internal behavior.

A Clear Field?

Although it is true that the United States no longer has the Soviet Union to worry about, it is not necessarily the case that the United States can intervene wherever it wishes without worrying about the involvement of third parties. The U.S. experience in Lebanon should have sobered those inclined to be bellicose. The Reagan administration, believing its own campaign rhetoric about the efficacy of force and the importance of political will, deployed U.S. troops in Lebanon without consideration of Syrian interests. It also believed that the actual use of force would intimidate the opponents of a government it had decided to favor in a vicious civil war. Those costly mistakes led to a humiliating withdrawal 17 months later.

Nor, as the crisis with North Korea has demonstrated clearly, does America have a completely free hand in Northeast Asia. There is a limit beyond which Washington cannot push North Korea without worrying about the reactions of communist China, Japan, and South Korea. China has not hesitated to clarify that its alliance with North

Korea remains in force. It has threatened to veto proposals for economic sanctions that may come before the Security Council. Japan and South Korea have indicated great unease with a policy that might bring conflict to the peninsula.

Along the periphery of Russia, the reaction of the Kremlin is one reason why the U.S. response to Russian peacekeeping efforts in the "near abroad" has been muted, to say the least. In South Asia, any outside military activity must take into account India's reaction. That reality was brought home to Americans when the Nixon administration ordered the USS *Enterprise* to enter the Bay of Bengal during the 1971 Bangladesh crisis. India's strong political reaction made many Americans aware for the first time that India was developing into a serious regional power.

Indeed, in most parts of the world except the Western Hemisphere and perhaps the Persian Gulf, there is a regional power whose opposition to U.S. intervention could make the exercise of force much more difficult to carry out successfully unless one assumes that air power alone would be sufficient. So while the disappearance of the Soviet Union is an important consideration in calculating the utility of the use of force, there are other actors whose policies Washington must take into account.

Nor does greater precision in delivery of weapons necessarily clear the way for a more ready resort to force. It is not at all certain that others calculate the costs of resistance as U.S. policymakers hope they will. As advanced countries have repeatedly learned, in a struggle between the technically sophisticated and unsophisticated, there is often a mismatch in political determination just as large as there is in technical capability. The West in general has a high capacity to kill but a low capacity to die. The equation is often reversed among the targets of the West's wrath. America learned about the differences between capacity and determination in Vietnam, the French learned in Algeria, and the Russians in Afghanistan. And that is the overlooked lesson of U.S. involvement in Somalia. The task the United States set for itself was not infeasible, but the Clinton administration grossly underestimated the price others were willing to pay to stop the U.S. Marines. CIA officials privately concede that the U.S. military may have killed from 7,000 to 10,000 Somalis during its engagement. America lost only 34 soldiers. Notwithstanding that extraordinary disparity, the decision was to withdraw.

Shifting Struggle

For most of history, wars have been a paying proposition. The victor gained land, wealth, or trade. Most of America's wars, in fact, have been over land. Washington was either seeking it or trying to bar others from taking it.

The Cold War was different. That war was a struggle over regimes. The Soviets wanted to change America's and America wanted to change theirs. Neither side sought more land, at least after the spoils of the Second World War had been distributed. Rather, each side sought more allies.

How can we characterize today's world? Today, despite several serious internal conflicts now raging at various points around the globe, the international system seems structurally stable for the first time since 1815. There are several reasons for the transformation.

The first is that none of the great powers seek additional land (though there remain small border disputes, like that between Russia and Japan over the Kurile Islands). Nor does any great power challenge the political legitimacy of the others. Some might say that Russia is a possible exception because so many Russians live in neighboring states and Russia is concerned about their fate. Yet the surprise has been that, thus far, Russia has accepted that its Russian or Russian-speaking brothers and sisters living in the near abroad should become citizens of those countries, even if it insists that neighboring states not discriminate against their Russian speakers and at times urges dual citizenship. China has minor border disputes with its neighbors, but none of them seem non-negotiable. And the decision of the Clinton administration to renew most-favored-nation trading status for China and end the policy link between trade and human rights was an acknowledgement that even if America is not comfortable with China's political system, it does not challenge it.

The second reason for the underlying stability in the international structure is that today most major states seek greater power not through external expansion—the historical route—but through internal development. The salient models for other countries are no longer expansionist countries like Great Britain or France during the age of colonialism but nonexpansionist states like Japan, the United States, or some of the Southeast Asian tigers.

The ideological crusades are over. The Clinton administration's proclaimed doctrine of democratic enlargement is a hope, not a policy. America today largely tends its own garden, its occasional indignation over human rights violations notwithstanding. So do other great powers.

Another reason for the historical discontinuity through which we are passing is that the recent record of states seeking greater power through external expansion is so poor. Argentina failed to seize the Falklands. Iraq failed to seize and hold part of Iran and subsequently all of Kuwait. Libya was forced to relinquish part of Chad. Somalia failed to seize part of Ethiopia.

Nor does the negative record on the use of force end there. More powerful states recently attempting to control the internal political structure of key countries through overt force also have failed—the United States in Vietnam, the Soviet Union in Afghanistan, India in Sri Lanka, and Israel and Syria in Lebanon. The only "successful" uses of large-scale military force in recent years for political purposes have been the U.S. conquests of Grenada and Panama, and even there press reports suggest that the internal situation is now worse, or no better, than before the intervention.

That record of repeated failure in the use of force is in part explained by the inability of conquering states to gain compliance from subject populations. For most of history, when a state conquered a new province, the inhabitants of that province respected the wishes of their new ruler. That practice could even extend into religion—"*cuius est regio, illius est religio*." But nowhere in today's world does such mass compliance take place. On the contrary, populations struggle on for years, even decades—the Tibetans against the Chinese, the East Timorese against the Indonesians, the Palestinians against the Israelis, the Kashmiris against the Indians. Of course, if states are allowed to carry out the kind of ethnic cleansing or forced integration that has been the norm in past centuries, then the seizure of land from a neighbor can turn out to be a rational decision. That is what the issues of settlements in the West Bank or ethnic cleansing in Bosnia have been all about. But if ethnic cleansing or forced integration is not possible, then one of the principal objectives of war disappears, because today, unlike yesterday, subjugated populations are not compliant.

Seven Categories of Force

Today, there appear to be seven distinct categories for the possible use of force by the United States:

- meeting alliance obligations
- promoting counterproliferation
- protecting key allies threatened with internal disorder
- protecting individual Americans
- supporting democracies abroad
- interdicting drugs and countering terrorism
- assisting peacekeeping and peace enforcement.

Ironically, the last, peacekeeping, is by far the most needed, yet it is the task that the United States is the least prepared to undertake. As a result, the United States suffers from a mismatch between capabilities and requirements.

Meeting Alliance Obligations

In theory the United States is obligated through treaties to protect most of Latin America, much of Europe, and a good part of Asia against external attack. The fact is that none of America's allies, except possibly South Korea, are threatened with attack. The Russian threat in Europe will not reappear for years even in the worst scenario. Because of draft-dodging, the Russian army may soon end up with more officers than enlisted personnel. Weapons procurement has been cut to a fraction of Cold War levels. The poor Russian military performance in Chechnya is revealing. Russia would need at least a decade to reestablish its internal cohesion before it could threaten America's treaty allies with a conventional conquest.

Nor does nuclear blackmail remain a serious worry. Blackmail must have a purpose. As long as the two superpowers engaged in a global struggle for influence, the United States had to worry that the Soviet Union would use nuclear blackmail to push European states into a neutral or pro-Soviet stand. But Russia has become a "normal" country seeking normal foreign policy objectives—security and economic development. It is difficult to imagine Russia's threatening France with a nuclear strike in order to gain trade privileges. It is true that the United States must worry about new nuclear states such as India, Israel, Pakistan, and perhaps North Korea, but none of those states have global ambitions. With the possible exception of India, none even have regional ambitions. Most have acquired nuclear weapons in order to combat the overwhelming military or demographic challenges of their neighbors.

What about other security threats to the United States? Say, subversion in Latin America? In the Western Hemisphere, the Cuban/Soviet threat has ended. Not only has Cuba lost the support of Moscow, which enabled Cuban officials to develop a continental or even transcontinental reach, but the country has lost its allure as an alternative model. There is no immediate security threat to the treaty allies of the United States in the Western Hemisphere.

Now, the purpose of threatening the use of force is not deterrence but compellence.

There is one clear security threat for the United States today. It is in Asia. North Korea's apparent nuclear ambitions together with America's treaty commitment to South Korea create an explosive situation. America has 37,000 troops stationed in South Korea. The United States is anxious to prevent North Korea from developing a major nuclear weapons program and has signed a sweeping agreement with North Korea to provide it with safer nuclear energy technology in return for North Korean abandonment of its nuclear weapons program. The inevitable difficulties in implementing this complicated agreement with a suspicious, well-armed opponent pose the most pressing crisis in the world for the United States, but it exists in part because recent administrations have allowed partisan politics at home to prevent the United States from looking out for its own security interests. It is preposterous that the United States should have to assist in the land defense of a country (South Korea) that is twice as populous and 10 times as rich as its northern brother. But ever since Jimmy Carter reversed his campaign pledge to remove U.S. troops from Korea, which was probably premature, the American ground commitment to South Korea has been politically inviolate. Clinton even went so far when he was in South Korea to tell that country's legislators that U.S. troops would remain in South Korea as long as the South Korean people "want" as well as "need" them. Once the current crisis is past, the United States should step back from this foolish statement, which places too much of the initiative in Seoul's hands, and press South Korea to assume, over time, full responsibility for land defense with the United States progressively fulfilling its treaty obligation through air and sea power.

Indeed, over the longer run there is now only one area of the world where the United States must be ready to fight a land war virtually unassisted by the states in the area, and that is the Persian Gulf. None of the states there will be prepared to confront Iraq or Iran for the foreseeable future; and in the wake of the most recent Gulf war, the United States has assumed the role of regional gendarme, a role it cannot abandon until the regimes in Tehran and Baghdad either fall or radically change policies.

Counterproliferation

The "Defense Counterproliferation Initiative" is an important policy priority of the Clinton administration. Clearly, with the end of the Cold War and of the Soviet-U.S. nuclear standoff, the most pressing long-run issue in international security for the United States is the proliferation of weapons of mass destruction. These could be the great equalizers of international relations, robbing the United States of the benefits of being the sole remaining superpower. If Libya, for example, had a handful of deliverable nuclear weapons, the entire diplomatic relationship between Washington and Tripoli might be transformed. Tripoli probably could not seriously threaten the United States, but it could threaten allies so that the United States would have to treat the Libyan regime with greater respect than it does now. The same could be said about a number of other states that are hostile to the United States.

Would nuclear weapons be more dangerous in the hands of Third World states than in those of the great powers? The principal assumption behind much counterproliferation concern is that the answer is yes, but the breakup of the Soviet Union should give pause. Nonetheless, the possession of nuclear weapons by new states would necessarily reduce the margin of U.S. power in the world. There is also the fear, whether valid or not, that a Kim Il Sung or Iranian ayatollah might not care about the fate of his own country or people and would someday decide to use a nuclear weapon against the

United States or one of its allies in a fit of irrationality. And, of course, the more widespread nuclear weapons become, the greater the risk of an accident or seizure of weapons by some outlaw or terrorist group. In short, in the post–Cold War period, any U.S. administration will have a very strong nonproliferation policy.

The issue is what one can realistically do about the issue of proliferation in a military sense. States have learned from the Israeli attack on the Iraqi nuclear facilities—which was only temporarily successful because it merely persuaded the Iraqis to move their program underground. Now all potential proliferants understand that they must not expose their programs to preemptive attack. In addition, according to most experts, a military answer in Korea is difficult. As Peter Rodman, former deputy assistant to the president for national security affairs in the Bush administration, pointed out in a November 1993 conference at the Carnegie Endowment for International Peace, "In the case of North Korea, the use of strikes is complicated by the difficulty of locating the right targets or preventing devastating retaliation by the North Koreans. Some people I respect, who are relatively hawkish on the issue in general, say that the military options are no good." Very senior Pentagon officials confirm that the North Koreans possess deeply protected artillery that could devastate Seoul in the event of war.

In a December 1993 briefing to the press, Pentagon officials hinted that American preemptive strikes against North Korea, similar to those of Israel against Iraq in June 1981, were being considered. But in March 1994, Ashton Carter, the assistant secretary of defense for international security policy, stated that those who believed that Washington might bomb nuclear facilities of potential proliferants had "misunderstood" Washington's intentions.

This author is not in a position to know the administration's true intentions. It is known that the administration is pressing ahead with efforts to develop special weapons that can penetrate the kind of concrete bunkers that are used to house nuclear facilities. Certainly, the United States will continue to keep open military options, however unpromising now, for a preemptive strike in the cause of counterproliferation. It will also continue to work on developing theater antiballistic weapons that could disarm a potential proliferant. But at this point a sensible nonproliferation policy would seem to rely more on diplomacy than force. The United States cannot police an uncooperative world. It is in the American interest to strengthen the nonproliferation regime in all its aspects, increasing the incentives for compliance while reducing the benefits from violation. Working for a comprehensive nuclear test ban, extending the nonproliferation treaty, and implementing the compromise with North Korea involving recognition and trade in exchange for a freeze in its nuclear weapons program seem better ways to serve U.S. interests than any early use of force to further the nonproliferation cause.

Protection of Key States Threatened with Internal Disorder

Some states in the world are so important to the United States that Washington would at least consider the use of military power to preserve the status quo domestically as well as internationally. Former secretary of defense James Schlesinger has suggested that the U.S. relationship with the Saudi Kingdom is now comparable in importance to the U.S. relationship with Germany. Although the United States has no treaty obligation to protect Saudi Arabia from external attack or internal disorder, President Ronald Reagan on October 1, 1981, did state that the United States would "never" let Saudi Arabia become another Iran: "There is no way that we could stand by and see that taken over by anyone that would shut off that oil." American policy during the Gulf war confirmed that, whatever the treaty obligations might be, the United States would use force if necessary to protect the Saudi Kingdom against external aggression. America may even be prepared to take military action to prevent internal change if a sensible option for the use of force seems available.

There are other states in the world that the United States, if it had the option, might consider using military force to protect even without treaty obligations. The United States has invested close to $100 billion in support of the Middle East peace process. The overthrow of the Egyptian government by Islamic forces would be a diplomatic setback for the United States comparable to the downfall of the Shah of Iran. Particularly with the memory of that setback in mind, the United States could be expected at least to consider using military power to help an imperiled Egyptian government if any option made sense. Of course, the Gulf countries should be added to that list. Since the Gulf war, the United States has become the defender of the status quo in the area. Washington certainly would react in the case of external aggression. What it would or could do in the case of an internal uprising is less clear.

There are other countries, such as a number of key states in Central and Eastern Europe, that the United States might judge sufficiently important to consider some form of military response if internal developments threatened to bring to power a government hostile to the United States. But the strong likelihood is that in the end Washington would do nothing of a significant military nature.

The ideal model for assisting an ally faced with internal disorder would be President George Bush's decision to save the Aquino regime in the Philippines by ordering U.S. aircraft to fly over Manila on December 1, 1989, in an implicit threat to those threatening to overthrow the government. The effort was low key and successful. No Americans died and few were even at risk. But it is doubtful if military intervention would be as successful in the other countries of special concern to the United States. It is even doubtful that the United States could carry out a similar operation in the Philippines today. When Bush gave his order, the United States still had military personnel stationed on Philippine soil. In addition, the United States enjoyed a positive reputation among the Filipino people. In most of the cases in question, the United States enjoys little or no advantage in terms of military intervention. It is revealing that when the Saudi monarch was threatened by religious riots in Mecca in 1979, the king drew on French commandos to help him restore order. Allowing Americans in the Holy City was seen as too risky.

So while it remains true that there are several countries of sufficient geopolitical interest for American officials to consider using force to preserve the status quo, a hard look at the realities suggests that U.S. options are few.

Support for Democracies Abroad

When U.N. ambassador Madeleine Albright delivered the Clinton administration's position on the "Use of Force in a Post–Cold War World" before the National War College on September 23, 1993, she mentioned four problems that might require the use of force: the spread of weapons of mass destruction, terrorism, ethnic violence, and the fall of democracy. She specifically mentioned Haiti as an example of the last.

Among the democracies abroad with which the United States has no formal security ties but that might well attract American forces in its defense is Israel. United by democratic values and intimate intergovernmental and societal ties, the two countries are as close to the status of allies as it is possible to be without the formal designation. Indeed, the lack of that formal designation continues because there are unbalanced advantages and disadvantages to the current arrangement. The lack of a treaty arrangement frees Israel from the obligation to consult with the United States about its own military actions. That deprives the United States of the ability to stop actions it opposes but also spares it the obligation to confront Israel publicly when the interests of the two countries diverge.

But the administration has suggested a grander commitment to democracy. Its off-and-on-again approach to Haiti has suggested that it is prepared in some circumstances to use force to reestablish democracy in a country where it has been overthrown. In Presidential Decision Directive 25, one justification for the dispatch of U.N. or other peacekeeping troops is the restoration of democracy. No doubt, if a viable military option existed, America would intervene to protect democratic forces in Mexico against an authoritarian alternative if that alternative threatened to become anti-American.

But a review of U.S. policy toward Haiti suggests that, official rhetoric notwithstanding, the United States will be very reluctant to use force to restore democracy to a friendly country. The Clinton administration did send troops to occupy Haiti and as of early 1995 the operation has gone much better than most observers expected, but congressional opposition to U.S. military action in Haiti has remained robust even though the Haitian government agreed to allow the U.S. troops to land unopposed. In light of congressional views, it is difficult to imagine how the executive branch can build a national consensus for a lengthy occupation of Haiti, yet that is what seems to be required. And if Washington finds it so difficult to act in Haiti, which is so close to U.S. shores and the source of thousands of unwanted refugees, it is unlikely to act elsewhere to "restore democracy." Beyond a very small circle of states, the use of force to restore democracy is going to be primarily through U.N. or other types of peacekeeping, and Presidential Decision Directive 25 makes it clear that U.S. participation in United Nations peacekeeping will be minimal.

Protecting Individuals and Countering Drugs and Terrorism

There will always be a military requirement for the United States to protect its citizens overseas. Approximately 2.5 million Americans live abroad, of whom nearly 100,000 reside outside the Organization for Economic Cooperation and Development countries where they can count on protection from the local government. But even in non-Western countries American citizens must depend on the local police. They cannot expect the Marines to help in more than a handful of situations.

Criminal acts of terrorism will be another concern of the U.S. military. But except on rare occasions where the U.S. government can trace a pattern of terrorist actions back to an accountable state—as Washington believes it has been able to do with Libya—there is no large-scale military response to terrorism. Good intelligence and police work are more important than military force.

Peacekeeping and Peace Enforcement

Ironically, the greatest requirement for the use of American force is in the one area where the United States is most skittish—namely peacekeeping and peace enforcement. There has been a veritable explosion of intrastate conflicts in recent years. According to U.N. figures, since the fall of the Berlin Wall, 82 conflicts have broken out around the world. But only three of those have been interstate. Seventy-nine were civil wars. And of the three interstate wars, Bosnia and Nagorno-Karabakh are regarded by many as civil wars.

In most of the internal conflicts one can imagine a constructive role for outside mediation and observation if not peace enforcement. Yet the recent evolution in U.S. policy has made it more and more unlikely that America will play a constructive role in that area.

The United States by some estimates will be spending more for defense in the coming four years than the rest of the world combined. Yet Washington's real defense needs do not seem to require that effort unless America wishes to become much more directly involved in curtailing intrastate ethnic strife and civil war.

In that regard, the position of the Clinton administration and the Congress on peacekeeping is scarcely reassuring. The early rhetoric suggested that the United States had a major interest in trying to intervene to manage such conflicts. But the recent Presidential Decision Directive 25 is greatly watered down from earlier versions and adopts criteria so restrictive that they would seem to bar the kind of U.N. force that has successfully monitored the ceasefire on the Golan Heights. Yet that very modest directive is facing major resistance in Congress, which has been hesitant to fund new peacekeeping operations. Both branches of government have been so timid about peacekeeping that using U.S. ground troops in NATO for European peacekeeping is ruled out unless they operate in circumstances that eliminate all risk. It is difficult to see how the United States is going to remain a European power if it refuses to participate in the one form of military activity that is the most needed in Europe today.

The Issue of Compellence

Yet even if the greatest need for U.S. forces is peacekeeping and peace enforcement in intrastate conflicts, that fact by itself does not help policymakers decide when it is appropriate and when it is not appropriate for the United States to intervene in ethnic disputes. What are the differences between interstate conflict and intrastate conflict that U.S. policymakers should understand before they consider the use of force?

For most American decision makers, the relevant paradigm for the use of force is the Cold War, with whose rules and regulations they are most familiar because they were similar to those of previous interstate conflicts. According to this paradigm, accountable governments maneuver around one another using the tools of diplomacy and deterrence. Each side attempts to influence the other through a series of veiled or open threats. Each side rationally calculates the odds and usually remains "deterred." Military power in steadily increasing amounts seems highly relevant to the conduct of policy because there is little danger that the weapons might be used; yet if deterrence fails, the more weapons the better. No effort is made to influence internal behavior. Indeed, it is not difficult to imagine how quickly the Cold War would have become a hot one had either Moscow or Washington threatened to use force to change the internal political order in either country—for instance, to end the Gulag or force immediate equal rights for black Americans.

Does that model for the use of force fit the situations American decision makers face today in places like Bosnia or Georgia or Somalia? Generally speaking, those conflicts do involve intrastate struggles. Statesmen are trying to change internal behavior, not external behavior. They often are not dealing with clearly accountable actors. Nor are the actors always rational. It was not rational for General Mohammad Farah Aidid to resist American demands at such a high price. But he and his people were willing to pay the price. It has not been rational for the Bosnian Serbs to carry out many of their actions, but the bitter memory of World War II, when so many Serbs died at the hands of Croats and Muslims, has driven them into a frenzy. It is not rational for Armenians to ethnically cleanse Azeris from Nagorno-Karabakh because it will prolong the war, but the outside world has little influence on the Armenian leadership.

In traditional interstate conflicts, the number of rational and accountable leaders on each side can be identified and is limited. A handful of officials at the top are able to give orders and have them obeyed. These officials order troops to fight and they order troops to lay down their arms. Usually, the troops follow orders. That fact dramatically influences the way that the international community orchestrates its efforts at preventive diplomacy or humanitarian aid. The United Nations, regional organizations, and neighboring states attempt to pressure the small circle of accountable leaders to persuade them to follow a conciliatory policy. Those efforts may or may not be successful, but no one doubts where pressure must be directed. That is what Washington has been trying to do in North Korea. But who are the real leaders in Bosnia or Haiti or Somalia? Can the Bosnian Serb leaders successfully order their troops to cease fighting? Can the Bosnian government command Muslim soldiers to stop struggling to return to homes from which they were driven by force?

In fact, in many intrastate conflicts, popular passions make elite compromise difficult. Conflicts become less a matter of calculation at the top than of mass emotion at the bottom. Leaders may rise up to exploit those emotions, but the kind of leadership they display resembles a man running ahead of a stampeding herd who maintains that he is in charge. He may be able to lead the herd to move to the right or the left but he cannot halt it. If he turns around to stop it, he will be trampled.

In intrastate conflicts, religious or ethnic hatred is often so strong that dialogue becomes virtually impossible. The opposing side is unfortunately viewed as almost subhuman. Extermination of the heretic, expulsion of the outsider is declared to be God's work or a patriot's duty. It is suggested that if the other side prevails, one's own side may well disappear. Only one way of life is likely to survive. In such situations, all individuals, old or young, male or female, are identified as combatants. The Indians in the American West knew that the arrival of an unarmed farm family was in effect a declaration of war. It was the advance troop of a larger army to follow that would make the traditional Indian way of life impossible.

Several centuries ago in Ireland, the Catholic inhabitants may well have viewed Protestant settlers as an even greater threat to the welfare and security of the Catholic Irish than the British soldiers who protected those settlers. The settlers represented another way of life that would suppress or even eradicate their own. The struggle was therefore to the knife.

Modern ethnic and religious conflicts regrettably have not lost this savage character. Palestinians and Israeli settlers on the West Bank or various ethnic groups in Bosnia struggle like the ancient Irish and for many of the same reasons. Each outsider, no matter how young or infirm, is seen as a mortal danger. That is the rationale for "ethnic cleansing," which has persisted throughout history.

Another characteristic of internal conflicts is that each side seeks total victory. Surrender is almost always unconditional. Victory for one means oblivion for the other. There is therefore a desperate quality to civil wars that makes them particularly hard to control once they start. In such struggles, when accountable actors do step forward and adopt unpopular positions, they often find that their own lives are in danger. The United States suffered terribly from its civil war, but it did have the good fortune that when one side prevailed, the losing army was commanded by a leader who could order his troops to cease fighting and gain compliance. Robert E. Lee deserves his reputation for greatness because he told his generals it was time to stop fighting and restore the nation. In many other civil wars such calming advice is not given or is not accepted. The leaders of the Irish uprising during and after World War I knew it was risky to seek a compromise with the British. Michael Collins, the Irish guerrilla leader, presciently stated that he had signed his own death warrant when he agreed to leave the six most northern counties under British control. He was assassinated eight months later. The Palestinians over the years have eliminated leaders who threatened to compromise with Israel. Today, Yasir Arafat may be in danger. Afghanistan, Somalia, and Bosnia suffer in part because it is difficult to identify accountable actors. There are too many who claim to be accountable but cannot deliver their people. Those who truly try may be pushed aside or eliminated. It is instructive that in Serbia, Slobodan Milošević is not the most extreme proponent of Serbian nationalism.

Since the main problem in the world today is not interstate aggression but ethnic or civil conflict, how can we deal with it? There are three options for the international community when a civil, ethnic, or religious war breaks out: victory by the stronger party, compelling all parties to compromise by the introduction of outside force, or an attempt to encourage power-sharing.

Letting the stronger side win is often the most effective option. It is, in fact, the option the international community traditionally has taken. Compellence is required, however, if outside powers are not prepared to see the stronger side win. Deterrence is unlikely to work precisely because the goal of the international community is to change internal behavior, not external behavior. Such an effort requires either peacekeeping or peace enforcement. In short, it entails risks. If the two sides acquiesce in the peacekeeping force, a ceasefire can be frozen in place and the risks are relatively low. An example is the U.N. peacekeeping force in Cyprus. If the two sides do not agree to the deployment, then a form of U.N. or other protectorate must be established and the risks begin to rise. Overall, compellence by military force is a daunting task that neither the international community nor the United States will often be willing to undertake. But if the task is never undertaken, then the international community is really saying that allowing the stronger to prevail is its only effective option. It is saying that there are no geopolitical consequences to internal change resulting from ethnic conflict that are sufficiently grave to merit the use of force. The 79 conflicts the U.N. secretariat has identified must simply be allowed to burn out.

A third option is power-sharing. But it must be recognized that parties in conflict usually will be reluctant to accept power-sharing until some rough balance of power has been achieved through either their own efforts or outside pressure. That is what happened in South Africa, when that country abandoned apartheid. There was no way to get a peaceful solution in South Africa except through power-sharing. Calling for winner-take-all democratic elections cannot solve such ethnic conflicts. Indeed, elections may even trigger conflict, as in Bosnia, where the West foolishly encouraged a referendum on independence that the Serb population boycotted.

Other approaches to ethnic conflict besides compellence must be explored. Ethnic problems in places like the Crimea or Kosovo cannot be solved with the approaches now under discussion. Secession in either case will bring on war. Ukraine will not permit Crimea to secede, and Serbia will not permit Kosovo to join Albania. But efforts to improve the human rights of Russians in Crimea or Albanians in Kosovo are also unlikely to work. Success in enhancing their rights is unlikely ever to be enough. To avoid permanent crisis, new, previously untouchable concepts like dual citizenship or shared sovereignty need to be introduced into the dialogue.

To avoid recurring conflict, the international community must also encourage closer economic and political ties among key states in the regions of conflict. In the case of Ukraine and Russia, fear of encouraging a restoration of the Soviet Union has prevented the West from encouraging closer ties between the two republics. But since neither will ever be allowed into the European Union and Ukrainian nationalism seems too strong to permit reabsorption in a Moscow-dominated polity, encouragement of closer ties seems prudent—both to prevent conflict and to improve the welfare of both countries. The Balkans seem even more resistant to peaceful solutions, but if the states there are to rise above the narrow confines of exclusionary and destructive nationalism, some form of Balkan confederation will be needed. The outside world could help by funding regional infrastructure projects that would improve life in all the countries in question. As expensive as those may be, they will be much cheaper than the continued costs of conflict in the area.

So far the established democracies have two unpalatable options in dealing with ethnic conflict. They can remain aloof and seem politically impotent, or they can become militarily engaged and risk embarrassing failure. A third path will require much bolder and more creative diplomacy than the world has seen so far in the post–Cold War period.

Redefining the National Interest

Joseph S. Nye, Jr.

CONFUSION AFTER KOSOVO

NATO'S MILITARY intervention in Kosovo dramatically raises a larger problem: how should the United States define its interests in today's world? After the collapse of the Soviet Union, what are the limits of America's concerns abroad? Can one define interests conventionally in the information age? The "national interest" is a slippery concept, used to describe as well as prescribe foreign policy. Hence the considerable debate about it. Some scholars have even regretted the waning of the very idea of a "national" interest today. Writing in these pages, Samuel P. Huntington argued recently that "without a sure sense of national identity, Americans have become unable to define their national interests, and as a result subnational commercial interests and transnational and nonnational ethnic interests have come to dominate foreign policy."

For almost five decades, the containment of Soviet power provided a North Star to guide American foreign policy. From a longer historical perspective, however, the Cold War was the anomalous period, and even it involved some bitter disputes over where our interests lay—during the Vietnam War, for example. Before World War II, confusion was more often the rule. For example, ethnic differences colored appraisals of whether the United States should enter World War I. Peter Trubowitz's recent study of American definitions of national interests

---

JOSEPH S. NYE, JR., is Dean of Harvard's Kennedy School of Government and served as Assistant Secretary of Defense for International Security Affairs in 1994 and 1995.

in the 1890s, 1930s, and 1980s concludes that "there is no single national interest. Analysts who assume that America has a discernible national interest whose defense should determine its relations with other nations are unable to explain the persistent failure to achieve domestic consensus on international objectives."

With all that said, it would be a mistake to discard the term. As the Commission on America's National Interests declared in 1996, "national interests are the fundamental building blocks in any discussion of foreign policy. . . . In fact, the concept is used regularly and widely by administration officials, members of Congress, and citizens at large." The commission goes on to identify five vital interests that most agree would justify the unilateral use of force. Not everyone would agree with this particular list. Economic and humanitarian interests are also widely thought important. Many experts argue that vital strategic concerns are more widely shared than other interests, and deserve priority because were we to fail to protect them, more Americans would be affected and in more profound ways. Leaders and experts are right to point out dangers to the public and to try to persuade it. Yet even "objective" threats are not always obvious. The connection between a particular event (Iraq's invasion of Kuwait or Serbia's rejection of the Rambouillet agreement) and an American interest may involve a long causal chain. Different people see different risks and dangers. And priorities vary: reasonable people can disagree, for example, about how much insurance to buy against remote threats and whether to do so before pursuing other values (such as human rights). In a democracy, such political struggles over the exact definition of national interests—and how to pursue them—are both inevitable and healthy. Foreign-policy experts can help clarify causation and tradeoffs in particular cases, but experts alone cannot decide. Nor should they. The national interest is too important to leave solely to the geopoliticians. Elected officials must play the key role.

In a democracy, the national interest is simply the set of shared priorities regarding relations with the rest of the world. It is broader than strategic interests, though they are part of it. It can include values such as human rights and democracy, if the public feels that those values are so important to its identity that it is willing to pay a price to promote them. The American people clearly think that their interests include certain values and their promotion abroad—such as opposition to ethnic cleansing in the Balkans. A democratic definition of the national interest does not accept the distinction between a morality-based and an interest-based foreign policy. Moral values are simply intangible interests. Leaders and experts may point out the costs of indulging these values. But if an informed public disagrees, experts cannot deny the legitimacy of public opinion. Polls show that the American people are neither isolationist nor eager to serve as the world's police. But finding a middle course is proving difficult and complex.

THE IMPACT OF THE INFORMATION AGE

STRATEGISTS ADVISE that interests should be defined in relation to power—but how would one describe the distribution of power in the information age? Some think the end of the bipolar world left multipolarity in its stead. But that is not a very good description of a world in which one country, the United States, is so much more powerful than all the others. On the other hand, unipolarity is not a very good description either, because it exaggerates the degree to and ease with which the United States is able to get what it wants—witness Kosovo.

Instead, power today is distributed like a three-dimensional chess game. The top, military board is unipolar, with the United States far outstripping all other states. The middle, economic board is multipolar, with the United States, Europe, and Japan accounting for two-thirds of world production. But the bottom—representing transnational relations that cross borders and lie outside the control of governments—has a more dispersed structure of power. This complexity makes policymaking today more difficult. It means playing on several boards at the same time. Moreover, although it is important not to ignore the continuing importance of military force for some purposes, it is equally important not to be misled into thinking that American power can always get its way in nonmilitary matters. The United States is a preponderant, but not a dominant, power.

Another distinction to keep in mind is that between "hard power" (a country's economic and military ability to buy and coerce) and "soft power" (the ability to attract through cultural and ideological appeal).

It is important that half a million foreign students want to study in the United States each year, that Europeans and Asians want to watch American films and TV, and that American liberties are attractive in many parts of the world. Our values are significant sources of soft power. Both hard and soft power remain vital, but in the information age soft power is becoming more compelling than ever before.

Massive flows of cheap information have expanded the number of contacts across national borders. In a deregulated world, global markets and nongovernmental actors play a larger role. States are more easily penetrated today and less like the classic realist model of solid billiard balls bouncing off each other. As a result, political leaders are finding it more difficult to maintain a coherent set of priorities in foreign policy, and more difficult to articulate a single national interest.

Yet the United States, with its democratic society, is well placed to benefit from the rapidly developing information age. Although greater pluralism may diminish the coherence of government policies, our institutions are attractive and the openness of our society enhances credibility—a crucial resource in an information age. Thus the United States is well placed to make use of soft power. At the same time, the soft power that comes from being a "city on the hill" does not provide the coercive capability that hard power does. Alone, it does not support a very venturesome foreign policy.

Hence different aspects of the information age mean different things for America's national interests. On the one hand, a good case can be made that the information revolution will have long-term benefits for democracies. Democratic societies can create credible information because they are not threatened by it. Authoritarian states will have more trouble. Governments can limit their citizens' access to the Internet and global markets, but they pay a high price if they do so. Singapore and China, for example, are currently wrestling with these problems. Moreover, transparency is becoming a key asset for countries seeking investments. Governments that want rapid development will have to give up some of the barriers to information flows.

On the other hand, some aspects of the information age are less benign. The free flow of broadcast information in open societies has always had an impact on public opinion and the formulation of foreign policy. But now the flow has increased in volume and shortened news cycles have reduced the time for deliberation. By focusing on certain conflicts and human rights problems, the media pressure politicians to respond to some foreign problems and not others—for example, Somalia rather than southern Sudan in 1992. The so-called CNN effect makes it hard to keep items that might otherwise warrant a lower priority off the top of the public agenda. Now, with the added interactivity of groups on the Internet, it will be harder than ever to maintain a consistent agenda.

Also problematic is the effect of transnational information flows on the stability of national communities. The Canadian media guru Marshall McLuhan once prophesied that communications technologies would turn the world into a global village. Instead of a single cosmopolitan community, however, they may have produced a congeries of global villages, each with all the parochial prejudices that the word implies, but with a greater awareness of global inequality. Transnational economic forces are disrupting traditional lifestyles, and this increases economic integration and communal disintegration at the same time. This is particularly true in the post-Soviet states and the old European-built empires of Africa. Political entrepreneurs use inexpensive information channels to mobilize the discontented on sub-national tribal levels: some to the cause of repressive nationalism, and some to transnational ethnic and religious communities. This in turn leads to increased demands for self-determination, increased violence, and other violations of human rights—all in the presence of television cameras and the Internet.

AMERICAN POWER AND PRIORITIES

WILLIAM PERRY and Ashton Carter have recently argued that we should rethink the way we understand risks to U.S. security. At the top of their new hierarchy they put "A list" threats like that the Soviet Union once presented to our survival. The "B list" features imminent threats to U.S. interests—but not to our survival—such as North Korea or Iraq. The "C list" includes important "contingencies that indirectly affect U.S. security but do not directly threaten U.S. interests": "the Kosovos, Bosnias, Somalias, Rwandas, and Haitis."

What is striking is how the "C list" has come to dominate today's foreign policy agenda. Carter and Perry speculate that this is because of the disappearance of "A list" threats since the end of the Cold War. But another reason is that "C list" issues dominate media attention in the information age. Dramatic visual portrayals of immediate human conflict and suffering are far easier to convey to the public than "A list" abstractions like the possibility of a "Weimar Russia," the rise of a hegemonic China and the importance of our alliance with Japan, or the potential collapse of the international system of trade and investment. Yet if these larger, more abstract strategic issues were to turn out badly, they would have a far greater impact on the lives of most Americans.

How should America set priorities in the information age?

How should Americans set priorities in such a world? We should start by understanding our power. On one hand, for reasons given above, American power is now less fungible and effective than it might first appear. On the other, the United States is likely to remain preponderant well into the next century. For a variety of reasons, the information revolution is likely to enhance rather than diminish American power.

As a wealthy status quo power, the United States has an interest in maintaining international order. Behind the abstractions about rising interdependence are changes that make it more difficult to isolate the United States from the effects of events in the rest of the world. More concretely, there are two simple reasons why Americans have a national interest in preventing disorder beyond our borders. First, events and actors out there can hurt us; and second, Americans want to influence distant governments and organizations on a variety of issues such as the proliferation of weapons of mass destruction, terrorism, drugs, shared resources, and the environment.

To do so, the United States cannot merely set a good example—it needs hard-power resources. Maintaining these will require an investment that Americans have recently been unwilling to make—witness the decline in the foreign affairs budget and the reluctance to take casualties. It is difficult to be a superpower on the cheap. Second, the United States has to recognize a basic proposition of public-goods theory: if

AP/WIDE WORLD PHOTOS

What should be our foreign policy priority? Russian soldiers . . .

the largest beneficiary of a public good (such as international order) does not provide disproportionate resources toward its maintenance, the smaller beneficiaries are unlikely to do so. This puts a different twist on Secretary of State Madeleine K. Albright's phrase that the United States is "the indispensable nation," and one less palatable to the public and to Congress.

Third, we should make sure that top priority is given to those aspects of the international system that, if not attended to properly, would have profound effects on the basic international order and therefore on the lives and welfare of Americans. Some analysts have suggested that we can learn something from the lesson of the United Kingdom in the nineteenth century, when it was also a preponderant but not dominating power. Three public goods that Britain attended to were maintaining the balance of power among the major states, promoting an open international economic system, and maintaining open international commons such as the freedom of the seas. All three translate relatively well to the current American case. In terms of

AP/WIDE WORLD PHOTOS

... or Kosovar refugees?

the distribution of power, we need to continue to "shape the environment" (in the words of the Pentagon's *Quadrennial Defense Review*), and that is why we keep 100,000 troops based in Europe, another 100,000 in Asia, and some 20,000 near the Persian Gulf. Our role as a stabilizer and a reassurance against the rise of hostile hegemons in important regions has to remain a top priority, an "A list" issue.

Meanwhile, promoting an open international economic system is good not just for America's economic growth but for other countries' as well. In the long term, economic growth is likely to foster stable democratic middle-class societies around the world. To keep the global system open, the United States must resist protectionism at home and strengthen international monitoring institutions such as the World Trade Organization, the International Monetary Fund, and the Bank for International Settlements. In regard to international commons, the United States, like nineteenth-century Britain, has an interest in freedom of the seas, but also in the environment, in the preservation of endangered species, and in the uses of outer space and of the new cyberspace.

Beyond the nineteenth-century analogy, in today's world the United States has a general interest in developing and maintaining the international laws and institutions that deal not just with trade and the environment, but with arms proliferation, peacekeeping, human rights, and other concerns. Those who denigrate the importance of law and institutions forget that the United States is a status quo power. They also ignore the extent to which legitimacy is a power reality. True realists would not make such a mistake.

Finally, as a preponderant power, the United States can provide an important public good by acting as a mediator and convener. By helping to organize coalitions of the willing and by using its good offices to mediate conflicts in places like Northern Ireland, the Middle East, or the Aegean Sea, the United States can help to shape the world in ways that are beneficial to us as well as to other nations.

THE C LIST

IF WE did not live in the information age, the foregoing strategy for prioritizing America's national interests might suffice. But the reality is that nonvital crises like Somalia, Bosnia, Haiti, and Kosovo continue to force their way to the foreground because of their ability to command massive media attention. Such crises raise moral concerns that the American people consistently include in their list of foreign policy interests. Policy experts may deplore such sympathies, but they are a democratic reality.

Some might object that a strategy based on "A list" issues does not take account of the ongoing erosion of Westphalian national sovereignty that is occurring today. It is true that old-fashioned state sovereignty is eroding—both de facto, through the penetration of national borders by transnational forces, and de jure, as seen in the imposition of sanctions against South Africa for apartheid, the development of an International Criminal Court, and the bombing of Yugoslavia over its policies in Kosovo. But the erosion of sovereignty is a long-term trend of decades and centuries, and it is a mixed blessing rather a clear good. Although the erosion may help advance human rights in repressive regimes by exposing them to international attention, it also portends considerable disorder. Recall that the seventeenth-century

Peace of Westphalia created a system of sovereign states to curtail vicious civil wars over religion. Although it is true that sovereignty stands in the way of national self-determination, such self-determination is not the unequivocal moral good it first appears. In a world where there are some two hundred states but many thousands of often overlapping entities that might eventually make a claim to nationhood, blind promotion of self-determination would have highly problematic consequences.

A human rights policy is not a foreign policy; it is an important part of a foreign policy.

So what do we do about the humanitarian concerns and strong moral preferences that Americans want to see expressed in their foreign policy? Americans have rarely accepted pure realpolitik as a guiding principle, and human rights and the alleviation of humanitarian disasters have long been important aspects of our foreign policy. But foreign policy involves trying to accomplish varied objectives in a complex and recalcitrant world. This entails tradeoffs. A human rights policy is not itself a foreign policy; it is an important *part* of a foreign policy. During the Cold War, this balancing act often meant tolerating human rights abuses by regimes that were crucial to balancing Soviet power—for example, in South Korea before its transition to democracy. Similar problems persist in the current period—witness our policy toward Saudi Arabia, or our efforts to balance human rights in China with our long-term strategic objectives.

In the information age, humanitarian concerns dominate attention to a greater degree than before, often at the cost of diverting attention from "A list" strategic issues. Since pictures are more powerful than words, arguments about tradeoffs become emotional and difficult. Of course, acting on humanitarian values is often appropriate. Few Americans can look at television pictures of starving people or miserable refugees and not say that their country should do something about them. And the United States often does respond to such catastrophes. Sometimes this is quite easily done, such as hurricane relief to Central America or the early stages of famine relief in Somalia. But apparently simple cases like Somalia can turn out to be extremely difficult to resolve, and others, like Kosovo, are difficult from the start.

The problem with such hard cases is that the humanitarian interest that instigates the action often turns out to be a mile wide and an inch deep. The American public's impulse to help starving Somalis (whose food supply was being interrupted by various warlords) vanished in the face of televised pictures of dead U.S. soldiers being dragged through the streets of Mogadishu. Such transience is sometimes attributed to popular reluctance to accept casualties. But that is too simple. Americans went into the Gulf War expecting and willing to accept some ten thousand casualties. As this suggests, Americans are reluctant to accept casualties only in cases where their *only* foreign policy goals are unreciprocated humanitarian interests. Ironically, when opinion turns against such cases, this may not only divert attention and limit willingness to support "A list" interests but may also undermine support for action in other, more serious humanitarian crises. One of the direct effects of the Somalia disaster was America's failure (along with other countries) to support and reinforce the United Nations peacekeeping force in Rwanda that could have limited a true genocide in 1994.

One effect of Somalia was America's failure to prevent true genocide in Rwanda in 1994.

There are no easy answers for such cases. We could not simply turn off the television or unplug our computers even if we wanted to. The "C list" cannot simply be ignored. But there are certain rules of prudence that may help the integration of such issues into the larger strategy for advancing the national interest. First, there are many degrees of humanitarian concern and many degrees of intervention to reflect them, such as condemnation, sanctions targeted on individuals, broad sanctions, and various uses of force. We should save violent options for the most egregious cases. When we do use force, it is worth remembering some principles of the "just war" doctrine: having a just cause in the eyes of others; discrimination in means so as to not unduly punish the innocent; proportionality of means to ends; and a high probability of good consequences (rather than wishful thinking).

We should generally avoid the use of force except in cases where our humanitarian interests are reinforced by the existence of other strong national interests. This was the case in the Gulf War, where the United States was concerned not only with the aggression against Kuwait, but also with energy supplies and regional allies. This was not the case in Somalia. In the former Yugoslavia (Bosnia and Kosovo), our interests combine both humanitarian values and the strategic concerns of European allies and NATO. We should try to involve other regional actors, preferably in the lead role when possible. In Africa after 1995, the United States offered to help with training, intelligence, logistics, and transportation if African countries provided the troops for a peacekeeping force. There were few takers. If African states are unwilling to do their part, we should be wary of going it alone. In Europe, we should welcome the idea of combined joint task forces that would be separable but not separate from NATO and encourage the Europeans to take the lead on such issues.

We should also be clearer about what are true cases of genocide. The American people have a real humanitarian interest in not letting another Holocaust occur. Yet we did just that in Rwanda in 1994. We therefore need to do more to organize prevention and response to real cases of genocide. Unfortunately, the Genocide Convention is written so loosely and the word is so abused for political purposes that there is danger of the term becoming trivialized. But a strict historical interpretation of the crime, based on the precedents of the Holocaust and Rwanda, can help to avoid such pitfalls.

Finally, Americans should be very wary about intervention in civil wars over self-determination. The principle is dangerously ambiguous; atrocities are often committed by activists on both sides and the precedents can have disastrous consequences.

How could these rules of prudence have helped in the case of Kosovo? At an earlier stage, they would have produced more caution. In December 1992, President Bush issued a vague threat that Serbia should not attack ethnic Albanians in its Kosovo province while he remained silent on Bosnia. A year later, the Clinton administration reiterated the warning. The United States was saved from having to back up these threats by the Kosovar Albanians' pacifist leader, Ibrahim Rugova, who espoused a Gandhian response to Serbian oppression. After 1996, the rise of the militantly pro-independence Kosovo Liberation Army undermined Rugova's leadership. According to journalist Chris Hedges, the radicals of the KLA, who combine "hints of fascism on one side and whiffs of communism on the other," have been labeled a terrorist organization by U.S. government officials. A KLA victory might well have involved atrocities and ethnic cleansing of the Serb minority in Kosovo. The KLA's refusal to sign the Rambouillet agreement in the first round of talks in February let the NATO alliance off the moral hook and should have been used as an opportunity to step back. Instead, the United States "fixed the problem" by pretending to believe the KLA's promise to accept autonomy within Yugoslavia. The United States then threatened to bomb Serbia. Milošević called the American bluff and initiated his planned ethnic cleansing of Kosovo.

At that point, new facts on the ground raised Kosovo from the "C list" to the "B list" of U.S. foreign policy concerns. The scale and ferocity of Milošević's ethnic cleansing could not be ignored. European allies such as the United Kingdom, France, and even Germany joined the United States in calling for NATO action. If the United States had then pulled the rug out from under its pro-interventionist allies, it would have produced a NATO crisis on the scale of Suez in 1956. The humanitarian impact had grown immensely and was now reinforced by a strategic interest in the future of the American alliance with Europe. Skeptics argue that one should never pursue "sunk costs." By this argument, if Kosovo was not worth intervention before, it is not worth it now. But history is path-dependent, since choices, once made, eliminate certain options and create others. In calculating the costs and benefits of future actions, policymakers must realistically assess the current situation, not the past. It does no good to lament the more prudent paths not taken at an earlier stage.

Kosovo illustrates how a "C list" issue can migrate to the "B list" of national interests that merit the use of force. Kosovo itself is not a vital American interest, and it only touches tangentially on an "A list" issue (the credibility of the NATO alliance). The "A list" also includes the future of Russia and of international laws and institutions such as the United Nations. NATO, Russia, and the United Nations must all figure in how we resolve the Kosovo crisis. And the rules of prudence must still be applied as we insist on the return of the refugees and the withdrawal of Serbian forces. If moral outrage or unilateralist temptations blind Americans to their other "A list" priorities, the

United States may dangerously overreach itself and turn a just cause into a counterproductive crusade.

Prudence alone cannot determine the national interest in the information age. But better consequences will flow if American values and goals are related to American power, and interests are rationally pursued within prudent limits. Determining the national interest has always been contentious throughout U.S. history. That is to be expected in a healthy democracy. But the debate about the American national interest in the information age should pay more attention to the peculiar nature of American power today; it should establish strategic priorities accordingly; and it should develop prudential rules that allow the United States to meld its strategic, economic, and humanitarian interests into an effective foreign policy.

The Rise of Illiberal Democracy

Fareed Zakaria

THE NEXT WAVE

THE AMERICAN diplomat Richard Holbrooke pondered a problem on the eve of the September 1996 elections in Bosnia, which were meant to restore civic life to that ravaged country. "Suppose the election was declared free and fair," he said, and those elected are "racists, fascists, separatists, who are publicly opposed to [peace and reintegration]. That is the dilemma." Indeed it is, not just in the former Yugoslavia, but increasingly around the world. Democratically elected regimes, often ones that have been reelected or reaffirmed through referenda, are routinely ignoring constitutional limits on their power and depriving their citizens of basic rights and freedoms. From Peru to the Palestinian Authority, from Sierra Leone to Slovakia, from Pakistan to the Philippines, we see the rise of a disturbing phenomenon in international life—illiberal democracy.

It has been difficult to recognize this problem because for almost a century in the West, democracy has meant *liberal* democracy—a political system marked not only by free and fair elections, but also by the rule of law, a separation of powers, and the protection of basic liberties of speech, assembly, religion, and property. In fact, this latter bundle of freedoms—what might be termed constitutional liberalism—is theoretically different and historically distinct

FAREED ZAKARIA is Managing Editor of *Foreign Affairs* and a Contributing Editor for *Newsweek*.

from democracy. As the political scientist Philippe Schmitter has pointed out, "Liberalism, either as a conception of political liberty, or as a doctrine about economic policy, may have coincided with the rise of democracy. But it has never been immutably or unambiguously linked to its practice." Today the two strands of liberal democracy, interwoven in the Western political fabric, are coming apart in the rest of the world. Democracy is flourishing; constitutional liberalism is not.

Today, 118 of the world's 193 countries are democratic, encompassing a majority of its people (54.8 percent, to be exact), a vast increase from even a decade ago. In this season of victory, one might have expected Western statesmen and intellectuals to go one further than E. M. Forster and give a rousing three cheers for democracy. Instead there is a growing unease at the rapid spread of multiparty elections across south-central Europe, Asia, Africa, and Latin America, perhaps because of what happens *after* the elections. Popular leaders like Russia's Boris Yeltsin and Argentina's Carlos Menem bypass their parliaments and rule by presidential decree, eroding basic constitutional practices. The Iranian parliament—elected more freely than most in the Middle East—imposes harsh restrictions on speech, assembly, and even dress, diminishing that country's already meager supply of liberty. Ethiopia's elected government turns its security forces on journalists and political opponents, doing permanent damage to human rights (as well as human beings).

Naturally there is a spectrum of illiberal democracy, ranging from modest offenders like Argentina to near-tyrannies like Kazakstan and Belarus, with countries like Romania and Bangladesh in between. Along much of the spectrum, elections are rarely as free and fair as in the West today, but they do reflect the reality of popular participation in politics and support for those elected. And the examples are not isolated or atypical. Freedom House's 1996-97 survey, *Freedom in the World*, has separate rankings for political liberties and civil liberties, which correspond roughly with democracy and constitutional liberalism, respectively. Of the countries that lie between confirmed dictatorship and consolidated democracy, 50 percent do better on political liberties than on civil ones. In other words, half of the "democratizing" countries in the world today are illiberal democracies.[1]

Illiberal democracy is a growth industry. Seven years ago only 22 percent of democratizing countries could have been so categorized; five years ago that figure had risen to 35 percent.[2] And to date few illiberal democracies have matured into liberal democracies; if anything, they are moving toward heightened illiberalism. Far from being a temporary or transitional stage, it appears that many countries are settling into a form of government that mixes a substantial degree of democracy with a substantial degree of illiberalism. Just as nations across the world have become comfortable with many variations of capitalism, they could well adopt and sustain varied forms of democracy. Western liberal democracy might prove to be not the final destination on the democratic road, but just one of many possible exits.

DEMOCRACY AND LIBERTY

FROM THE TIME of Herodotus democracy has meant, first and foremost, the rule of the people. This view of democracy as a process of selecting governments, articulated by scholars ranging from Alexis de Tocqueville to Joseph Schumpeter to Robert Dahl, is now widely used by social scientists. In *The Third Wave*, Samuel P. Huntington explains why:

> Elections, open, free and fair, are the essence of democracy, the inescapable sine qua non. Governments produced by elections may be

---

[1]Roger Kaplan, ed., *Freedom Around the World, 1997*, New York: Freedom House, 1997, pp. 21-22. The survey rates countries on two 7-point scales, for political rights and civil liberties (lower is better). I have considered all countries with a combined score of between 5 and 10 to be democratizing. The percentage figures are based on Freedom House's numbers, but in the case of individual countries I have not adhered strictly to its ratings. While the *Survey* is an extraordinary feat—comprehensive and intelligent—its methodology conflates certain constitutional rights with democratic procedures, which confuses matters. In addition, I use as examples (though not as part of the data set) countries like Iran, Kazakstan, and Belarus, which even in procedural terms are semi-democracies at best. But they are worth highlighting as interesting problem cases since most of their leaders were elected, reelected, and remain popular.

[2]*Freedom in the World: The Annual Survey of Political Rights and Civil Liberties, 1992-1993*, pp. 620-26; *Freedom in the World, 1989-1990*, pp. 312-19.

inefficient, corrupt, shortsighted, irresponsible, dominated by special interests, and incapable of adopting policies demanded by the public good. These qualities make such governments undesirable but they do not make them undemocratic. Democracy is one public virtue, not the only one, and the relation of democracy to other public virtues and vices can only be understood if democracy is clearly distinguished from the other characteristics of political systems.

This definition also accords with the commonsense view of the term. If a country holds competitive, multiparty elections, we call it democratic. When public participation in politics is increased, for example through the enfranchisement of women, it is seen as more democratic. Of course elections must be open and fair, and this requires some protections for freedom of speech and assembly. But to go beyond this minimalist definition and label a country democratic only if it guarantees a comprehensive catalog of social, political, economic, and religious rights turns the word democracy into a badge of honor rather than a descriptive category. After all, Sweden has an economic system that many argue curtails individual property rights, France until recently had a state monopoly on television, and England has an established religion. But they are all clearly and identifiably democracies. To have democracy mean, subjectively, "a good government" renders it analytically useless.

Constitutional liberalism, on the other hand, is not about the procedures for selecting government, but rather government's goals. It refers to the tradition, deep in Western history, that seeks to protect an individual's autonomy and dignity against coercion, whatever the source—state, church, or society. The term marries two closely connected ideas. It is *liberal* because it draws on the philosophical strain, beginning with the Greeks, that emphasizes individual liberty.[3] It is *constitutional* because it rests on the tradition, beginning with the Romans, of the rule of law. Constitutional liberalism developed in Western Europe and the United States as a defense of the individual's right to life and property, and freedom of religion and speech. To secure these rights, it emphasized checks on the power of each branch of government, equality under the law, impartial courts and tribunals, and separation of church and state. Its canonical figures include the poet John Milton, the jurist William Blackstone, statesmen such as Thomas Jefferson and James Madison, and philosophers such as Thomas Hobbes, John Locke, Adam Smith, Baron de Montesquieu, John Stuart Mill, and Isaiah Berlin. In almost all of its variants, constitutional liberalism argues that human beings have certain natural (or "inalienable") rights and that governments must accept a basic law, limiting its own powers, that secures them. Thus in 1215 at Runnymede, England's barons forced the king to abide by the settled and customary law of the land. In the American colonies these laws were made explicit, and in 1638 the town of Hartford adopted the first written constitution in modern history. In the 1970s, Western nations codified standards of behavior for regimes across the globe. The Magna Carta, the Fundamental Orders of Connecticut, the American Constitution, and the Helsinki Final Act are all expressions of constitutional liberalism.

THE ROAD TO LIBERAL DEMOCRACY

SINCE 1945 Western governments have, for the most part, embodied both democracy and constitutional liberalism. Thus it is difficult to imagine the two apart, in the form of either illiberal democracy or liberal autocracy. In fact both have existed in the past and persist in the present. Until the twentieth century, most countries in

[3] The term "liberal" is used here in its older, European sense, now often called classical liberalism. In America today the word has come to mean something quite different, namely policies upholding the modern welfare state.

Western Europe were liberal autocracies or, at best, semi-democracies. The franchise was tightly restricted, and elected legislatures had little power. In 1830 Great Britain, in some ways the most democratic European nation, allowed barely 2 percent of its population to vote for one house of Parliament; that figure rose to 7 percent after 1867 and reached around 40 percent in the 1880s. Only in the late 1940s did most Western countries become full-fledged democracies, with universal adult suffrage. But one hundred years earlier, by the late 1840s, most of them had adopted important aspects of constitutional liberalism—the rule of law, private property rights, and increasingly, separated powers and free speech and assembly. For much of modern history, what characterized governments in Europe and North America, and differentiated them from those around the world, was not democracy but constitutional liberalism. The "Western model" is best symbolized not by the mass plebiscite but the impartial judge.

Democracy does not necessarily bring about constitutional liberalism.

The recent history of East Asia follows the Western itinerary. After brief flirtations with democracy after World War II, most East Asian regimes turned authoritarian. Over time they moved from autocracy to liberalizing autocracy, and, in some cases, toward liberalizing semi-democracy.[4] Most of the regimes in East Asia remain only semi-democratic, with patriarchs or one-party systems that make their elections ratifications of power rather than genuine contests. But these regimes have accorded their citizens a widening sphere of economic, civil, religious, and limited political rights. As in the West, liberalization in East Asia has included economic liberalization, which is crucial in promoting both growth and liberal democracy. Historically, the factors most closely associated with full-fledged liberal democracies are capitalism, a bourgeoisie, and a high

[4]Indonesia, Singapore, and Malaysia are examples of liberalizing autocracies, while South Korea, Taiwan, and Thailand are liberal semi-democracies. Both groups, however, are more liberal than they are democratic, which is also true of the region's only liberal democracy, Japan; Papua New Guinea, and to a lesser extent the Philippines, are the only examples of illiberal democracy in East Asia.

per capita GNP. Today's East Asian governments are a mix of democracy, liberalism, capitalism, oligarchy, and corruption—much like Western governments circa 1900.

Constitutional liberalism has led to democracy, but democracy does not seem to bring constitutional liberalism. In contrast to the Western and East Asian paths, during the last two decades in Latin America, Africa, and parts of Asia, dictatorships with little background in constitutional liberalism have given way to democracy. The results are not encouraging. In the western hemisphere, with elections having been held in every country except Cuba, a 1993 study by the scholar Larry Diamond determined that 10 of the 22 principal Latin American countries "have levels of human rights abuse that are incompatible with the consolidation of [liberal] democracy."[5] In Africa, democratization has been extraordinarily rapid. Within six months in 1990 much of Francophone Africa lifted its ban on multiparty politics. Yet although elections have been held in most of the 45 sub-Saharan states since 1991 (18 in 1996 alone), there have been setbacks for freedom in many countries. One of Africa's most careful observers, Michael Chege, surveyed the wave of democratization and drew the lesson that the continent had "overemphasized multiparty elections . . . and correspondingly neglected the basic tenets of liberal governance." In Central Asia, elections, even when reasonably free, as in Kyrgyzstan and Kazakstan, have resulted in strong executives, weak legislatures and judiciaries, and few civil and economic liberties. In the Islamic world, from the Palestinian Authority to Iran to Pakistan, democratization has led to an increasing role for theocratic politics, eroding long-standing traditions of secularism and tolerance. In many parts of that world, such as Tunisia, Morocco, Egypt, and some of the Gulf States, were elections to be held tomorrow, the resulting regimes would almost certainly be more illiberal than the ones now in place.

Many of the countries of Central Europe, on the other hand, have moved successfully from communism to liberal democracy,

---

[5] Larry Diamond, "Democracy in Latin America," in Tom Farer, ed., *Beyond Sovereignty: Collectively Defending Democracy in a World of Sovereign States*, Baltimore: Johns Hopkins University Press, 1996, p. 73.

having gone through the same phase of liberalization without democracy as other European countries did during the nineteenth century. Indeed, the Austro-Hungarian empire, to which most belonged, was a classic liberal autocracy. Even outside Europe, the political scientist Myron Weiner detected a striking connection between a constitutional past and a liberal democratic present. He pointed out that, as of 1983, "every single country in the Third World that emerged from colonial rule since the Second World War with a population of at least one million (and almost all the smaller colonies as well) with a continuous democratic experience is a former British colony."[6] British rule meant not democracy—colonialism is by definition undemocratic—but constitutional liberalism. Britain's legacy of law and administration has proved more beneficial than France's policy of enfranchising some of its colonial populations.

While liberal autocracies may have existed in the past, can one imagine them today? Until recently, a small but powerful example flourished off the Asian mainland—Hong Kong. For 156 years, until July 1, 1997, Hong Kong was ruled by the British Crown through an appointed governor general. Until 1991 it had never held a meaningful election, but its government epitomized constitutional liberalism, protecting its citizens' basic rights and administering a fair court system and bureaucracy. A September 8, 1997, editorial on the island's future in *The Washington Post* was titled ominously, "Undoing Hong Kong's Democracy." Actually, Hong Kong has precious little democracy to undo; what it has is a framework of rights and laws. Small islands may not hold much practical significance in today's world, but they do help one weigh the relative value of democracy and constitutional liberalism. Consider, for example, the question of where you would rather live, Haiti, an illiberal democracy, or Antigua, a liberal semi-democracy. Your choice would probably relate not to the weather, which is pleasant in both, but to the political climate, which is not.

---

[6]Myron Weiner, "Empirical Democratic Theory," in Myron Weiner and Ergun Ozbudun, eds., *Competitive Elections in Developing Countries*, Durham: Duke University Press, 1987, p. 20. Today there are functioning democracies in the Third World that are not former British colonies, but the majority of the former are the latter.

ABSOLUTE SOVEREIGNTY

JOHN STUART MILL opened his classic *On Liberty* by noting that as countries became democratic, people tended to believe that "too much importance had been attached to the limitation of power itself. That . . . was a response against rulers whose interests were opposed to those of the people." Once the people were themselves in charge, caution was unnecessary. "The nation did not need to be protected against its own will." As if confirming Mill's fears, consider the words of Alexandr Lukashenko after being elected president of Belarus with an overwhelming majority in a free election in 1994, when asked about limiting his powers: "There will be no dictatorship. I am of the people, and I am going to be for the people."

The tension between constitutional liberalism and democracy centers on the scope of governmental authority. Constitutional liberalism is about the limitation of power, democracy about its accumulation and use. For this reason, many eighteenth- and nineteenth-century liberals saw in democracy a force that could undermine liberty. James Madison explained in *The Federalist* that "the danger of oppression" in a democracy came from "the majority of the community." Tocqueville warned of the "tyranny of the majority," writing, "The very essence of democratic government consists in the absolute sovereignty of the majority."

The tendency for a democratic government to believe it has absolute sovereignty (that is, power) can result in the centralization of authority, often by extraconstitutional means and with grim results. Over the last decade, elected governments claiming to represent the people have steadily encroached on the powers and rights of other elements in society, a usurpation that is both horizontal (from other branches of the national government) and vertical (from regional and local authorities as well as private businesses and other nongovernmental groups). Lukashenko and Peru's Alberto Fujimori are only the worst examples of this practice. (While Fujimori's actions—disbanding the legislature and suspending the constitution, among others—make it difficult to call his regime democratic, it is worth noting that he won two elections and was extremely popular until recently.) Even a bona fide reformer like Carlos Menem has passed close to 300 presidential decrees in his eight years in office, about three times as many as all previous Argentinean presidents put together, going back to 1853. Kyrgyzstan's Askar Akayev, elected with 60 percent of the vote, proposed enhancing his powers in a referendum that passed easily in 1996. His new powers include appointing all top officials except the prime minister, although he can dissolve parliament if it turns down three of his nominees for the latter post.

Horizontal usurpation, usually by presidents, is more obvious, but vertical usurpation is more common. Over the last three decades, the Indian government has routinely disbanded state legislatures on flimsy grounds, placing regions under New Delhi's direct rule. In a less dramatic but typical move, the elected government of the Central African Republic recently ended the long-standing independence of its university system, making it part of the central state apparatus.

Usurpation is particularly widespread in Latin America and the states of the former Soviet Union, perhaps because both regions mostly have presidencies. These systems tend to produce strong leaders who believe that they speak for the people—even when they have been elected by no more than a plurality. (As Juan Linz points out, Salvador Allende was elected to the Chilean presidency in 1970 with only 36 percent of the vote. In similar circumstances, a prime minister would have had to share power in a coalition government.) Presidents appoint cabinets of cronies, rather than senior party figures, maintaining few internal checks on their power. And when their views conflict with those of the legislature, or even the courts, presidents tend to "go to the nation," bypassing the dreary tasks of bargaining and coalition-building. While scholars debate the merits of presidential versus parliamentary forms of government, usurpation can occur under either, absent well-developed alternate centers of power such as strong legislatures, courts, political parties, regional governments, and independent universities and media. Latin America actually combines presidential systems with proportional representation, producing populist leaders and multiple parties—an unstable combination.

Many Western governments and scholars have encouraged the creation of strong and centralized states in the Third World. Leaders in these countries have argued that they need the authority to break down feudalism, split entrenched coalitions, override vested interests, and bring order to chaotic societies. But this confuses the need for a legitimate government with that for a powerful one. Governments that are seen as legitimate can usually maintain order and pursue tough policies, albeit slowly, by building coalitions. After all, few claim that governments in developing countries should not have adequate police powers; the trouble comes from all the other political, social, and economic powers that they accumulate. In crises like civil wars, constitutional governments might not be able to rule effectively, but the alternative—states with vast security apparatuses that suspend constitutional rights—has usually produced neither order nor good government. More often, such states have become predatory, maintaining some order but also arresting opponents, muzzling dissent, nationalizing industries, and confiscating property. While anarchy has its dangers, the greatest threats to human liberty and happiness in this century have been caused not by disorder but by brutally strong, centralized states, like Nazi Germany, Soviet Russia, and Maoist China. The Third World is littered with the bloody handiwork of strong states.

Historically, unchecked centralization has been the enemy of liberal democracy. As political participation increased in Europe over the nineteenth century, it was accommodated smoothly in countries such as England and Sweden, where medieval assemblies, local governments, and regional councils had remained strong. Countries like France and Prussia, on the other hand, where the monarchy had effectively centralized power (both horizontally and vertically), often ended up illiberal and undemocratic. It is not a coincidence that in twentieth-century Spain, the beachhead of liberalism lay in Catalonia, for centuries a doggedly independent and autonomous region. In America, the presence of a rich variety of institutions—state, local, and private—made it much easier to accommodate the rapid and large extensions in suffrage that took place in the early nineteenth century. Arthur Schlesinger Sr.

has documented how, during America's first 50 years, virtually every state, interest group and faction tried to weaken and even break up the federal government.[7] More recently, India's semi-liberal democracy has survived because of, not despite, its strong regions and varied languages, cultures, and even castes. The point is logical, even tautological: pluralism in the past helps ensure political pluralism in the present.

Fifty years ago, politicians in the developing world wanted extraordinary powers to implement then-fashionable economic doctrines, like nationalization of industries. Today their successors want similar powers to privatize those very industries. Menem's justification for his methods is that they are desperately needed to enact tough economic reforms. Similar arguments are made by Abdalá Bucarem of Ecuador and by Fujimori. Lending institutions, such as the International Monetary Fund and the World Bank, have been sympathetic to these pleas, and the bond market has been positively exuberant. But except in emergencies like war, illiberal means are in the long run incompatible with liberal ends. Constitutional government is in fact the key to a successful economic reform policy. The experience of East Asia and Central Europe suggests that when regimes—whether authoritarian, as in East Asia, or

[7]Arthur Schlesinger, Sr., *New Viewpoints in American History*, New York: Macmillan, 1922, pp. 220-40.

liberal democratic, as in Poland, Hungary, and the Czech Republic—protect individual rights, including those of property and contract, and create a framework of law and administration, capitalism and growth will follow. In a recent speech at the Woodrow Wilson International Center in Washington, explaining what it takes for capitalism to flourish, Federal Reserve chairman Alan Greenspan concluded that, "The guiding mechanism of a free market economy. . . is a bill of rights, enforced by an impartial judiciary"

The democratic peace is actually the liberal peace.

Finally, and perhaps more important, power accumulated to do good can be used subsequently to do ill. When Fujimori disbanded parliament, his approval ratings shot up to their highest ever. But recent opinion polls suggest that most of those who once approved of his actions now wish he were more constrained. In 1993 Boris Yeltsin famously (and literally) attacked the Russian parliament, prompted by parliament's own unconstitutional acts. He then suspended the constitutional court, dismantled the system of local governments, and fired several provincial governors. From the war in Chechnya to his economic programs, Yeltsin has displayed a routine lack of concern for constitutional procedures and limits. He may well be a liberal democrat at heart, but Yeltsin's actions have created a Russian super-presidency. We can only hope his successor will not abuse it.

For centuries Western intellectuals have had a tendency to view constitutional liberalism as a quaint exercise in rule-making, mere formalism that should take a back seat to battling larger evils in society. The most eloquent counterpoint to this view remains an exchange in Robert Bolt's play *A Man For All Seasons*. The fiery young William Roper, who yearns to battle evil, is exasperated by Sir Thomas More's devotion to the law. More gently defends himself.

MORE: What would you do? Cut a great road through the law to get after the Devil?
ROPER: I'd cut every law in England to do that!
MORE: And when the last law was down, and the Devil turned on you—where would you hide Roper, the laws all being flat?

ETHNIC CONFLICT AND WAR

ON DECEMBER 8, 1996, Jack Lang made a dramatic dash to Belgrade. The French celebrity politician, formerly minister of culture, had been inspired by the student demonstrations involving tens of thousands against Slobodan Milošević, a man Lang and many Western intellectuals held responsible for the war in the Balkans. Lang wanted to lend his moral support to the Yugoslav opposition. The leaders of the movement received him in their offices—the philosophy department—only to boot him out, declare him "an enemy of the Serbs," and order him to leave the country. It turned out that the students opposed Milošević not for starting the war, but for failing to win it.

Lang's embarrassment highlights two common, and often mistaken, assumptions—that the forces of democracy are the forces of ethnic harmony and of peace. Neither is necessarily true. Mature liberal democracies can usually accommodate ethnic divisions without violence or terror and live in peace with other liberal democracies. But without a background in constitutional liberalism, the introduction of democracy in divided societies has actually fomented nationalism, ethnic conflict, and even war. The spate of elections held immediately after the collapse of communism were won in the Soviet Union and Yugoslavia by nationalist separatists and resulted in the breakup of those countries. This was not in and of itself bad, since those countries had been bound together by force. But the rapid secessions, without guarantees, institutions, or political power for the many minorities living within the new countries, have caused spirals of rebellion, repression, and, in places like Bosnia, Azerbaijan, and Georgia, war.

Elections require that politicians compete for peoples' votes. In societies without strong traditions of multiethnic groups or assimilation, it is easiest to organize support along racial, ethnic, or religious lines. Once an ethnic group is in power, it tends to exclude other ethnic groups. Compromise seems impossible; one can bargain on material issues like housing, hospitals, and handouts, but how does one split the difference on a national religion? Political competition that is so divisive can rapidly degenerate into violence. Opposition movements, armed rebellions, and coups in Africa have often been directed against ethnically based regimes, many of which came to power through elections. Surveying the breakdown of African and Asian democracies in the 1960s, two scholars concluded that democracy "is simply not viable in an environment of intense ethnic preferences." Recent studies, particularly of Africa and Central Asia, have confirmed this pessimism. A distinguished expert on ethnic conflict, Donald Horowitz, concluded, "In the face of this rather dismal account . . . of the concrete failures of democracy in divided societies . . . one is tempted to throw up one's hands. What is the point of holding elections if all they do in the end is to substitute a Bemba-dominated regime for a Nyanja regime in Zambia, the two equally narrow, or a southern regime for a northern one in Benin, neither incorporating the other half of the state?"[8]

Over the past decade, one of the most spirited debates among scholars of international relations concerns the "democratic peace"—the assertion that no two modern democracies have gone to war with each other. The debate raises interesting substantive questions (does the American Civil War count? do nuclear weapons better explain the peace?) and even the statistical findings have raised interesting dissents. (As the scholar David Spiro points out, given the small number of both democracies and wars over the last two hundred years, sheer chance might explain the absence of war between democracies. No member of his family has ever won the lottery, yet few offer explanations for this impressive correlation.) But even if the statistics are correct, what explains them? Kant, the original proponent of the democratic peace, contended that in democracies, those who pay for wars—that is, the public—make the decisions, so they are understandably cautious. But that claim suggests that democracies are more pacific than other states. Actually they are more warlike, going to war more often and with greater intensity than most states. It is only with other democracies that the peace holds.

When divining the cause behind this correlation, one thing becomes clear: the democratic peace is actually the liberal peace. Writing in the

---

[8] Alvin Rabushka and Kenneth Shepsle, *Politics in Plural Societies: A Theory of Democratic Instability*, Columbus: Charles E. Merill, pp. 62-92; Donald Horowitz, "Democracy in Divided Societies," in Larry Diamond and Mark F. Plattner, eds., *Nationalism, Ethnic Conflict and Democracy*, Baltimore: The Johns Hopkins University Press, 1994, pp. 35-55.

eighteenth century, Kant believed that democracies were tyrannical, and he specifically excluded them from his conception of "republican" governments, which lived in a zone of peace. Republicanism, for Kant, meant a separation of powers, checks and balances, the rule of law, protection of individual rights, and some level of representation in government (though nothing close to universal suffrage). Kant's other explanations for the "perpetual peace" between republics are all closely linked to their constitutional and liberal character: a mutual respect for the rights of each other's citizens, a system of checks and balances assuring that no single leader can drag his country into war, and classical liberal economic policies—most importantly, free trade—which create an interdependence that makes war costly and cooperation useful. Michael Doyle, the leading scholar on the subject, confirms in his 1997 book *Ways of War and Peace* that without constitutional liberalism, democracy itself has no peace-inducing qualities:

> Kant distrusted unfettered, democratic majoritarianism, and his argument offers no support for a claim that all participatory polities—democracies—should be peaceful, either in general or between fellow democracies. Many participatory polities have been non-liberal. For two thousand years before the modern age, popular rule was widely associated with aggressiveness (by Thucydides) or imperial success (by

> Machiavelli) . . . The decisive preference of [the] median voter might well include "ethnic cleansing" against other democratic polities.

The distinction between liberal and illiberal democracies sheds light on another striking statistical correlation. Political scientists Jack Snyder and Edward Mansfield contend, using an impressive data set, that over the last 200 years democratizing states went to war significantly more often than either stable autocracies or liberal democracies. In countries not grounded in constitutional liberalism, the rise of democracy often brings with it hyper-nationalism and war-mongering. When the political system is opened up, diverse groups with incompatible interests gain access to power and press their demands. Political and military leaders, who are often embattled remnants of the old authoritarian order, realize that to succeed that they must rally the masses behind a national cause. The result is invariably aggressive rhetoric and policies, which often drag countries into confrontation and war. Noteworthy examples range from Napoleon III's France, Wilhelmine Germany, and Taisho Japan to those in today's newspapers, like Armenia and Azerbaijan and Milošević's Serbia. The democratic peace, it turns out, has little to do with democracy.

THE AMERICAN PATH

AN AMERICAN SCHOLAR recently traveled to Kazakstan on a U.S. government-sponsored mission to help the new parliament draft its electoral laws. His counterpart, a senior member of the Kazak parliament, brushed aside the many options the American expert was outlining, saying emphatically, "We want our parliament to be just like your Congress." The American was horrified, recalling, "I tried to say something other than the three words that had immediately come screaming into my mind: 'No you don't!'" This view is not unusual. Americans in the democracy business tend to see their own system as an unwieldy contraption that no other country should put up with. In fact, the adoption of some aspects of the American constitutional framework could ameliorate many of the problems associated with illiberal democracy. The philosophy behind the U.S. Constitution, a fear of accumulated power, is as relevant today as it was in 1789. Kazakstan, as it happens, would be particularly well-served by a strong parliament—like the American Congress—to check the insatiable appetite of its president.

It is odd that the United States is so often the advocate of elections and plebiscitary democracy abroad. What is distinctive about the American system is not how democratic it is but rather how undemocratic it is, placing as it does multiple constraints on electoral majorities. Of its three branches of government, one—arguably paramount—is headed by nine unelected men and women with life tenure. Its Senate is the most unrepresentative upper house in the world, with the lone exception of the House of Lords, which is powerless. (Every state sends two senators to Washington regardless of its population—California's 30 million people have as many votes in the Senate as Arizona's 3.7 million—which means that senators representing about 16 percent of the country can block any proposed law.) Similarly, in legislatures all over the United States, what is striking is not the power of majorities but that of minorities. To further check national power, state and local governments are strong and fiercely battle every federal intrusion onto their turf. Private businesses and other nongovernmental groups, what Tocqueville called intermediate associations, make up another stratum within society.

The American system is based on an avowedly pessimistic conception of human nature, assuming that people cannot be trusted with power. "If men were angels," Madison famously wrote, "no government would be necessary." The other model for democratic governance in Western history is based on the French Revolution. The French model places its faith in the goodness of human beings. Once the people are the source of power, it should be unlimited so that they can create a just society. (The French revolution, as Lord Acton observed, is not about the limitation of sovereign power but the abrogation of all intermediate powers that get in its way.) Most non-Western countries have embraced the French model—not least because political elites like the prospect of empowering the state, since that means empowering themselves—and most have descended into bouts of chaos, tyranny, or both. This should have come as no surprise. After all, since its revolution France itself has run through two monarchies, two empires, one proto-fascist dictatorship, and five republics.[9]

---

[9]Bernard Lewis, "Why Turkey Is the Only Muslim Democracy," *Middle East Quarterly,* March 1994, pp. 47-48.

Of course cultures vary, and different societies will require different frameworks of government. This is not a plea for the wholesale adoption of the American way but rather for a more variegated conception of liberal democracy, one that emphasizes both parts of that phrase. Before new policies can be adopted, there lies an intellectual task of recovering the constitutional liberal tradition, central to the Western experience and to the development of good government throughout the world. Political progress in Western history has been the result of a growing recognition over the centuries that, as the Declaration of Independence puts it, human beings have "certain inalienable rights" and that "it is to secure these rights that governments are instituted." If a democracy does not preserve liberty and law, that it is a democracy is a small consolation.

LIBERALIZING FOREIGN POLICY

A PROPER appreciation of constitutional liberalism has a variety of implications for American foreign policy. First, it suggests a certain humility. While it is easy to impose elections on a country, it is more difficult to push constitutional liberalism on a society. The process of genuine liberalization and democratization is gradual and long-term, in which an election is only one step. Without appropriate preparation, it might even be a false step. Recognizing this, governments and nongovernmental organizations are increasingly promoting a wide array of measures designed to bolster constitutional liberalism in developing countries. The National Endowment for Democracy promotes free markets, independent labor movements, and political parties. The U.S. Agency for International Development funds independent judiciaries. In the end, however, elections trump everything. If a country holds elections, Washington and the world will tolerate a great deal from the resulting government, as they have with Yeltsin, Akayev, and Menem. In an age of images and symbols, elections are easy to capture on film. (How do you televise the rule of law?) But there is life after elections, especially for the people who live there.

Conversely, the absence of free and fair elections should be viewed as one flaw, not the definition of tyranny. Elections are an important virtue of governance, but they are not the only virtue. Governments should be judged by yardsticks related to constitutional liberalism as well. Economic, civil, and religious liberties are at the core of human autonomy and dignity. If a government with limited democracy steadily expands these freedoms, it should not be branded a dictatorship. Despite the limited political choice they offer, countries like Singapore, Malaysia, and Thailand provide a better environment for the life, liberty, and happiness of their citizens than do either dictatorships like Iraq and Libya or illiberal democracies like Slovakia or Ghana. And the pressures of global capitalism can push the process of liberalization forward. Markets and morals can work together. Even China, which remains a deeply repressive regime, has given its citizens more autonomy and economic liberty than they have had in generations. Much more needs to change before China can even be called a liberalizing autocracy, but that should not mask the fact that much has changed.

Finally, we need to revive constitutionalism. One effect of the overemphasis on pure democracy is that little effort is given to creating imaginative constitutions for transitional countries. Constitutionalism, as it was understood by its greatest eighteenth century exponents, such as Montesquieu and Madison, is a complicated system of checks and balances designed to prevent the accumulation of power and the abuse of office. This is done not by simply writing up a list of rights but by constructing a system in which government will not violate those rights. Various groups must be included and empowered because, as Madison explained, "ambition must be made to counteract ambition." Constitutions were also meant to tame the passions of the public, creating not simply democratic but also deliberative government. Unfortunately, the rich variety of unelected bodies, indirect voting, federal arrangements, and checks and balances that characterized so many of the formal and informal constitutions of Europe are now regarded with suspicion. What could be called the Weimar syndrome—named after interwar Germany's beautifully constructed constitution, which failed to avert fascism—has made people regard constitutions as simply paperwork that cannot make much difference. (As if any political system in Germany would have easily weathered military defeat, social revolution, the Great Depression, and hyperinflation.) Procedures that inhibit direct democracy are seen as inauthentic, muzzling the voice of the people. Today around the world we see variations on the same majoritarian theme. But the trouble with these winner-take-all systems is that, in most democratizing countries, the winner really does take all.

DEMOCRACY'S DISCONTENTS

WE LIVE IN a democratic age. Through much of human history the danger to an individual's life, liberty and happiness came from the absolutism of monarchies, the dogma of churches, the terror of dictatorships, and the iron grip of totalitarianism. Dictators and a few straggling totalitarian regimes still persist, but increasingly they are anachronisms in a world of global markets, information, and media. There are no longer respectable alternatives to democracy; it is part of the fashionable attire of modernity. Thus the problems of governance in the 21st century will likely be problems *within* democracy. This makes them more difficult to handle, wrapped as they are in the mantle of legitimacy.

Illiberal democracies gain legitimacy, and thus strength, from the fact that they are reasonably democratic. Conversely, the greatest danger that illiberal democracy poses—other than to its own people—is that it will discredit liberal democracy itself, casting a shadow on democratic governance. This would not be unprecedented. Every wave of democracy has been followed by setbacks in which the system was seen as inadequate and new alternatives were sought by ambitious leaders and restless masses. The last such period of disenchantment, in Europe during the interwar years, was seized upon by demagogues, many of whom were initially popular and even elected. Today, in the face of a spreading virus of illiberalism, the most useful role that the international community, and most importantly the United States, can play is—instead of searching for new lands to democratize and new places to hold elections—to consolidate democracy where it has taken root and to encourage the gradual development of constitutional liberalism across the globe. Democracy without constitutional liberalism is not simply inadequate, but dangerous, bringing with it the erosion of liberty, the abuse of power, ethnic divisions, and even war. Eighty years ago, Woodrow Wilson took America into the twentieth century with a challenge, to make the world safe for democracy. As we approach the next century, our task is to make democracy safe for the world.

Defending Democracy

Why Democrats Trump Autocrats

John Shattuck and J. Brian Atwood

Fareed Zakaria observes that an increasing number of democratically elected governments are abusing their powers and repressing civil rights ("The Rise of Illiberal Democracy," November/December 1997). He contends that instead of promoting elections, U.S. policy should concentrate on consolidating existing democracies that respect civil liberties, the rule of law, and a separation of powers between government institutions. Proclaiming constitutional liberalism to be a necessary precondition for "liberal democracy," Zakaria asserts that without it, elections will inevitably lead to what he calls "illiberal democracy," bringing extreme nationalism, ethnic conflict, and war. He proposes that instead of coddling illiberal democrats, the United States should endorse "liberal autocracies" in less developed nations—governments that, though not democratically elected, respect individual rights.

There are three flaws in Zakaria's argument. First, he mischaracterizes current U.S. democracy assistance, suggesting that it is aimed only at promoting elections. Second, he downplays the political repression of seemingly benevolent autocratic regimes. Third, he relies on questionable evidence to demonstrate that democratization exacerbates rather than reduces social tensions.

OPEN IS BETTER

Over the last decade, indigenous forces in Central Europe, Latin America, and parts of Africa and Asia have succeeded in pressuring their governments to democratize by demanding more political rights, less arbitrary rule, and free elections. U.S. diplomacy and assistance programs

---

JOHN SHATTUCK is Assistant Secretary of State for Democracy, Human Rights and Labor. J. BRIAN ATWOOD is Administrator of the U.S. Agency for International Development.

have supported this process, promoting not only elections, but also the creation of legislatures, judiciaries, executive agencies, independent media, trade unions, and a plethora of nongovernmental organizations (NGOs). In fact, the United States Agency for International Development, the primary U.S. vehicle for funding democracy promotion, spends less than 25 percent of its democracy funds on elections.

U.S. democracy assistance helps governments and NGOs in Africa, Central America, the Balkans, the Caucasus, Haiti, and elsewhere to institutionalize the rule of law and foster greater respect for human rights, which means building independent judiciaries and public support for their role. These and other institutions are essential to safeguarding basic freedoms, protecting ethnic and religious minorities, promoting decision-making according to rules rather than by fiat, and providing social stability and reliable methods of dispute resolution.

U.S. democracy-promotion policy is based on the realistic premise that in today's global market, open societies with democratic governance have the best chance to produce stable and equitable economic development. But Zakaria argues that because liberal autocracies are insulated from interest-group politics, they have greater freedom to act on behalf of economic development than democracies. Enlightened autocrats are purportedly able to ignore short-term interests in favor of the long-term welfare of society as a whole. They can pursue the disciplined fiscal and monetary policies needed for sustained economic growth. It is certainly true that some autocratic regimes, particularly in Asia, have produced impressive economic gains, but the current Asian economic crisis underlines the need for greater transparency and openness in these societies as a bulwark against corruption and economic mismanagement.

Political pluralism, including a free press and a political opposition, generates more and better information for use in economic decision-making. Consider, for example, economist Amartya Sen's research on government responses to economic calamities such as drought. According to Sen, democratic governments are better than autocratic governments at mitigating the effects of drought because they are open to receiving negative information and political pressure to respond with appropriate policies. One need only compare the modest economic effect of the recent drought in democratic Botswana with the famines that occurred under similar circumstances in Sudan and North Korea to verify this observation.

Democratic competition can also increase the incentive for officials to resist corruption. Facing regular elections, an organized opposition, and a free media, political leaders in democratizing societies have less room for wheeling and dealing. In addition, the legitimacy that elected leaders gain through the democratic process enables them to appeal to the electorate to endure the temporary hardships brought by economic reform. Many of the current economic problems in East Asian countries stem from a lack of government accountability and transparency in the management of banks and other financial institutions. Not surprisingly, Thailand and the Republic of Korea, with their increasingly democratic cultures, have begun to embrace the reforms needed to address these problems. Indonesia, with one of the least open political systems in the region, was initially reluctant to reform.

Zakaria greatly underestimates the high costs of authoritarianism. Examples abound. Poverty has skyrocketed under Burma's military junta, and autocratic leaders such as Ferdinand Marcos and Mobutu Sese Seko presided over economic decline and egregious maldistributions of wealth. While better than these regimes, Zakaria's liberal autocrats look liberal only in comparison with the totalitarian rulers that preceded them. The abuse of human rights and repression of political choice make these autocracies poor alternatives to governments committed to democratization. Of course, emerging democracies are far from perfect, but as messy and complex as the growth of democratic culture is, the United States should be more willing to err on the side of those who are struggling for democracy than to throw in its lot with autocratic leaders who are likely to abuse their powers.

ROADS TO DEMOCRACY

Equally fallacious is the claim that democracy develops from some preconceived formula, with one ingredient preceding another. Zakaria's view that the development of constitutional liberalism must come before electoral democracy simply ignores the facts. There are many countries in which representative government predated the protection of civil and political liberties. South Korea and Taiwan are recent examples. The related argument that economic development must precede democracy ignores the fact that many countries, from Costa Rica and Poland to the Philippines and Botswana, have found that the road to democracy also leads to economic prosperity. The successful democratic transitions in African nations such as Benin, Mali, South Africa, and Namibia further demonstrate that neither a tradition of equal opportunity nor widely distributed wealth must come before political freedom. In short, political liberalization, economic development, and the protection of human rights are all tied together. For this reason, U.S. policy addresses them simultaneously, not in sequence.

Finally, Zakaria and others have contended that without constitutional liberalism, electoral democracy invariably leads to ethnic strife. This argument is belied by the effects of electoral pluralism in providing a safety valve for ethnic differences in many central and east European states and the newly independent states of the former Soviet Union. By the same token, some degree of pluralism and more moderate leadership have resulted from the series of elections in Bosnia over the last two years. In fact, in January 1998, Milorad Dodik, an avowed moderate with Western sympathies, was elected prime minister of the Bosnian Serb Republic. Elections have also allowed Bosnian Serb President Biljana Plavsić to stake out more moderate positions, breaking with the Pale leadership. Opposition parties have won as much as 30 percent of the vote in municipal elections, a sign that the extreme hard-line nationalists loyal to wartime Serb leader Radovan Karadžić are losing ground.

Democratization is a long and complex struggle, constantly marked by advances and setbacks. Elections, of course, are only part of the process of developing democratic culture, and they are certainly not a panacea for societies torn by conflict or countries wracked by poverty or economic crisis. But this does not mean that the United States should pull back from efforts to promote elections abroad; rather, it means that it should provide long-term assistance, in a wide variety of ways, to foster the growth of civil society, basic freedoms, the rule of law, and democratic culture wherever they have a reasonable chance of taking hold. Building democratic culture and institutions is worthwhile not because it is easy, but because the long-term rewards—increased stability, prosperity, and enrichment of the human spirit—make it worth the effort.

THE STRATEGY OF TERRORISM

By David Fromkin

THE grim events at the Athens airport on August 5, 1973, were in a sense symbolic. Dreadfully real to those who were involved, the occurrences of that day also transcended their own reality, somewhat as myths do, epitomizing an entire aspect of contemporary existence in one specific drama.

When the hand grenades were hurled into the departure lounge and the machine gunners simultaneously mowed down the passengers waiting to embark for New York City, it seemed incomprehensible that so harmless a group should be attacked. The merest glance at their hand-luggage, filled with snorkels and cameras, would have shown that they had spent their time in such peaceful pursuits as swimming, sunbathing, and snapping photos of the Parthenon.

The raid had been undertaken on behalf of an Arab Palestine. Yet the airport passengers had done the Arabs no harm. Their journey had only been to Greece. Palestine had nothing to do with them; it was another country, across the sea, and its problems were not of their making. Moreover, Athens was a capital friendly to the Arab cause—as was Paris, the scene of more recent airline attacks.

Similar incidents have occurred with terrible frequency throughout the 1960s and 1970s. The generations that have come to maturity in Europe and America since the end of the Second World War have asked only to bask in the sunshine of a summertime world; but increasingly they have been forced instead to live in the fearful shadow of other people's deadly quarrels. Gangs of politically motivated gunmen have disrupted everyday life, intruding and forcing their parochial feuds upon the unwilling attention of everybody else.

True, other ages have suffered from crime and outrage, but what we are experiencing today goes beyond such things. Too small to impose their will by military force, terrorist bands nonetheless are capable nowadays of causing enough damage to intimidate and blackmail the governments of the world. Only modern technology makes this possible—the bazooka, the plastic bomb, the submachine gun, and perhaps, over the horizon, the nuclear mini-bomb. The transformation has enabled terrorism to enter the political arena on a new scale, and to express ideological goals of an organized sort rather than mere crime, madness, or emotional derangement as in the past.

Political terrorism is a distinctive disorder of the modern world. It originated as a term and, arguably, as a practice, less than two centuries ago and has come into the spotlight of global conflict in our lifetime. Whereas both organized and irregular (or guerrilla) warfare began with the human race, political terrorism emerged as a concept only in 1793. As a political strategy, it is both new and original; and if I am correct, its nature has not yet fully been appreciated.

Of course nobody can remain unaware of the upsurge of global terrorism that has occurred in recent years. But the novelty of it has not been perceived. Force usually generates fear, and fear is usually an additional weapon. But terrorism employs the weapon of fear in a special and complicated sort of way.

II

The disassociation of fear from force in the context of organized politics emerged first in the Reign of Terror, the episode (1793–1794) during the history of revolutionary France from which the English and French words for terrorism derive. The terrorists in question were, of course, Robespierre and his satellites, St. Just and Couthon. Sitting as a faction in the Committee of Public Safety, their accusations of treason sent victims to the guillotine in droves. By the mere threat of accusation against their fellow Committee members, they used the entire Committee, thus united, in order to dominate the National Convention and the other public bodies of the French Republic.

Robespierre was overthrown when his system was used against him. His mistake was in letting Joseph Fouché know that he was the next intended victim; and Fouché, the wily intriguer who later became Napoleon's minister of police, made the best possible use of his few remaining days. He persuaded the feuding, rival politicians of his day that they had to unite against the triumvirs or else face execution one by one; fear of the regime should cause them not to serve it, but to overthrow it. On 8 Thermidor (July 26, 1794) Robespierre made another mistake when he told the Convention that he had prepared a new list of traitors in their midst—and then refused to tell them whose names were on the list. Fouché's warnings were confirmed, and his counsel was heeded. When Robespierre entered the National Convention late in the stormy summer morning of 9 Thermidor, he found a mob of delegates united by the determination to murder him before he could murder them; and that was the end of him.

Robespierre had coerced a nation of 27 million people into accepting his dictatorship. His followers sent many thousands either to jail or to their deaths; one scholar's estimate is 40,000 deaths and 300,000 arrests. Yet when retribution came and Robespierre and his group of supporters were executed, it turned out that in all there were only 22 of them.

Of course it is not meant to suggest that this is the whole story of the French Terror. Yet what emerges most strongly from any account of these events is the dramatic disparity between the objective weakness of the Robespierre faction, whose numbers were few and whose military resources were limited, and their immense subjective power, which allowed them to kill, imprison, or control so many. There was no need to fear the triumvirs other than the fact that other people feared them and therefore would execute their orders. Their power was unreal; it was an illusionist's trick. No citadels had to be stormed, no armies had to be crushed, in order to overthrow them. If the public ignored what they said, then the terrorists went back to being political nobodies. Their dictatorship vanished in an instant when Robespierre and his colleagues were prevented from reaching the speakers' platform on 9 Thermidor.

In the end, the terrorists overreached themselves, and men saw through them and stood up to them. Then—and only then—it became clear that France had never had anything to fear from them other than fear itself.

III

Perhaps the closest parallel to Robespierre's method was that followed by the late Senator Joseph McCarthy in 1950–54. Like Robespierre, McCarthy claimed to have lists of traitors whose names he would not immediately reveal, and many did his will in order to avoid being accused by him of treason or of lack of patriotism. And, like Robespierre's, his power stopped when he went too far and Joseph Welch, his Fouché, stood up to him on television. But McCarthy never seized supreme power in the country, nor did his accusations send people to the guillotine. In that sense it can be said that Robespierre has had no successors.

Since his time, in fact, political terrorism has become especially notorious in a different cause from that in which Robespierre used it. It has been used to destroy governments rather than to sustain them. This changed the way in which many people thought of it as a political strategy and how they viewed its adherents. As revolutionaries, terrorists have come to seem romantic figures to many. Their life of dangers and disguises, risks and betrayals, conspiracies and secret societies, exerted a powerful fascination. As torn and tormented characters, they provided authors with the stuff of which complex and interesting novels can be made.

Though the terrorists seemed romantic, until recently they also seemed ineffective. Until the Irish Treaty of 1921, they scored no significant political successes. The most famous of the terrorist groups up to that time was the Terrorist Brigade of the Russian Socialists-Revolutionists; and not merely did they fail to change the Tsarist government in the ways in which they desired, they also failed to pick up the pieces when it was overthrown by others. Plekhanov, Lenin, Trotsky and the other Russian disciples of Marx had seen more clearly in placing their emphasis on mass organization rather than on individual terrorism. The Bolsheviks came to power by winning the metropolitan workmen, the sailors of the Baltic fleet, and the soldiers to their side. Organization proved to be the key to victory. It was not individual gunmen but armed masses who seized power in Russia. Revolution, like war, is the strategy of the strong; terrorism is the strategy of the weak.

It is an uncertain and indirect strategy that employs the weapon of fear in a special sort of way in which to make governments react. Is fear an effective method? Is fright any kind of weapon at all? What can terrorists hope to accomplish by sowing fear? How can it help their side to vanquish its opponents? Clearly it can do so in many ways. Fright can paralyze the will, befuddle the mind, and exhaust the strength of an adversary. Moreover, it can persuade an opponent that a particular political point of view is taken with such deadly seriousness by its few adherents that it should be accommodated, rather than suffering casualties year after year in a campaign to suppress it.

All of these elements came together, for example, in the struggle that led to the independence of southern Ireland. It is difficult to disentangle the role of terrorism in this achievement from the other elements that were involved, for the Irish also had put in motion what was, in effect, a guerrilla warfare campaign. Moreover, the Liberal members of the coalition that then governed the United Kingdom had a political commitment that went back more than a quarter of a century to the cause of Irish Home Rule. Yet there can be little doubt that terrorism played a major role in causing Britain to tire of the struggle.

Terrorism can also make heroes out of gunmen, and thereby rally popular support to their cause. The problem this creates for them is that when the time comes to make the compromises necessary in order to negotiate the terms of their victory, the glamour wanes, and with it, the political support. Michael Collins was a romantic figure who captured the imagination of all Ireland as long as he was an outlaw; but when he sat down to make peace, he was seen by many in a much different light. As he signed the Irish Treaty of 1921 on Britain's behalf, Lord Birkenhead remarked to Collins, "I may have signed my political death-warrant tonight"; to which Collins replied, "I may have signed my actual death-warrant." Eight months later Michael Collins lay dead on an Irish roadway with a bullet through his head.

Just as it can make gangsters into heroes, terrorist provocations can also make policemen into villains. The Black-and-Tans who fought the Irish revolutionists were, in an objective sense, so successful at repression that Michael Collins told an English official afterwards, in regard to the July 1921 peace negotiations: "You had us dead beat. We could not have lasted another three weeks." Yet Black-and-Tan methods made the cause of repression so odious that Britain was induced to choose another course of action.

Brutality is an induced governmental response that can boomerang. It is this ability to use the strength of repression against itself, in many different ways, that has enabled terrorist strategies to succeed in many situations that have, rightly or wrongly, been described as colonialist in the modern world.

IV

Sophisticated approaches have been developed along these lines. One of these was explained to me and to others at a meeting in New York City sometime in 1945 by one of the founders of the Irgun Zvai Leumi, a tiny group of Jewish militants in what was then the British-mandated territory of Palestine. His organization had no more than 1,000 or 1,500 members, and it was at odds with the Palestinian Jewish community almost as much as it was with the mandatory regime. Yet he proposed to combat Great Britain, then a global power whose armed forces in the Second World War numbered in the millions, and to expel Great Britain from Palestine.

How could such a thousand-to-one struggle be won? To do so, as he explained it, his organization would attack property interests. After giving advance warning to evacuate them, his small band of followers would blow up buildings. This, he said, would lead the British to overreact by garrisoning the country with an immense army drawn from stations in other parts of the world. But postwar Britain could not afford financially to maintain so great an army either there or anywhere else for any extended period of time. Britain urgently needed to demobilize its armed forces. The strain would tell; and eventually economic pressure would drive the Attlee-Bevin government either to withdraw from Palestine or else to try some reckless and possibly losing gamble in an effort to retrieve the situation.

It can be argued that such is in fact what happened. Of course Britain might have withdrawn anyway, at some other time or for some other reason. But that is really beside the point, for the Irgun wanted independence then and there, in order to open up the country to refugees from Hitler's Europe. They got what they wanted when they wanted it by doing it in their own way.

There were two flaws in the Irgun strategy. It would have failed had the British not reacted to the destruction of buildings as they were expected to do. If instead they had done nothing at all, maintained only a modest military garrison, and sent for no reinforcements, all that would have happened would have been that a few more buildings would have been blown up and the owners would have collected the insurance money and would have rebuilt them; and the Irgun would have proved a failure.

In the second place, the plan of attacking property without hurting people proved to be unrealistic. Accidents inevitably occur when violence is unleashed. Almost a hundred persons were killed when the Irgun blew up the King David Hotel in Jerusalem. According to the plan, they should have been evacuated before the blast, but in actual life people misunderstand, or their telephone line is busy, or somebody forgets to give them the message in time. Moreover, terrorism generates its own momentum, and before long the killing becomes deliberate. The bloodshed caused by the Irgun isolated it politically and alienated the rest of the Palestinian Jewish community. The British failed to perceive or exploit this situation. But Ben-Gurion did; in 1948 he made use of it to crush the Irgun, for the Israeli army might have been unwilling to carry out orders to attack those unloading the Irgun ship the *Altalena,* if the Irgun had not used up its political credit before then by the taking of too many lives.

Yet despite its flaws, the strategy was sufficiently ingenious so that the Irgun played a big part in getting the British to withdraw. Its ingenuity lay in using an opponent's own strength against him. It was a sort of jujitsu. First the adversary was made to be afraid, and then, predictably, he would react to his fear by increasing the bulk of his strength, and then the sheer weight of that bulk would drag him down. Another way of saying this is that the Irgun, seeing that it was too small to defeat Great Britain, decided, as an alternative approach, that Britain was big enough to defeat itself.

V

In the 1950s, the nationalist rebel group in Algeria developed yet another method of using the strength of an occupying power against itself. Their method was to induce that strength to be used as a form of persuasion.

For, in Algeria, the whole question was one of persuasion. The problem initially faced by the miniscule band of Algerian nationalists that called itself the National Liberation Front (or, in its French initials, FLN) was that Algeria at that time had little sense of national identity. Its population was not homogeneous; and the Berbers, the Arabs, and the settlers of European descent were peoples quite different from one another. The name and separate existence of Algeria were only of recent origin. For most of recorded history, Algeria had been no more than the middle part of North Africa, with no distinct history of its own. Legally it was merely the southern part of France. The French had treated Morocco and Tunisia as protectorates, with separate identities, but not Algeria, which was absorbed into France herself. With sarcasm, Frenchmen used to reply to Americans who urged independence for Algeria by saying that, on the same basis, the United States should set Wisconsin free or give back independence to South Carolina.

It was a jibe that went to the heart of the matter. Colonial empires were coming to an end in the 1950s and 1960s. If Algeria was a nation, then inevitably it would be set free to govern itself. Only if it were genuinely a part of France could it continue to be ruled from Paris. All depended, therefore, on whether the indigenous population could be convinced by the French government that Algeria was not a separate country, or upon whether they could be persuaded by the FLN to change their minds so as to think of themselves as a nation.

The FLN strategy of terrorism addressed itself to this central and decisive issue. By itself, as has been said, terror can accomplish nothing in terms of political goals; it can only aim at obtaining a response that will achieve those goals for it. What the FLN did was to goad the French into reacting in such a way as to demonstrate the unreality of the claim that there was no distinct Algerian nation. Unlike the Irgun, the FLN did not set out to campaign merely against property; it attacked people. It used random violence, planting bombs in market places and in other crowded locations. The instinctive French reaction was to treat all persons of non-European origin as suspects; but, as Raymond Aron was to write, "As suspects, all the Muslims felt excluded from the existing community." Their feeling was confirmed when, in the middle 1950s, the authorities further reacted by transferring the French army units composed of Muslim Algerian troops out of Algeria and into mainland France, and replacing them in Algeria by European troops. By such actions they showed in the most unmistakable way that they regarded no Algerians as Frenchmen except for the European settlers. They spoke of we and us, and of they and them, and did not realize that their doing so meant the end of Algérie Française.

Thus the French conceded the issue of the war at its very outset. They threw away the potential support of Muslim Algeria because they were skeptical of the possibility that it could be obtained. From that moment the conclusion of the conflict was foregone. Once the sympathies of the population had shifted to its side, the FLN was able to outgrow mere terrorism and to organize a campaign of guerrilla warfare. It also was enabled to appeal to world sympathies on behalf of a people fighting for its freedom. From the French point of view all had become hopeless; for no amount of force can keep an unwilling population indefinitely in subjection. Even though the FLN had written the script, the French, with suicidal logic, went ahead to play the role for which they had been cast.

The FLN success was therefore a special case. It required a particular kind of opponent. It could not be duplicated in other circumstances and conditions.

VI

Revolutionist-terrorists of the last decade have failed to perceive the special characteristics of the colonialist situation that facilitated success for Irish, Irgun, and Algerian terrorists. They have tried to apply the strategy of terrorism in situations that are essentially different. This has been true, for example, of extremist groups seeking to overthrow liberal-pluralistic regimes during the 1960s. Their theory has been that their terrorist attacks would force hitherto liberal regimes to become repressive, a change which in turn would alienate the masses, thus setting the stage for revolution. But it has not worked out that way in practice. In the United States, for example, terrorist bomb attacks have not led to any change at all in the form of government, much less to a transformation of America into a police state. On the other hand, in Uruguay, once the model democracy of Latin America, the terror of the Tupamaro bands has led to a military dictatorship that brutally destroyed the Tupamaros, but that does not seem, at least as yet, to have led to the predicted reaction by the masses in favor of revolutionary action.

Other revolutionary groups have taken a somewhat different approach. They have argued that liberal democracies are already police states. Thus, the object of revolutionary terrorist action should be to reveal this hidden reality to the population at large. Unthinking reaction by the authorities to terrorist provocation would accomplish the desired result. Thus the aim of terrorism would be to trick the government into taking off its mask.

In open societies such as Great Britain and the United States, the liberal democratic features have proved to be a face and not a mask: there is nothing to take off, and the strategy failed because its factual premise proved to be untrue.

In closed societies, the strategy has been to show that authoritarian regimes are actually impotent despite their outward show of virility. In such circumstances, supposedly, by demonstrating that the public authorities are powerless to enforce law and order, a campaign of terror can cause a government to collapse; but the flaw in the theory is that the terrorists usually are not strong enough to take its place. Either some more broadly based group will seize power, or else, as in Argentina, private groups will take the law into their own hands and retaliate in kind against murder and extortion, so that society relapses into a semi-anarchic state of reprisals and blood feuds, where terrorists are buried with their victims.

VII

It is against this background that Arab Palestinian terrorism has seized the attention of the contemporary world. It is aimed at Israel; it is aimed at the Arabs who live within Israel; and it is aimed at the world outside. It is, in other words, a mixed strategy. Each of its mixed aspects has to be considered separately. All that Arab terrorism can accomplish in the land that has been promised to so many is to frighten and to threaten the Arab inhabitants of Israel in order to keep them from cooperating with the Israeli authorities. Israel itself, however, cannot be terrorized into disappearing of its own accord; yet removing Israel from the map has long been the proclaimed goal of the Arab terrorist movement.

Terrorism can be employed more successfully in colonialist situations than in Palestine because a colonial power suffers the disadvantage of fighting the battle away from its own base, and also because a colonial power, having a country of its own to which it can withdraw, is under no compulsion to fight to the bitter end. The Israelis, though termed colonialist by the Arabs, are fighting on home territory, and they have no other country to which they can withdraw; they fight with their backs to the sea. They can be goaded into a self-defeating reaction, but unless they permit that to happen, nothing can be done to their domestic public opinion that is likely to destroy them.

The Arab terrorists therefore have turned elsewhere, and have attacked the arteries of world transportation in hopes that a world indifferent to the merits of the Arab-Israeli dispute will turn against the Israelis in order to end the annoyance of a disrupted airline service.

In doing so they have strayed across a frontier and into the eerie world of Mr. McLuhan, and they have transformed terrorism into a form of mass communication—but communication aimed at the whole world and not, as in the case of Algeria, mostly at the indigenous population. Theirs is a campaign that needs publicity in order to succeed, and therefore they have come to operate within the ambit of contemporary public relations and communications arts: the world of cinema, camp fashion, and pop art, in which deadlines and prime-time are the chief realities and in which shock value is the chief virtue. If audiences throughout the world react with horror, and turn against the political cause in whose name so many innocent people have been harmed and killed, the strategy will have backfired. So far they have not done so and it has not done so.

It is a corruption of the human spirit for which all political sides are responsible. The left-wing journalist Paul Johnson wrote an article some months back arguing that left-wing movements are as much at fault as anybody else for accepting the murder of the innocent as a legitimate means for the pursuit of political ends. He quoted the sixteenth-century humanist Castellio, "who was lucky to escape burning by both Catholics and Protestants, and who pointed out in his tract for toleration, *Whether Heretics Are To Be Persecuted?,* that no certitude of righteousness justifies violence: 'To kill a man is not to defend a doctrine, it is to kill a man'." Appalled at the welcome accorded by the United Nations to the leader of the Arab terrorists, Johnson wrote that, "Step by step, almost imperceptibly, without anyone being aware that a fatal watershed has been crossed, mankind has descended into the age of terror."

VIII

If this is an age of terror, then it has become all the more important for us to understand exactly what it is that terrorism means. Terrorism, as has been seen, is the weapon of those who are prepared to use violence but who believe that they would lose any contest of sheer strength. All too little understood, the uniqueness of the strategy lies in this: that it achieves its goal not through its acts but through the response to its acts. In any other such strategy, the violence is the beginning and its consequences are the end of it. For terrorism, however, the consequences of the violence are themselves merely a first step and form a stepping stone toward objectives that are more remote. Whereas military and revolutionary actions aim at a physical result, terrorist actions aim at a psychological result.

But even that psychological result is not the final goal. Terrorism is violence used in order to create fear; but it is aimed at creating fear in order that the fear, in turn, will lead somebody else—not the terrorist—to embark on some quite different program of action that will accomplish whatever it is that the terrorist really desires. Unlike the soldier, the guerrilla fighter, or the revolutionist, the terrorist therefore is always in the paradoxical position of undertaking actions the immediate physical consequences of which are not particularly desired by him. An ordinary murderer will kill somebody because he wants the person to be dead, but a terrorist will shoot somebody even though it is a matter of complete indifference to him whether that person lives or dies. He would do so, for example, in order to provoke a brutal police repression that he believes will lead to political conditions propitious to revolutionary agitation and organization aimed at overthrowing the government. The act of murder is the same in both cases, but its purpose is different, and each act plays a different role in the strategies of violence.

Only an understanding of the purpose for which such an act is undertaken can enable us to know the nature of the act. When Julius Caesar was murdered in the Roman Senate, it was an assassination of the traditional sort, intended to eliminate a specific figure from the political scene; but had he been killed there by the representative of a subversive sect, intent on plunging his dagger into the first Roman leader he encountered in order to provoke a certain political response from the Senate, it would instead have been an act of political terrorism.

It is because an action of the same sort may be undertaken by two different groups with two quite different ends in view that terrorism is so often confused with guerrilla warfare, for terrorists and guerrillas often seem to be doing the same sorts of things. Both of them, for example, often sabotage transportation facilities. When T. E. Lawrence led his classic guerrilla warfare campaign against Turkish rule in Arabia, he systematically dynamited railway tracks and bridges. Lawrence's strategy was later explained by Winston Churchill as follows: "The Turkish armies operating against Egypt depended upon the desert railway. This slender steel track ran through hundreds of miles of blistering desert. If it were permanently cut the Turkish armies must perish." And Lawrence therefore rode on camelback across the sands to destroy the enemy army by blowing up its transportation facilities. In recent years those who say that they wish to destroy the state of Israel have also blown up transportation facilities in the Arab desert; in this case, jet airplanes belonging to civil aviation companies. Yet if thereby they were to permanently cut the airline networks of TWA or BOAC they would not cause the Israeli army to perish. Indeed the fate of such civil aviation companies is a matter of indifference to the terrorists. Lawrence the guerrilla leader attacked a railway because he wanted to destroy it, whereas Arab terrorists attack an airline even though they do not want to destroy it.

The distinction is of more than academic importance. The French lost their empire over Algeria when they mistook terrorism for guerrilla warfare. They thought that when the FLN planted a bomb in a public bus, it was in order to blow up the bus; whereas the real FLN purpose in planting the bomb was not to blow up the bus, but to lure authorities into reacting by arresting all the non-Europeans in the area as suspects.

The terrorist is like a magician who tricks you into watching his right hand while his left hand, unnoticed, makes the switch. It is understandable that the French authorities in Algeria became totally obsessed by the need to stamp out criminal attacks, but it was fatal to their policy to do so, for the violent attacks were merely a subsidiary issue. The tiny FLN band of outlaws could have blown up every bus in all of Algeria and never won a convert to their cause of independence. Failing to understand the strategy of terrorism, the French did not see that it was not the FLN's move, but rather the French countermove, that would determine whether the FLN succeeded or failed.

It may be the case that the current Israeli policy of attacking Arab terrorist bases in southern Lebanon is another example of concentrating too much attention on preventing terrorist actions and too little attention on foiling terrorist purposes. The Israeli policy is certainly understandable on many grounds, and valid arguments can be adduced in its support; but the weakening of an essentially benevolent Lebanese government, as well as the further estrangement of world opinion, are results of the Israeli raids into Lebanon that may outweigh the value of using that particular approach to the problem of combating terrorism.

For the Israelis, threatened by enemies outside of their society, the problem is an enormously difficult one. For societies threatened only by enemies from within, it is considerably less so. The very wickedness of terrorism makes it a vulnerable strategy in such a society. Other strategies sometimes kill the innocent by mistake. Terrorism kills the innocent deliberately; for not even the terrorist necessarily believes that the particular person who happens to become his victim deserves to be killed or injured. It is horrifying not merely because of the deed that is done but also because at first the deed seems pointless. If you want to make war on the United States on behalf of Puerto Rican independence, why blow up a historic tavern in New York's financial district? What has Fraunces Tavern got to do with Puerto Rico? Why not attack the alleged forces of occupation in Puerto Rico instead? If you opposed by force and violence the continuation of U.S. aid to South Vietnam, why threaten to destroy the Smithsonian Institution? What had its plant collections and its ichthyological specimens to do with American policy in Southeast Asia? The destruction seems so purposeless that it is a natural reaction to turn on those who perpetrate it in hatred and in anger.

The tragedies that befall great public figures can sometimes seem to have been deserved; but when a man on the street is killed at random on behalf of a cause with which he had nothing to do, it is a different matter and provokes a different reaction. In a homogeneous society, at any rate, it leads to a reaction against the terrorism, and it renders it vulnerable to a campaign that politically isolates it in order to physically destroy it, for the nature of the attacks tends to demonstrate that terrorists are enemies of the people rather than merely of the government. It is for this reason that Che Guevara, as a theoretician and practitioner of guerrilla warfare, warned against the strategy of terrorism, arguing that it hinders "contact with the masses and makes impossible unification for actions that will be necessary at a critical moment."

Even in the international arena, terrorist movements are vulnerable when their actions alienate support. This was tacitly recognized by the Palestine Liberation Organization (PLO) when on January 29, 1975, it announced that henceforth it had decided to treat hijacking of airplanes, ships, or trains as crimes and would impose death penalties on hijackers if their actions led to the loss of life. Whether the PLO will indeed abandon its campaign of terror against international transportation remains to be seen. Yet the declaration of its intention to do so is in itself significant, for it suggests a realization that a point has arrived when a public identification with terrorist activity will harm rather than help. This is because terrorism is so much more evil than other strategies of violence that public opinion sometimes can be rallied against it.

Indeed, in view of its inherent weakness, it is remarkable how many political successes have been scored by the strategy of terrorism in the last few decades. Its success seems to be due in large part to a miscomprehension of the strategy by its opponents. They have neglected the more important of the two levels on which terrorism operates. They have failed to focus on the crucial issue of how the manner in which they, as opponents, respond affects the political goals of the terrorists. Discussion instead has centered on the criminal justice aspects of the question: prevention and punishment.

Much has been written, for example, about the technological defenses that have been developed or could be developed against terrorism in order to prevent it from occurring. This can be a highly useful line of approach, as the successful use of electronic surveillance devices at airports seems to have demonstrated. It may even be advisable to require that any new technologies that are developed from time to time should incorporate some sort of internal defense against attack, much as environmentalists argue that pollution control devices should be incorporated in equipment and its cost charged to the manufacturers. Yet no technology is perfect, and there will always be somebody who will manage to slip by any defenses that can be created.

Prevention of terrorism in non-technological ways scarcely merits discussion. Perhaps one day the social sciences will teach us how to drain the swamps of misery in which hatred and fanaticism breed, but at the moment that day seems far distant. The hollow formalism of the law offers, if anything, even less help. Ingenious schemes for new international tribunals and procedures have been proposed, and they completely miss the point. The manifest unwillingness of many governments to use existing legal remedies against terrorism shows that the real problem is the lack of a will and not the lack of a way. For example, it was only when an attack was staged at the Paris airport that the French Minister of the Interior, in January of 1975, proposed to negotiate an international convention to provide for the punishment of terrorist acts. It is not any kind of genuine solution, in any event, but it will be interesting to see if Michel Poniatowski perseveres in even so ritualistic a response as this after the fleeting memory of injured national pride fades from view. There are all too many who object to terrorism only when they are its victims.

Far more effective than the reaction of M. Poniatowski was that of the French press. There were suggestions in the newspapers that the pro-Arab policy of the French government should be reversed because it had failed to prevent the attack at Orly airport. Within days

promoting sectarianism in Pakistan. The movements share madrasahs, camps, bureaucracies, and operatives. The JUI, the SSP's founding party, also helped create both the Taliban and Harkat. Deobandi madrasahs issue anti-Shi'a *fatwas* (edicts), and boys trained to fight in Kashmir are also trained to call Shi'a *kafirs* (infidels). Jaesh-e-Mohammad, an offshoot of Harkat and the newest Pakistani militant group in Kashmir, reportedly used SSP personnel during a fundraising drive in early 2000. And the SSP's Inqalabi, who was recently released after four years in jail for his alleged involvement in sectarian killings, told me that whenever "one of our youngsters wants to do jihad," they join up with the Taliban, Harkat, or Jaesh-e-Mohammad—all Deobandi groups that he claims are "close" to the SSP.

Sectarian clashes have killed or injured thousands of Pakistanis since 1990. As the American scholar Vali Nasr explains, the largely theological differences between Shi'a and Sunni Muslims have been transformed into full-fledged political conflict, with broad ramifications for law and order, social cohesion, and government authority. The impotent Pakistani government has essentially allowed Sunni Saudi Arabia and Shi'a Iran to fight a proxy war on Pakistani soil, with devastating consequences for the Pakistani people.

WHITHER PAKISTAN?

PAKISTAN is a weak state, and government policies are making it weaker still. Its disastrous economy, exacerbated by a series of corrupt leaders, is at the root of many of its problems. Yet despite its poverty, Pakistan is spending hundreds of millions of dollars on weapons instead of schools and public health. Ironically, the government's "cost-saving" measures are even more troubling. In trying to save money in the short run by using irregulars in Kashmir and relying on madrasahs to educate its youth, Pakistan is pursuing a path that is likely to be disastrous in the long run, allowing a culture of violence to take root.

The United States has asked Pakistan to crack down on the militant groups and to close certain madrasahs, but America must do more than just scold. After all, the United States, along with Saudi Arabia, helped create the first international "jihad" to fight the Soviet Union during the Afghan war. "Does America expect us to send in the troops and shut the madrasahs down?" one official asks. "Jihad is a mindset. It developed over many years during the Afghan war. You can't change a mindset in 24 hours."

The most important contribution the United States can make, then, is to help strengthen Pakistan's secular education system. Because so much international aid to Pakistan has been diverted through corruption, both public and private assistance should come in the form of relatively nonfungible goods and services: books, buildings, teachers, and training, rather than money. Urdu-speaking teachers from around the world should be sent to Pakistan to help. And educational exchanges among students, scholars, journalists, and military officials should be encouraged and facilitated. Helping Pakistan educate its youth will not only cut off the culture of violence by reducing ignorance and poverty, it will also promote long-term economic development.

Moreover, assisting Pakistan will make the world a safer place. As observers frequently note, conflict between India and Pakistan over Kashmir is one of the most likely routes to nuclear war in the world today. The Pakistani militants' continued incursions into Indian-held Kashmir escalate the conflict, greatly increasing the risk of nuclear war between the two countries.

Although the United States can help, Pakistan must make its own changes. It must stamp out corruption, strengthen democratic institutions, and make education a much higher priority. But none of this can happen if Pakistan continues to devote an estimated 30 percent of its national budget to defense.

Most important, Pakistan must recognize the militant groups for what they are: dangerous gangs whose resources and reach continue to grow, threatening to destabilize the entire region. Pakistan's continued support of religious militant groups suggests that it does not recognize its own susceptibility to the culture of violence it has helped create. It should think again.

The Taliban: Exporting Extremism

Ahmed Rashid

REWRITING THE RULES OF THE GREAT GAME

"TALIBANIZATION," the destabilizing export of Afghan-style radical Islam, may be a new term in the American political lexicon. But in Central and South Asia, where the repercussions of the superstrict Taliban rule of Afghanistan have been widely felt, the word has become all too familiar. As political fragmentation, economic meltdown, ethnic and sectarian warfare, and Islamic fundamentalism tighten their grip on Pakistan and much of the rest of the region, the dangerous behavior of Afghanistan's new leaders is no longer a local affair.

More and more, chaos in Afghanistan is seeping through its porous borders. The ongoing civil war has polarized the region, with Pakistan and Saudi Arabia backing the Taliban regime while Iran, Russia, India, and four former Soviet Central Asian republics support the opposition Northern Alliance. The confrontation is producing enormous economic disruption throughout the area, as the Afghan warlords' dependence on smuggling and drug trafficking grows insatiable.

Into the political vacuum left by 20 years of war and the collapse of stable government has marched a new generation of violent fundamentalists, nurtured and inspired by the Taliban's unique Islamist model. Thousands of foreign radicals now fighting alongside the Taliban in

---

AHMED RASHID has covered the war in Afghanistan for 20 years. He is Pakistan, Afghanistan, and Central Asia Correspondent for the *Far Eastern Economic Review* and author of *The Resurgence of Central Asia: Islam or Nationalism?* and the forthcoming *Taliban: Militant Islam, Oil, and Fundamentalism in Central Asia*.

Afghanistan are determined to someday overthrow their own regimes and carry out Taliban-style Islamist revolutions in their homelands. For example, the Chechnya-based militants who took over parts of Dagestan in July included in their ranks Arabs, Afghans, and Pakistanis, most of whom had fought in Afghanistan. So had the 800 Uzbek and Tajik gunmen who took over parts of southern Kyrgyzstan in August. The state breakdown in Afghanistan offers militants from Pakistan, Iran, the Central Asian republics, and China's predominantly Muslim Xinjiang province a tempting package deal: sanctuary and financial support through smuggling.

Meanwhile, Washington's sole response so far has been its single-minded obsession with bringing to justice the Saudi-born terrorist Usama bin Ladin—hardly a comprehensive policy for dealing with this increasingly volatile part of the world.

For Western nations to presume that they can safely exploit the vast oil and gas riches of Central Asia without first helping bring peace to Afghanistan is unrealistic to the extreme. A new Great Game is being played in the region. At stake, however, are no longer questions of mere political influence or who gets to build oil and gas pipelines where. These issues will be irrelevant unless the West figures out how to stop the spreading conflagration in Afghanistan—and fast.

THE STUDENTS WHO CAME IN FROM THE COLD

FOR AFGHANISTAN to be at the center of both dialogue and conflict between civilizations is nothing new. The country's location at the crossroads between Iran, Central Asia, the Arabian Sea, and India has given its mountain passes a strategic significance for centuries. At certain times, Afghanistan has acted as a buffer between competing empires and ideologies; at others it has served as a corridor through which armies marched. Repeated efforts to colonize the country, most recently by the British and the Soviets, have failed and in the process given the Afghans a fierce sense of independence and pride.

The United States, patron of the Afghan rebellion against the Soviet invaders, walked away after the Soviet Union withdrew its last troops in 1989. The Afghans, once on the frontline of the Cold War, were left with a devastated country. One million had died during the ten-year occupation. But only three years later, when Kabul fell to the mujahideen who had fought off the Soviets, gory civil war again gripped the country, fueled by neighboring countries trying to carve out areas of influence. The civil war has pitted the majority Pushtun population in the south and east against the ethnic minorities of the north—Tajik, Uzbek, Hazara, and Turkmen.

The predominantly Pushtun Taliban emerged in late 1994 as a messianic movement made up of *taliban* (literally, students) from Islamic *madrasahs* (seminaries) who were living as refugees in Pakistan. They vowed to bring peace to Afghanistan, establish law and order, disarm the population, and impose *sharia* (Islamic law). Welcomed by a war-weary Pushtun population, the Taliban were at first remarkably successful and popular. Until they captured Kabul in 1996 they expressed no desire to rule the country. But ever since then—abetted by their Pakistani and Saudi backers and inspired by ideological mentors such as bin Ladin—the Taliban have committed themselves to conquering the entire country and more.

In 1998, the Taliban overran much of northern Afghanistan, pushing the Northern Alliance (made up of non-Pushtun minorities) into a thin sliver of territory in the northeast. This victory further polarized the region, as Iran threatened to invade and accused Pakistan of supporting the Taliban.

The nature of the Taliban—who they are and what they represent—has been difficult for outsiders to understand because of the excessive secrecy that surrounds their leaders and political structure. The Taliban do not issue policy statements or hold regular press conferences. There is no Taliban manifesto. Because of the ban on photography and television, Afghans do not even know what their new leaders look like. The one-eyed Taliban religious leader, Mullah Muhammad Umar, does not meet with non-Muslims and so remains a mystery.

Historically, Afghanistan was a deeply conservative Muslim country where *sharia*, as interpreted by Afghan tribal custom, prevailed for centuries. But the Islam traditionally practiced in Afghanistan was also immensely tolerant—of other Muslim sects, other religions, and different lifestyles. Until 1992, Hindus, Sikhs, and Jews all played a significant role in the country's bazaar economy and sectarianism was not an issue.

Since 1992, however, the bloody civil war has destroyed this tolerance, setting sects and ethnic groups against one another in a way formerly unimaginable. The once-unifying factor of Islam has become a lethal weapon in the hands of extremists and a force for division and fragmentation.

Ninety percent of Afghans are Sunni Muslims, although Shiites predominate among the Hazaras and some Tajik clans settled in central Afghanistan. Traditional Islam in Afghanistan believed in minimum government with as little state interference as possible. Another key factor contributing to Afghan tolerance was the enormous popularity of Sufism, a mystical and undogmatic branch of Islam.

Before the Taliban arrived, none of Islam's extreme orthodox sects—such as the conservative Wahhabis from Saudi Arabia—had ever found a home in Afghanistan. But the Taliban emerged at a critical juncture, as the country was fractured by warlords, Pushtun hegemony dissipated, and an ideological vacuum grew within the Islamist movement. The Taliban began as reformers, following a well-worn tradition in Muslim history based on the familiar notion of jihad—holy war against infidels. Jihad, however, does not sanction the killing of fellow Muslims on the basis of ethnicity or sect. Yet the Taliban has used it to do just that. This appalls non-Pushtuns, who accuse the Taliban of using jihad as a cover to exterminate them.

The Taliban have created a new radical model for Islamic revolution.

The Taliban's anomalous interpretation of Islam emerged from an extreme and perverse interpretation of Deobandism, preached by Pakistani mullahs (clerics) in Afghan refugee camps. Deobandism, a branch of Sunni Islam, arose in British India as a reform movement that aimed to regenerate Muslim society as it struggled to live within the confines of a colonized state. The Deobandis sought to harmonize classical Islamic texts with current realities—an aim the Taliban has ignored.

Early on, a few Deobandi *madrasahs* were established in Afghanistan, but they were not hugely popular. They were more successful in Pakistan, however. Pakistani Deobandis set up a political party, the Jamiat-ul-Ulema-e-Islam (JUI), with a strong anti-American stance.

During the war against the Soviets, the few Deobandi Afghan groups that then existed were ignored. Across the border, however, the JUI used the war to set up hundreds of *madrasahs* in Pakistan's Pushtun belt, offering Afghan refugees and young Pakistanis free education, food, shelter, and military training. These Deobandi *madrasahs,* however, were run by barely literate mullahs untutored in the original reformist Deobandi agenda. Saudi funds and scholarships brought them closer to ultraconservative Wahhabism.

Still, the JUI remained politically isolated until Pakistan's 1993 elections, when it allied itself with the victorious Prime Minister Benazir Bhutto, becoming a part of her ruling coalition. For the first time the JUI gained access to the corridors of power, establishing close links with the army, the Inter-Services Intelligence agency (ISI) and the Interior Ministry. In 1996 the Taliban handed control of training camps in Afghanistan over to JUI factions, thus enhancing their image among the new generation of Pakistani and Arab militants who studied there.

The JUI and its many breakaway factions have become the main recruiters of Pakistani and foreign students to fight for the Taliban. Between 1994 and 1999, an estimated 80,000 to 100,000 Pakistanis trained and fought in Afghanistan. These battle-hardened militants now gravely threaten Pakistan's own stability, and the support the Taliban receives from Pakistan's Deobandi network, quite separate from military supplies it gets from the government, ensures even greater Taliban penetration into Pakistani society.

The joint venture between the Taliban and the JUI, funded by Saudi Wahhabis and supported by the Pakistani ISI, has become an ever-expanding enterprise, seeking new markets in Central Asia and beyond. The Taliban may have debased Deobandi traditions—but in doing so they have promoted a new, radical model for Islamist revolution. Unlike their predecessors, the Taliban have little knowledge of Islamic and Afghan history, of *sharia* or the Quran. Their exposure to the radical Islamic debate around the world is minimal; indeed, they are so rigid in their beliefs that they admit no discussion.

THE NEXT TO FALL: PAKISTAN AND KASHMIR

THE TALIBAN'S purist ideology and the Pakistani recruits it has nurtured have had immense cross-border repercussions in Pakistan. An already fragile nation in the midst of an identity crisis, economic meltdown, ethnic and sectarian division, and suffering under a rapacious ruling elite unable to provide good governance, Pakistan could easily be submerged by a new Islamist wave—one led not by established, more mature Islamist parties but by neo-Taliban groups.

By 1998, such neo-Taliban parties had become a major influence in the Pakistani provinces of Baluchistan and the North West Frontier Province. In those regions, they had begun banning television and videos, imposing *sharia* punishments such as stoning and amputation, assassinating Pakistani Shiites, and forcing women to adopt the restrictive Taliban dress code. Their influence is now starting to creep outside the Pushtun belt to Punjab and Sind. Of the 6,000–8,000 Pakistani militants who joined the Taliban for their July 1999 offensive against the Northern Alliance, the majority were, for the first time, not Pushtuns but Punjabis. The Pakistani government's support for the Taliban is thus coming back to haunt it, even as Pakistan's leaders remain oblivious of the danger and continue their support.

The contradictions in Pakistan's Afghan policy have become even more acute due to the support given to the Taliban by two extremist JUI splinter groups, the Sipah-Sahaba Pakistan and the Lashkar-e-Jhangvi. Both groups have killed hundreds of Pakistani Shiites and allegedly twice tried to assassinate Prime Minister Muhammad Nawaz Sharif. When Sharif responded with a crackdown against them in Punjab, their leaders took refuge in Kabul and came under Taliban protection—the same Taliban still backed by Islamabad.

Pakistan believes that a Taliban-controlled Afghanistan will be an ally and give its army strategic depth in its ongoing conflict with India. In particular, Islamabad considers support for the Taliban necessary because of its dispute with India over Kashmir. The Taliban, Deobandi groups in Pakistan, and bin Ladin's terrorist network all give major support to Kashmiri insurgents resisting New Delhi's control of Indian Kashmir. Islamabad therefore cannot drop its support for them without affecting the Kashmir cause it espouses.

Yet the increasing Islamicization of the Kashmiri struggle has undermined both the Kashmiris' own demand for self-determination from India and Pakistan's bid to win international mediation of the dispute. The Kashmiri independence movement is losing world sympathy as more and more Pakistani and Arab recruits join the fight and turn it into a Taliban jihad. The longer this goes on, the less chance there will be that the territorial dispute will ever be peacefully resolved. Day by day, the danger grows for Pakistan, Kashmir, and India itself.

DOMINOES: CENTRAL ASIA, IRAN, AND CHINA

WITH THEIR POROUS BORDERS, weak security apparatuses, and crisis-torn economies, the five former Soviet Central Asian republics—Kazakhstan, Kyrgyzstan, Tajikistan, Turkmenistan, and Uzbekistan—have every reason to fear the turmoil emanating from Afghanistan. The threats include the flow of drugs and weapons and a possible flood of refugees if the Northern Alliance is defeated.

But Central Asia's leaders, who have not changed since the Soviet era, are growing increasingly authoritarian. Their rigged elections and

AP/WIDE WORLD PHOTOS

Putting a new face on radical Islam: Afghan women in Taliban-mandated burqas, Kabul, November 1998

restrictions on political parties have undermined democratic alternatives, leaving underground Islamist movements as the only political opposition. Widespread poverty and unemployment provide a fertile recruiting base for young militants.

During the recent Afghan civil war, the newly independent Central Asian states supported their ethnic kin in northern Afghanistan, who provided a buffer against the spread of Pushtun fundamentalism. That buffer has now been virtually eliminated. The Taliban control Afghan territory bordering Uzbekistan, Turkmenistan, and Tajikistan. Yet apart from Turkmenistan, which has declared itself neutral in the Afghan conflict, these states continue to support the weakened Northern Alliance. Ahmad Shah Masud, the alliance's ethnic Tajik military commander, keeps a major resupply base in southern Tajikistan, where he receives arms from Russia and Iran.

Meanwhile, earlier this year, Tahir Yuldashev, the leader of the Islamic Movement of Uzbekistan (IMU), fled to Afghanistan. Yuldashev is allegedly one of the masterminds behind the assassination attempt against Uzbek President Islam A. Karimov in February, when six bombs in Tashkent killed 16 people and wounded 128. In May, the Taliban allowed Yuldashev to set up a military training camp in northern Afghanistan, just a few miles from the border. Multiple sources in the region say he is training several hundred Islamist militants from Uzbekistan, Tajikistan, and Kyrgyzstan, as well as Uighurs from Xinjiang province in China.

By harboring dissidents, Kabul gets its revenge.

Taliban officials deny helping the IMU. Yet in June, the Taliban rejected a request to extradite Yuldashev to Uzbekistan. And in late August, Juma Namangani, another IMU leader, entered southern Kyrgyzstan with some 800 militants, seized villages and hostages, and threatened to invade Uzbekistan. For Central Asians, the war in Afghanistan is now truly coming home.

Although the IMU are not Deobandis, they are influenced by Wahhabism and have tried to impose the Taliban code in their areas of influence. Although Uzbeks have historically been suspicious of the Pushtuns, the Taliban offer the IMU a sanctuary from Karimov's crackdown, weapons, and the means to finance themselves through the drug trade.

Iran is also threatened by the Taliban. The Shiite regime in Tehran has long opposed Pushtun fundamentalism because it is backed by a regional rival—Pakistan—and because it is Sunni-dominated. Moreover, the Taliban are virulently and violently anti-Shiite. During the Afghan war against the Soviets, the Iranians backed the Shiite Hazaras. They have now extended military support to all non-Pushtun groups in the Northern Alliance. Matters came to a head in late 1998, when the Taliban executed 11 Iranian diplomats in Mazar-i-Sharif. Iran threatened to invade Afghanistan, and war was narrowly avoided.

The Taliban now harbor various Iranian dissidents. They have given sanctuary to the small Ahl-e-Sunnah Wal Jamaat, made up of Sunni Iranians opposed to the Tehran regime. And leaders of the principal

Iranian opposition group, the Iraq-based Mujahideen-e-Khalq, frequently visit Kandahar and have asked the Taliban for an operational base.

China, too, has been affected by the ascendance of the Taliban. Beijing shunned the civil war in Afghanistan until February 1999, when it first made overtures to the Taliban in an attempt to stem the tide of Afghan heroin flooding Xinjiang. The heroin was helping fund Islamist and nationalist opposition to Beijing among the Uighurs and other Muslim ethnic groups. Uighur militants have trained and fought with the Afghan mujahideen since 1986, and Chinese officials say the arms and explosives the rebels have used against Chinese security forces come from Afghanistan. Taliban officials have assured China that they are not harboring fugitive Uighurs, but some Uighur militants are known to be involved with Yuldashev and with bin Ladin—if not the Taliban itself.

The Taliban's reasons for this regional adventurism are a mixture of naiveté, frustration, and ideology. At one level, the Taliban insist that Afghan tribal tradition obliges them to give sanctuary to guests such as the Uighur rebels or bin Ladin. But the Taliban are also furious with Iran and Uzbekistan for their military support of the Northern Alliance. And Kabul is deeply frustrated with its rejection by the international community and the Muslim world, which has refused to recognize the Taliban government. By harboring dissidents, Afghanistan gets its revenge.

"Our prestige is spreading across the region because we have truly implemented Islam, and this makes the Americans and some neighbors very nervous," says Afghan Information Minister Amir Khan Muttaqi. That is putting it lightly. As militants from around the world flock to it for sanctuary, Kabul only increases its support for the wave of Talibanization it hopes to unleash on the region and beyond.

BLOWBACK

WITH the active encouragement of the CIA and Pakistan's ISI, who wanted to turn the Afghan jihad into a global war waged by all Muslim states against the Soviet Union, some 35,000 Muslim radicals from 40 Islamic countries joined Afghanistan's fight between 1982 and 1992. Tens of thousands more came to study in Pakistani *madrasahs*. Eventually more than 100,000 foreign Muslim radicals were directly influenced by the Afghan jihad.

The camps in Pakistan and Afghanistan where they trained became virtual universities for promoting pan-Islamic radicalism in Algeria, Egypt, Yemen, Sudan, Jordan, the Philippines, and Bangladesh. Americans woke up to the danger only in 1993, when Afghan-trained Arab militants blew up the World Trade Center in New York, killing six people and injuring 1,000. The bombers believed that, just as Afghanistan had defeated one superpower—the Soviet Union—they would defeat a second.

One of the main recruiters of Arab militants for the Afghan jihad was bin Ladin. As the richest and highest-ranking Saudi to participate in the struggle, he was heavily patronized by the ISI and Saudi intelligence. Bin Ladin left Afghanistan in 1990 but returned in May 1996. Soon he turned on his former patrons and issued his first "Declaration of Jihad" against the Saudi royal family and the Americans, whom he accused of occupying his homeland.

Striking up a friendship with Umar, the Taliban chief, bin Ladin moved to Umar's base in Kandahar in early 1997. Bin Ladin reunited and rearmed the Arab militants still remaining in Afghanistan after the war against the Soviets, creating the "055" brigade. The Taliban had no contact with Arab Afghans or pan-Islamic ideology until then. But Umar was quickly influenced by his new friend and became increasingly vociferous in his attacks on Americans, the United Nations, and the Saudis and other pro-Western Muslim regimes. Recent Taliban statements reflect a bin Ladin–style outrage, defiance, and pan-Islamism that the Taliban had never used before his arrival.

After the August 1998 bombings of U.S. embassies in Kenya and Tanzania, the United States accused bin Ladin of financing terrorist camps in Somalia, Egypt, Sudan, Yemen, Egypt, and Afghanistan. A few days later, America fired cruise missiles at bin Ladin's camps in eastern Afghanistan, killing nearly 20 militants but leaving his network unharmed. Washington demanded bin Ladin's extradition; the Taliban refused to comply.

Bin Ladin's notoriety has created major problems for Pakistan and Saudi Arabia—two key American allies in the region who have recognized the Taliban government. Pakistan is reluctant to help the United States capture bin Ladin; the Saudi terrorist gives valuable help to the Kashmiris and the JUI would protest if Islamabad was seen to do Washington's bidding. Already in July the JUI issued death threats to all Americans in Pakistan, to be carried out if bin Ladin is extradited to the United States.

The Saudi dilemma is even worse. Saudi Arabia has helped finance the Taliban and has provided crucial military support for their offensives. But this all ended after the U.S. embassy bombings in Africa. The Saudis suspended diplomatic relations with the Taliban and ostensibly ceased all aid, although they did not withdraw diplomatic recognition and private donations continue to flow. Like Pakistan, Saudi Arabia would like to leave bin Ladin in Afghanistan. His arrest and trial in the United States could be highly embarrassing, exposing his continuing relationship with sympathetic members of the ruling elites and intelligence services of both countries.

FLOWER POWER

AROUND KANDAHAR, poppy fields stretch as far as the horizon. In Herat, the Taliban have set up model farms where farmers learn the best methods of heroin cultivation. The U.N. Drug Control Program reports that Afghanistan produced 4,600 metric tons of opium in 1999—twice as much as in the previous year. Afghanistan now produces three times more opium than the rest of the world put together. Ninety-six percent of it is cultivated in Taliban-controlled areas, making the Taliban the largest heroin producer in the world.

The Taliban collect a 20 percent tax from opium dealers and transporters—money that goes straight to the Taliban war chest. The Northern Alliance imposes a similar tax on opium shipments crossing into Uzbekistan and Tajikistan. Drug dealers operate the only banking system in the country—offering farmers credit in advance of their poppy crop. This criminalized economy has weakened states throughout the region.

Whereas Afghan opium was exported to the West through Pakistan in the 1980s, there are now multiple export routes through Iran, the Persian Gulf states, and Central Asia. As these routes expand, so do the beneficiaries. U.S. officials claim that, with most of his bank accounts frozen, bin Ladin now finances his operations through opium. Chinese officials report that drug smuggling from Afghanistan is similarly funding the Uighur opposition. Uzbekistan's government has drawn a direct drug-smuggling link between Afghanistan and the Ferghana Valley, where the IMU is based. The civil war in Tajikistan was partly fueled by Afghan drugs, and Pakistan's economy has been crippled by them. Furthermore, according to governments in the region, heroin addiction is growing: there are now five million addicts in Pakistan, three million in Iran, and one million in China, largely in Xinjiang.

Meanwhile, the smuggling of consumer goods, fuel, and foodstuffs through Afghanistan is wreaking further havoc. The contraband trade developed in the 1950s, when Pakistan granted landlocked Afghanistan the right to import duty-free goods through the port of Karachi under the Afghan Transit Trade Agreement (ATTA). Many of these imported goods were resold in Pakistani bazaars, but with the opening of Central Asia and Iran and the arrival of the Taliban in 1994, this trade has expanded enormously.

Today Afghan and Pakistani truckers smuggle goods across a huge swath of territory that includes Russia, the Caucasus, Central Asia, Iran, and Pakistan. ATTA was worth only $50 million in the 1980s, but it increased to $128 million in 1992–93 and then jumped to $266 million in 1994–95—the first year of Taliban conquests. A 1999 World Bank study estimates that the smuggling trade between Pakistan and Afghanistan alone amounted to $2.5 billion in 1997, equivalent to more than half of Afghanistan's estimated GDP. Add to that the smuggling to and from the rest of the region and the total rises to $5 billion.

This smuggling has crippled local industry in all the affected states; local factories cannot compete with smuggled, foreign-made, duty-free consumer goods. The smuggling also creates huge losses in customs revenue and sales taxes. According to Pakistan's Central Board of Revenue, Pakistan's losses in 1998 amounted to 30 percent of the government's total revenues of $6 billion. The Taliban tax on the smuggling trade was its second-largest source of income after drugs.

New transport and smuggling mafias have developed in Turkmenistan, Uzbekistan, Tajikistan, and Iran. They are ignored by their governments, due to a web of corruption that benefits everyone from border guards to cabinet ministers. Not surprisingly, all these transport mafias are keen supporters and major funders of the Taliban. And this illegal economy is only expanding, since Afghanistan's formal one remains nonexistent. The Afghan infrastructure is devastated, health care and education are virtually absent, and abject poverty is rampant. Afghanistan today has 6 working factories, compared to 220 in 1979. Fighting and smuggling offer the only employment.

AND THE WEST SLEEPS ON

AFTER PROVIDING billions of dollars' worth of arms and ammunition to the mujahideen, the United States abandoned Afghanistan once Soviet troops withdrew. America gave its allies in the region, Pakistan and Saudi Arabia, a free hand to direct the ensuing Afghan civil war.

After the end of the Cold War, Washington never developed a new strategic framework for the area. The United States dealt with issues as they came up in a haphazard, piecemeal fashion, pursuing constantly changing single-issue agendas that were driven more by domestic American politics than the goal of ending the civil war. Afghanistan's neighbors took note of U.S. reluctance to get involved and stepped up arms supplies to their Afghan proxies.

What the United States needed and still needs to do is to put serious pressure on neighboring states to halt the supply of arms into Afghanistan—beginning with local U.S. allies such as Pakistan, Saudi Arabia, and Uzbekistan. That may convince Iran and Russia to do the same. If the flow of weapons ceases and drug exports are curtailed by united regional resolve, the Afghan warlords will see their main sources of support dry up and may then be forced to negotiate an end to the war.

This is the track that the U.N. mediator for Afghanistan, Lakhdar Brahimi, has pursued for the past two years. His lack of success has been directly related to the lack of Western pressure on neighboring states to end their interference. Most Afghan civilians still believe that Americans hold the key to ending foreign interference. Despite Washington's record, there is still enormous goodwill for America among ordinary Afghans. But until the United States demonstrates that it has the determination to mobilize an international effort for ending outside interference, Afghanistan's chaos will only spread. Terrorism will develop new adherents there. The drug trade will expand. These are costs that no country—not Afghanistan, the United States, its allies, China, or Iran—can hope to bear.

The New Threat of Mass Destruction

Richard K. Betts

WHAT IF MCVEIGH HAD USED ANTHRAX?

DURING THE Cold War, weapons of mass destruction were the centerpiece of foreign policy. Nuclear arms hovered in the background of every major issue in East-West competition and alliance relations. The highest priorities of U.S. policy could almost all be linked in some way to the danger of World War III and the fear of millions of casualties in the American homeland.

Since the Cold War, other matters have displaced strategic concerns on the foreign policy agenda, and that agenda itself is now barely on the public's radar screen. Apart from defense policy professionals, few Americans still lose sleep over weapons of mass destruction (WMD). After all, what do normal people feel is the main relief provided by the end of the Cold War? It is that the danger of nuclear war is off their backs.

Yet today, WMD present more and different things to worry about than during the Cold War. For one, nuclear arms are no longer the only concern, as chemical and biological weapons have come to the fore. For another, there is less danger of complete annihilation, but more danger of mass destruction. Since the Cold War is over and American and Russian nuclear inventories are much smaller, there is less chance of an apocalyptic exchange of many thousands of weapons. But the probability that some smaller number of WMD will

---

RICHARD K. BETTS is Director of National Security Studies at the Council on Foreign Relations and Professor of Political Science and Director of the Institute for War and Peace Studies at Columbia University.

be used is growing. Many of the standard strategies and ideas for coping with WMD threats are no longer as relevant as they were when Moscow was the main adversary. But new thinking has not yet congealed in as clear a form as the Cold War concepts of nuclear deterrence theory.

The new dangers have not been ignored inside the Beltway. "Counterproliferation" has become a cottage industry in the Pentagon and the intelligence community, and many worthwhile initiatives to cope with threats are under way. Some of the most important implications of the new era, however, have not yet registered on the public agenda. This in turn limits the inclination of politicians to push some appropriate programs. Even the defense establishment has directed its attention mainly toward countering threats WMD pose to U.S. military forces operating abroad rather than to the more worrisome danger that mass destruction will occur in the United States, killing large numbers of civilians.

The points to keep in mind about the new world of mass destruction are the following. First, the roles such weapons play in international conflict are changing. They no longer represent the technological frontier of warfare. Increasingly, they will be weapons of the weak—states or groups that militarily are at best second-class. The importance of the different types among them has also shifted. Biological weapons should now be the most serious concern, with nuclear weapons second and chemicals a distant third.

Second, the mainstays of Cold War security policy—deterrence and arms control—are not what they used to be. Some new threats may not be deterrable, and the role of arms control in dealing with WMD has been marginalized. In a few instances, continuing devotion to deterrence and arms control may have side effects that offset the benefits.

Third, some of the responses most likely to cope with the threats in novel ways will not find a warm welcome. The response that should now be the highest priority is one long ignored, opposed, or ridiculed: a serious civil defense program to blunt the effects of WMD if they are unleashed within the United States. Some of the most effective measures to prevent attacks within the United States may also challenge traditional civil liberties if pursued to the maximum. And the most troubling conclusion for foreign policy as a whole is that reducing the odds of attacks in the United States might require pulling back from involvement in some foreign conflicts. American activism to guarantee international stability is, paradoxically, the prime source of American vulnerability.

This was partly true in the Cold War, when the main danger that nuclear weapons might detonate on U.S. soil sprang from strategic engagement in Europe, Asia, and the Middle East to deter attacks on U.S. allies. But engagement then assumed a direct link between regional stability and U.S. survival. The connection is less evident today, when there is no globally threatening superpower or transnational ideology to be contained—only an array of serious but entirely local disruptions. Today, as the only nation acting to police areas outside its own region, the United States makes itself a target for states or groups whose aspirations are frustrated by U.S. power.

FROM MODERN TO PRIMITIVE

WHEN NUCLEAR weapons were born, they represented the most advanced military applications of science, technology, and engineering. None but the great powers could hope to obtain them. By now, however, nuclear arms have been around for more than half a century, and chemical and biological weapons even longer. They are not just getting old. In the strategic terms most relevant to American security, they have become primitive. Once the military cutting edge of the strong, they have become the only hope for so-called rogue states or terrorists who want to contest American power. Why? Because the United States has developed overwhelming superiority in conventional military force—something it never thought it had against the Soviet Union.

The Persian Gulf War of 1991 demonstrated the American advantage in a manner that stunned many abroad. Although the U.S. defense budget has plunged, other countries are not closing the gap. U.S. military spending remains more than triple that of any potentially hostile power and higher than the combined defense budgets of Russia, China, Iran, Iraq, North Korea, and Cuba.

More to the point, there is no evidence that those countries' level of military professionalism is rising at a rate that would make them competitive even if they were to spend far more on their forces. Rolling along in what some see as a revolution in military affairs, American forces continue to make unmatched use of state-of-the-art weapons, surveillance and information systems, and the organizational and doctrinal flexibility for managing the integration of these complex innovations into "systems of systems" that is the key to modern military effectiveness. More than ever in military history, brains are brawn. Even if hostile countries somehow catch up in an arms race, their military organizations and cultures are unlikely to catch up in the competence race for management, technology assimilation, and combat command skills.

The primary risk is that enemies might trigger catastrophes in American cities.

If it is infeasible for hostile states to counter the United States in conventional combat, it is even more daunting for smaller groups such as terrorists. If the United States is lucky, the various violent groups with grievances against the American government and society will continue to think up schemes using conventional explosives. Few terrorist groups have shown an interest in inflicting true mass destruction. Bombings or hostage seizures have generally threatened no more than a few hundred lives. Let us hope that this limitation has been due to a powerful underlying reason, rather than a simple lack of capability, and that the few exceptions do not become more typical.

There is no sure reason to bet on such restraint. Indeed, some have tried to use WMD, only to see them fizzle. The Japanese Aum Shinrikyo cult released sarin nerve gas in Tokyo in 1995 but killed only a few people, and some analysts believe that those who attacked the World Trade Center in 1993 laced their bomb with cyanide, which burned up in the explosion (this was not confirmed, but a large amount of cyanide was found in the perpetrators' possession). Eventually such a group will prove less incompetent. If terrorists decide that they want to stun American policymakers by inflicting enormous damage, WMD become more attractive at the same time that they are becoming more accessible.

Finally, unchallenged military superiority has shifted the attention of the U.S. military establishment away from WMD. During the Cold War, nuclear weapons were the bedrock of American war capabilities. They were the linchpin of defense debate, procurement programs, and arms control because the United States faced another superpower—

one that conventional wisdom feared could best it in conventional warfare. Today, no one cares about the MX missile or B-1 bomber, and hardly anyone really cares about the Strategic Arms Reduction Treaty. In a manner that could only have seemed ludicrous during the Cold War, proponents now rationalize the $2 billion B-2 as a weapon for conventional war. Hardly anyone in the Pentagon is still interested in how the United States could use WMD for its own strategic purposes.

What military planners are interested in is how to keep adversaries from using WMD as an "asymmetric" means to counter U.S. conventional power, and how to protect U.S. ground and naval forces abroad from WMD attacks. This concern is all well and good, but it abets a drift of attention away from the main danger. The primary risk is not that enemies might lob some nuclear or chemical weapons at U.S. armored battalions or ships, awful as that would be. Rather, it is that they might attempt to punish the United States by triggering catastrophes in American cities.

CHOOSE YOUR WEAPONS WELL

UNTIL THE past decade, the issue was nuclear arms, period. Chemical weapons received some attention from specialists, but never made the priority list of presidents and cabinets. Biological weapons were almost forgotten after they were banned by the 1972 Biological Weapons Convention. Chemical and biological arms have received more attention in the 1990s. The issues posed by the trio lumped under the umbrella of mass destruction differ, however. Most significantly, biological weapons have received less attention than the others but probably represent the greatest danger.

Chemical weapons have been noticed more in the past decade, especially since they were used by Iraq against Iranian troops in the 1980-88 Iran-Iraq War and against Kurdish civilians in 1988. Chemicals are far more widely available than nuclear weapons because the technology required to produce them is far simpler, and large numbers of countries have undertaken chemical weapons programs. But chemical weapons are not really in the same class as other weapons of mass destruction, in the sense of ability to inflict a huge number of civilian casualties in a single strike. For the tens of thousands of fatalities as in, say, the biggest strategic bombing raids of World War II, it would be very difficult logistically and operationally to deliver chemical weapons in necessary quantities over wide areas.

Nevertheless, much attention and effort have been lavished on a campaign to eradicate chemical weapons. This may be a good thing, but the side effects are not entirely benign. For one, banning chemicals means that for deterrence, nuclear weapons become even more important than they used to be. That is because a treaty cannot assuredly prevent hostile nations from deploying chemical weapons, while the United States has forsworn the option to retaliate in kind.

In the past, the United States had a no-first-use policy for chemical weapons but reserved the right to strike back with them if an enemy used them first. The 1993 Chemical Weapons Convention (CWC), which entered into force last April, requires the United States to destroy its stockpile, thus ending this option. The United States did the same with biological arms long ago, during the Nixon administration. Eliminating its own chemical and biological weapons practically precludes a no-first-use policy for nuclear weapons, since they become the only WMD available for retaliation.

Would the United States follow through and use nuclear weapons against a country or group that had killed several thousand Americans with deadly chemicals? It is hard to imagine breaking the post-Nagasaki taboo in that situation. But schemes for conventional military retaliation would not suffice without detracting from the force of American deterrent threats. There would be a risk for the United States in setting a precedent that someone could use WMD against Americans without suffering similar destruction in return. Limiting the range of deterrent alternatives available to U.S. strategy will not necessarily cause deterrence to fail, but it will certainly not strengthen it.

The ostensible benefit of the CWC is that it will make chemical arms harder to acquire and every bit as illegal and stigmatized as biological weapons have been for a quarter-century. If it has that benefit, what effect will the ban have on the choices of countries or groups who want some kind of WMD in any case, whether for purposes of deterrence, aggression, or revenge? At the margin, the ban will reduce the disincentives to acquiring biological weapons, since they will be no less illegal, no harder to obtain or conceal, and far more damaging than chemical weapons. If major reductions in the chemical threat produce even minor increases in the biological threat, it will be a bad trade.

One simple fact should worry Americans more about biological than about nuclear or chemical arms: unlike either of the other two, biological weapons combine maximum destructiveness and easy availability. Nuclear arms have great killing capacity but are hard to get; chemical weapons are easy to get but lack such killing capacity; biological agents have both qualities. A 1993 study by the Office of Technology Assessment concluded that a single airplane delivering 100 kilograms of anthrax spores—a dormant phase of a bacillus that multiplies rapidly in the body, producing toxins and rapid hemorrhaging—by aerosol on a clear, calm night over the Washington, D.C., area could kill between one million and three million people, 300 times as many fatalities as if the plane had delivered sarin gas in amounts ten times larger.[1]

Like chemical weapons but unlike nuclear weapons, biologicals are relatively easy to make. Innovations in biotechnology have obviated many of the old problems in handling and preserving biological agents, and many have been freely available for scientific research. Nuclear weapons are not likely to be the WMD of choice for non-state terrorist groups. They require huge investments and targetable infrastructure, and are subject to credible threats by the United States. An aggrieved group that decides it wants to kill huge numbers of Americans will find the mission easier to accomplish with anthrax than with a nuclear explosion.

Inside the Pentagon, concern about biological weapons has picked up tremendously in the past couple of years, but there is little serious attention to the problem elsewhere. This could be a good thing if nothing much can be done, since publicity might

[1]U.S. Congress, Office of Technology Assessment, *Proliferation of Weapons of Mass Destruction: Assessing the Risks,* Washington: Government Printing Office, 1993, p. 54.

only give enemies ideas. But it is a bad thing if it impedes efforts to take steps—such as civil defense—that could blunt nuclear, chemical, or biological attacks.

DETERRENCE AND ARMS CONTROL IN DECLINE

AN OLD vocabulary still dominates policy discussion of WMD. Rhetoric in the defense establishment falls back on the all-purpose strategic buzzword of the Cold War: deterrence. But deterrence now covers fewer of the threats the United States faces than it did during the Cold War.

The logic of deterrence is clearest when the issue is preventing unprovoked and unambiguous aggression, when the aggressor recognizes that it is the aggressor rather than the defender. Deterrence is less reliable when both sides in a conflict see each other as the aggressor. When the United States intervenes in messy Third World conflicts, the latter is often true. In such cases, the side that the United States wants to deter may see itself as trying to deter the United States. Such situations are ripe for miscalculation.

For the country that used to be the object of U.S. deterrence—Russia—the strategic burden has been reversed. Based on assumptions of Soviet conventional military superiority, U.S. strategy used to rely on the threat to escalate—to be the first to use nuclear weapons during a war—to deter attack by Soviet armored divisions. Today the tables have turned. There is no Warsaw Pact, Russia has half or less of the military potential of the Soviet Union, and its current conventional forces are in disarray, while NATO is expanding eastward. It is now Moscow that has the incentive to compensate for conventional weakness by placing heavier reliance on nuclear capabilities. The Russians adopted a nuclear no-first-use policy in the early 1980s, but renounced it after their precipitous post–Cold War decline.

Today Russia needs to be reassured, not deterred. The main danger from Russian WMD is leakage from vast stockpiles to anti-American groups elsewhere—the "loose nukes" problem. So long as the United States has no intention of attacking the Russians, their greater reliance on nuclear forces is not a problem. If the United States has an interest in reducing nuclear stockpiles, however, it is.

The traditional American approach—thinking in terms of its own deterrence strategies—provides no guidance. Indeed, noises some Americans still make about deterring the Russians compound the problem by reinforcing Moscow's alarm.

Similarly, U.S. conventional military superiority gives China an incentive to consider more reliance on an escalation strategy. The Chinese have a long-standing no-first-use policy but adopted it when their strategic doctrine was that of "people's war," which relied on mass mobilization and low-tech weaponry. Faith in that doctrine was severely shaken by the American performance in the Persian Gulf War. Again, the United States might assume that there is no problem as long as Beijing only wants to deter and the United States does not want to attack. But how do these assumptions relate to the prospect of a war over Taiwan? That is a conflict that no one wants but that can hardly be ruled out in light of evolving tensions. If the United States decides openly to deter Beijing from attacking Taiwan, the old lore from the Cold War may be relevant. But if Washington continues to leave policy ambiguous, who will know who is deterring whom? Ambiguity is a recipe for confusion and miscalculation in a time of crisis. For all the upsurge of attention in the national security establishment to the prospect of conflict with China, there has been remarkably little discussion of the role of nuclear weapons in a Sino-American collision.

Deterrence requires knowledge of who has launched an attack.

The main problem for deterrence, however, is that it still relies on the corpus of theory that undergirded Cold War policy, dominated by reliance on the threat of second-strike retaliation. But retaliation requires knowledge of who has launched an attack and the address at which they reside. These requirements are not a problem when the threat comes from a government, but they are if the enemy is anonymous. Today some groups may wish to punish the United States without taking credit for the action—a mass killing equivalent to the 1988 bombing of Pan Am Flight 103 over Lockerbie, Scotland. Moreover, the options the defense establishment favors have shifted over entirely from deterrence to preemption. The majority of those who dealt with nuclear weapons policy during the Cold War adamantly opposed developing first-strike options. Today, scarcely anyone looks to that old logic when thinking about rogues or terrorists, and most hope to be able to mount a disarming action against any group with WMD.

Finally, eliminating chemical weapons trims some options for deterrence. Arms control restrictions on the instruments that can be used for deterrent threats are not necessarily the wrong policy, but they do work against maximizing deterrence. Overall, however, the problem with arms control is not that it does too much but that it now does relatively little.

From the Limited Test Ban negotiations in the 1960s through the Strategic Arms Limitation Talks, Strategic Arms Reduction Talks, and Intermediate-range Nuclear Forces negotiations in the 1970s and 1980s, arms control treaties were central to managing WMD threats. Debates about whether particular agreements with Moscow were in the United States' interest were bitter because everyone believed that the results mattered. Today there is no consensus that treaties regulating armaments matter much. Among national security experts, the corps that pays close attention to START and Conventional Forces in Europe negotiations has shrunk. With the exception of the Chemical Weapons Convention, efforts to control WMD by treaty have become small potatoes. The biggest recent news in arms control has not been any negotiation to regulate WMD, but a campaign to ban land mines.

The United States' Cold War partner in arms control, Russia, has disarmed a great deal voluntarily. But despite standard rhetoric, the United States has not placed a high priority on convincing Moscow to divest itself of more of its nuclear weapons; the Clinton administration has chosen to promote NATO expansion, which pushes the Russians in the opposite direction.

The 1968 Nuclear Nonproliferation Treaty remains a hallowed institution, but it has nowhere new to go. It will not convert the problem countries that want to obtain WMD—unless, like Iraq and North Korea in the 1980s, they sign and accept the legal obligation and then simply cheat. The NPT regime will continue to impede access to fissile materials on the open market, but it will not do so in novel or more effective ways. And it does not address the problem of Russian "loose nukes" any better than the Russian and American governments do on their own.

CIVIL DEFENSE

DESPITE ALL the new limitations, deterrence remains an important aspect of strategy. There is not much the United States needs to do to keep up its deterrence capability, however, given the thousands of nuclear weapons and the conventional military superiority it has. Where capabilities are grossly underdeveloped, however, is the area of responses for coping should deterrence fail.

Enthusiasts for defensive capability, mostly proponents of the Strategic Defense Initiative from the Reagan years, remain fixated on the least relevant form of it: high-tech active defenses to intercept ballistic missiles. There is still scant interest in what should now be the first priority: civil defense preparations to cope with uses of WMD within the United States. Active defenses against missiles would be expensive investments that might or might not work against a threat the United States probably will not face for years, but would do nothing against the threat it already faces. Civil defense measures are extremely cheap and could prove far more effective than they would have against a large-scale Soviet attack.

During the Cold War, debate about antimissile defense concerned whether it was technologically feasible or cost-effective and whether it would threaten the Soviets and ignite a spiraling arms race between offensive and defensive weapons. One need not refight the battles over SDI to see that the relevance to current WMD threats is tenuous. Iraq, Iran, or North Korea will not be able to deploy intercontinental missiles for years. Nor, if they are strategically cunning, should they want to. For the limited number of nuclear warheads these countries are likely to have, and especially for biological weapons, other means of delivery are more easily available. Alternatives to ballistic missiles include aircraft, ship-launched cruise missiles, and unconventional means, such as smuggling, at which the intelligence agencies of these countries have excelled. Non-state perpetrators like those who bombed the World Trade Center will choose clandestine means of necessity.

A ballistic missile defense system, whether it costs more or less than the $60 billion the Congressional Budget Office recently estimated would be required for one limited option, will not counter these modes of attack. Indeed, if a larger part of the worry about WMD these days is about their use by terrorist states or groups, the odds are higher that sometime, somewhere in the country, some of these weapons will go off, despite the best efforts to stop them. If that happens, the United States should have in place whatever measures can mitigate the consequences.

By the later phases of the Cold War it was hard to get people interested in civil defense against an all-out Soviet attack that could detonate thousands of high-yield nuclear weapons in U.S. population centers. To many, the lives that would have been saved seemed less salient than the many millions that would still have been lost. It should be easier to see the value of civil defense, however, in the context of more limited attacks, perhaps with only a few low-yield weapons. A host of minor measures can increase protection or recovery from biological, nuclear, or chemical effects. Examples are stockpiling or distribution of protective masks; equipment and training for decontamination; standby programs for mass vaccinations and emergency treatment with antibiotics; wider and deeper planning of emergency response procedures; and public education about hasty sheltering and emergency actions to reduce individual vulnerability.

Stockpiling gas masks and antibiotics could reduce the death toll.

Such programs would not make absorbing a WMD attack tolerable. But inadequacy is no excuse for neglecting actions that could reduce death and suffering, even if the difference in casualties is small. Civil defenses are especially worthwhile considering that they are extraordinarily cheap compared with regular military programs or active defense systems. Yet until recently, only half a billion dollars—less than two-tenths of one percent of the defense budget and less than $2 a head for every American—went to chemical and biological defense, while nearly $4 billion was spent annually on ballistic missile defense.[2] Why haven't policymakers attended to first things first—cheap programs that can cushion the effects of a disaster—before undertaking expensive programs that provide no assurance they will be able to prevent it?

One problem is conceptual inertia. The Cold War accustomed strategists to worrying about an enemy with thousands of WMD, rather than foes with a handful. For decades the question of strategic defense

[2]John F. Sopko, "The Changing Proliferation Threat," *Foreign Policy*, Spring 1997, pp. 3-20.

was also posed as a debate between those who saw no alternative to relying on deterrence and those who hoped that an astrodome over the United States could replace deterrence with invulnerability. None of these hoary fixations address the most probable WMD threats in the post–Cold War world.

Opposition to Cold War civil defense programs underlies psychological aversion to them now. Opponents used to argue that civil defense was a dangerous illusion because it could do nothing significant to reduce the horror of an attack that would obliterate hundreds of cities, because it would promote a false sense of security, and because it could even be destabilizing and provoke attack in a crisis. Whether or not such arguments were valid then, they are not now. But both then and now, there has been a powerful reason that civil defense efforts have been unpopular: they alarm people. They remind them that their vulnerability to mass destruction is not a bad dream, not something that strategic schemes for deterrence, preemption, or interception are sure to solve.

Civil defense can limit damage but not minimize it. For example, some opponents may be able to develop biological agents that circumvent available vaccines and antibiotics. (Those with marginal technical capabilities, however, might be stopped by blocking the easier options.) Which is worse—the limitations of defenses, or having to answer for failure to try? The moment that WMD are used somewhere in a manner that produces tens of thousands of fatalities, there will be hysterical outbursts of all sorts. One of them will surely be, "Why didn't the government prepare us for this?" It is not in the long-term interest of political leaders to indulge popular aversion. If public resistance under current circumstances prevents widespread distribution, stockpiling, and instruction in the use of defensive equipment or medical services, the least that should be done is to optimize plans and preparations to rapidly implement such activities when the first crisis ignites demand.

As threats of terrorism using WMD are taken more seriously, interest will grow in preemptive defense measures—the most obvious of which is intensified intelligence collection. Where this involves targeting groups within the United States that might seem to be potential breeding grounds for terrorists (for example, supporters of Palestinian militants, home-grown militias or cults, or radicals with ties to Iran, Iraq, or Libya), controversies will arise over constitutional limits on invasion of

FRANCES ROBERTS/NYT PICTURES

Better safe than sarin: New York City conducts a nerve gas attack drill, November 9, 1997

privacy or search and seizure. So long as the WMD danger remains hypothetical, such controversies will not be easily resolved. They have not come to the fore so far because U.S. law enforcement has been unbelievably lucky in apprehending terrorists. The group arrested in 1993 for planning to bomb the Lincoln Tunnel happened to be infiltrated by an informer, and Timothy McVeigh happened to be picked up in 1995 for driving without a license plate. Those who fear compromising civil liberties with permissive standards for government snooping should consider what is likely to happen once such luck runs out and it proves impossible to identify perpetrators. Suppose a secretive radical Islamic group launches a biological attack, kills 100,000 people, and announces that it will do the same thing again if its terms are not met. (The probability of such a scenario may not be high, but it can no longer be consigned to science fiction.) In that case, it is hardly unthinkable that a panicked legal system would roll over and treat Arab-Americans as it did the Japanese-Americans who were herded into concentration camps after Pearl Harbor. Stretching limits on domestic surveillance to reduce the chances of facing such choices could be the lesser evil.

IS RETREAT THE BEST DEFENSE?

NO PROGRAMS aimed at controlling adversaries' capabilities can eliminate the dangers. One risk is that in the more fluid politics of the post–Cold War world, the United States could stumble into an unanticipated crisis with Russia or China. There are no well-established rules of the game to brake a spiraling conflict over the Baltic states or Taiwan, as there were in the superpower competition after the Cuban missile crisis. The second danger is that some angry group that blames the United States for its problems may decide to coerce Americans, or simply exact vengeance, by inflicting devastation on them where they live.

If steps to deal with the problem in terms of capabilities are limited, can anything be done to address intentions—the incentives of any foreign power or group to lash out at the United States? There are few answers to this question that do not compromise the fundamental strategic activism and internationalist thrust of U.S. foreign policy over the past half-century. That is because the best way to keep people from believing that the United States is responsible for their problems is to avoid involvement in their conflicts.

Ever since the Munich agreement and Pearl Harbor, with only a brief interruption during the decade after the Tet offensive, there has been a consensus that if Americans did not draw their defense perimeter far forward and confront foreign troubles in their early stages, those troubles would come to them at home. But because the United States is now the only superpower and weapons of mass destruction have become more accessible, American intervention in troubled areas is not so much a way to fend off such threats as it is what stirs them up.

Will U.S. involvement in unstable situations around the former U.S.S.R. head off conflict with Moscow or generate it? Will making NATO bigger and moving it to Russia's doorstep deter Russian pressure on Ukraine and the Baltics or provoke it? With Russia and China, there is less chance that either will set out to conquer Europe or Asia than that they will try to restore old sovereignties and security zones by reincorporating new states of the former Soviet Union or the province of Taiwan. None of this means that NATO expansion or support for Taiwan's autonomy will cause nuclear war. It does mean that to whatever extent American activism increases those countries' incentives to rely on WMD while intensifying political friction between them and Washington, it is counterproductive.

The other main danger is the ire of smaller states or religious and cultural groups that see the United States as an evil force blocking their legitimate aspirations. It is hardly likely that Middle Eastern radicals would be hatching schemes like the destruction of the World Trade Center if the United States had not been identified for so long as the mainstay of Israel, the shah of Iran, and conservative Arab regimes and the source of a cultural assault on Islam. Cold War triumph magnified the problem. U.S. military and cultural hegemony—the basic threats to radicals seeking to challenge the status quo—are directly linked to the imputation of American responsibility for maintaining world order. Playing Globocop feeds the urge of aggrieved groups to strike back.

Is this a brief for isolationism? No. It is too late to turn off foreign resentments by retreating, even if that were an acceptable course. Alienated groups and governments would not stop blaming Washington for their problems. In addition, there is more to foreign policy than dampening incentives to hurt the United States. It is not automatically sensible to stop pursuing other interests for the sake of uncertain reductions in a threat of uncertain probability. Security is not all of a piece, and survival is only part of security.

But it is no longer prudent to assume that important security interests complement each other as they did during the Cold War. The interest at the very core—protecting the American homeland from attack—may now often be in conflict with security more broadly conceived and with the interests that mandate promoting American political values, economic interdependence, social Westernization, and stability in regions beyond Western Europe and the Americas. The United States should not give up all its broader political interests, but it should tread cautiously in areas—especially the Middle East—where broader interests grate against the core imperative of preventing mass destruction within America's borders.

License to Kill

Usama bin Ladin's Declaration of Jihad

Bernard Lewis

On February 23, 1998, *Al-Quds al-Arabi,* an Arabic newspaper published in London, printed the full text of a "Declaration of the World Islamic Front for Jihad against the Jews and the Crusaders." According to the paper, the statement was faxed to them under the signatures of Usama bin Ladin, the Saudi financier blamed by the United States for masterminding the August bombings of its embassies in East Africa, and the leaders of militant Islamist groups in Egypt, Pakistan, and Bangladesh. The statement—a magnificent piece of eloquent, at times even poetic Arabic prose—reveals a version of history that most Westerners will find unfamiliar. Bin Ladin's grievances are not quite what many would expect.

The declaration begins with an exordium quoting the more militant passages in the Quran and the sayings of the Prophet Muhammad, then continues:

> Since God laid down the Arabian peninsula, created its desert, and surrounded it with its seas, no calamity has ever befallen it like these Crusader hosts that have spread in it like locusts, crowding its soil, eating its fruits, and destroying its verdure; and this at a time when the nations contend against the Muslims like diners jostling around a bowl of food.

The statement goes on to talk of the need to understand the situation and act to rectify it. The facts, it says, are known to everyone and fall under three main headings:

> First—For more than seven years the United States is occupying the lands of Islam in the holiest of its territories, Arabia, plundering its riches, overwhelming its rulers, humiliating its people, threatening its neighbors, and using its bases in the peninsula as a spearhead to fight against the neighboring Islamic peoples.
>
> Though some in the past have disputed the true nature of this occupation, the people of Arabia in their entirety have now recognized it.
>
> There is no better proof of this than the continuing American aggression against the Iraqi people, launched from

BERNARD LEWIS is Cleveland E. Dodge Professor Emeritus of Near Eastern Studies at Princeton University. His books include *The Arabs in History, The Emergence of Modern Turkey,* and, most recently, *The Middle East: A Brief History of the Last 2,000 Years.*

> Arabia despite its rulers, who all oppose the use of their territories for this purpose but are subjugated.
>
> Second—Despite the immense destruction inflicted on the Iraqi people at the hands of the Crusader-Jewish alliance and in spite of the appalling number of dead, exceeding a million, the Americans nevertheless, in spite of all this, are trying once more to repeat this dreadful slaughter. It seems that the long blockade following after a fierce war, the dismemberment and the destruction are not enough for them. So they come again today to destroy what remains of this people and to humiliate their Muslim neighbors.
>
> Third—While the purposes of the Americans in these wars are religious and economic, they also serve the petty state of the Jews, to divert attention from their occupation of Jerusalem and their killing of Muslims in it.
>
> There is no better proof of all this than their eagerness to destroy Iraq, the strongest of the neighboring Arab states, and their attempt to dismember all the states of the region, such as Iraq and Saudi Arabia and Egypt and Sudan, into petty states, whose division and weakness would ensure the survival of Israel and the continuation of the calamitous Crusader occupation of the lands of Arabia.

These crimes, the statement declares, amount to "a clear declaration of war by the Americans against God, his Prophet, and the Muslims." In such a situation, the declaration says, the *ulema*—authorities on theology and Islamic law, or *sharia*—throughout the centuries unanimously ruled that when enemies attack the Muslim lands, jihad becomes every Muslim's personal duty.

In the technical language of the *ulema,* religious duties may be collective, to be discharged by the community as a whole, or personal, incumbent on every individual Muslim. In an offensive war, the religious duty of jihad is collective and may be discharged by volunteers and professionals. When the Muslim community is defending itself, however, jihad becomes an individual obligation.

After quoting various Muslim authorities, the signatories then proceed to the final and most important part of their declaration, the *fatwa,* or ruling. It holds that

> To kill Americans and their allies, both civil and military, is an individual duty of every Muslim who is able, in any country where this is possible, until the Aqsa Mosque [in Jerusalem] and the Haram Mosque [in Mecca] are freed from their grip and until their armies, shattered and broken-winged, depart from all the lands of Islam, incapable of threatening any Muslim.

After citing some further relevant Quranic verses, the document continues:

> By God's leave, we call on every Muslim who believes in God and hopes for reward to obey God's command to kill the Americans and plunder their possessions wherever he finds them and whenever he can. Likewise we call on the Muslim *ulema* and leaders and youth and soldiers to launch attacks against the armies of the American devils and against those who are allied with them from among the helpers of Satan.

The declaration and *fatwa* conclude with a series of further quotations from Muslim scripture.

INFIDELS

Bin Ladin's view of the Gulf War as American aggression against Iraq may seem a little odd, but it is widely—though by no means universally—accepted in the Islamic world. For holy warriors of any faith, the faithful are always right and the infidels always wrong, whoever the protagonists and whatever the circumstances of their encounter.

The three areas of grievance listed in the declaration—Arabia, Iraq, and Jerusalem—will be familiar to observers of the Middle Eastern scene. What may be less familiar is the sequence and emphasis. For Muslims, as we in the West sometimes tend to forget but those familiar with Islamic history and literature know, the holy land par excellence is Arabia—Mecca, where the Prophet was born; Medina, where he established the first Muslim state; and the Hijaz, whose people were the first to rally to the new faith and become its standard-bearers. Muhammad lived and died in Arabia, as did the Rashidun caliphs, his immediate successors at the head of the Islamic community. Thereafter, except for a brief interlude in Syria, the center of the Islamic world and the scene of its major achievements was Iraq, the seat of the caliphate for half a millennium. For Muslims, no piece of land once added to the realm of Islam can ever be finally renounced, but none compares in significance with Arabia and Iraq.

Of these two, Arabia is by far the more important. The classical Arabic historians tell us that in the year 20 after the *hijra* (Muhammad's move from Mecca to Medina), corresponding to 641 of the Christian calendar, the Caliph Umar decreed that Jews and Christians should be removed from Arabia to fulfill an injunction the Prophet uttered on his deathbed: "Let there not be two religions in Arabia." The people in question were the Jews of the oasis of Khaybar in the north and the Christians of Najran in the south. Both were ancient and deep-rooted communities, Arab in their speech, culture, and way of life, differing from their neighbors only in their faith.

The saying attributed to the Prophet was impugned by some earlier Islamic authorities. But it was generally accepted as authentic, and Umar put it into effect. The expulsion of religious minorities is extremely rare in Islamic history—unlike medieval Christendom, where evictions of Jews and (after the reconquest of Spain) Muslims were normal and frequent. Compared with European expulsions, Umar's decree was both limited and compassionate. It did not include southern and southeastern Arabia, which were not seen as part of Islam's holy land. And unlike the Jews and Muslims driven out of Spain and other European countries to find what refuge they could elsewhere, the Jews and Christians of Arabia were resettled on lands assigned to them—the Jews in Syria, the Christians in Iraq. The process was also gradual rather than sudden, and there are reports of Jews and Christians remaining in Khaybar and Najran for some time after Umar's edict.

But the decree was final and irreversible, and from then until now the holy land of the Hijaz has been forbidden territory for non-Muslims. According to the Hanbali school of Islamic jurisprudence, accepted by both the Saudis and the declaration's signatories, for a non-Muslim even to set foot on the sacred soil is a major offense. In the rest of the kingdom, non-Muslims, while admitted as temporary visitors, were not permitted to establish residence or practice their religion.

The history of the Crusades provides a vivid example of the relative importance

MAGNUM PHOTOS/ABBAS

Defenders or defilers?: U.S. troops in Saudi Arabia, 1990

of Arabia and other places in Islamic perceptions. The Crusaders' capture of Jerusalem in 1099 was a triumph for Christendom and a disaster for the city's Jews. But to judge by the Arabic historiography of the period, it aroused scant interest in the region. Appeals for help by local Muslims to Damascus and Baghdad went unanswered, and the newly established Crusader principalities from Antioch to Jerusalem soon fitted into the game of Levantine politics, with cross-religious alliances forming a pattern of rivalries between and among Muslim and Christian princes.

The great counter-Crusade that ultimately drove the Crusaders into the sea did not begin until almost a century later. Its immediate cause was the activities of a freebooting Crusader leader, Reynald of Châtillon, who held the fortress of Kerak, in southern Jordan, between 1176 and 1187 and used it to launch a series of raids against Muslim caravans and commerce in the adjoining regions, including the Hijaz. Historians of the Crusades are probably right in saying that Reynald's motive was primarily economic—the desire for loot. But Muslims saw his campaigns as a provocation, a challenge directed against Islam's holy places. In 1182, violating an agreement between the Crusader king of Jerusalem and the Muslim leader Saladin, Reynald attacked and looted Muslim caravans, including one of pilgrims bound for Mecca. Even more heinous, from a Muslim point of view, was his threat to Arabia and a memorable buccaneering expedition in the Red Sea, featuring attacks on Muslim shipping and the Hijaz ports that served

Mecca and Medina. Outraged, Saladin proclaimed a jihad against the Crusaders.

Even in Christian Europe, Saladin was justly celebrated and admired for his chivalrous and generous treatment of his defeated enemies. His magnanimity did not extend to Reynald of Châtillon. The great Arab historian Ibn al-Athir wrote, "Twice, [Saladin said,] I had made a vow to kill him if I had him in my hands; once when he tried to march on Mecca and Medina, and again when he treacherously captured the caravan." After Saladin's triumph, when many of the Crusader princes and chieftains were taken captive, he separated Reynald of Châtillon from the rest and beheaded him with his own hands.

After the success of the jihad and the recapture of Jerusalem, Saladin and his successors seem to have lost interest in the city. In 1229, one of them even ceded Jerusalem to the Emperor Frederick II as part of a general compromise agreement between the Muslim ruler and the Crusaders. Jerusalem was retaken in 1244 after the Crusaders tried to make it a purely Christian city, then eventually became a minor provincial town. Widespread interest in Jerusalem was reawakened only in the nineteenth century, first by the European powers' quarrels over custody of the Christian holy places and then by new waves of Jewish immigration after 1882.

In Arabia, however, the next perceived infidel threat came in the eighteenth century with the consolidation of European power in South Asia and the reappearance of Christian ships off the shores of Arabia. The resulting sense of outrage was at least one of the elements in the religious revival inspired in Arabia by the puritanical Wahhabi movement and led by the House of Saud, the founders of the modern Saudi state. During the period of Anglo-French domination of the Middle East, the imperial powers ruled Iraq, Syria, Palestine, Egypt, and Sudan. They nibbled at the fringes of Arabia, in Aden and the trucial sheikhdoms of the Gulf, but were wise enough to have no military and minimal political involvement in the affairs of the peninsula.

Oil made that level of involvement totally inadequate, and a growing Western presence, predominantly American, began to transform every aspect of Arabian life. The Red Sea port of Jiddah had long served as a kind of religious quarantine area in which foreign diplomatic, consular, and commercial representatives were allowed to live. The discovery and exploitation of oil—and the consequent growth of the Saudi capital, Riyadh, from small oasis town to major metropolis—brought a considerable influx of foreigners. Their presence, still seen by many as a desecration, planted the seeds for a growing mood of resentment.

As long as this foreign involvement was exclusively economic, and as long as the rewards were more than adequate to soothe every grievance, the alien presence could be borne. But in recent years both have changed. With the fall in oil prices and the rise in population and expenditure, the rewards are no longer adequate and the grievances have become more numerous and more vocal. Nor is the involvement limited to economic activities. The revolution in Iran and the wars of Saddam Hussein have added political and military dimensions to the foreign involvement and have lent some plausibility to the increasingly heard cries of "imperialism." Where their holy land is involved, many Muslims tend to define the struggle—and sometimes also the enemy—in religious terms, seeing the American troops sent to free Kuwait and save Saudi Arabia from Saddam Hussein as infidel invaders and occupiers. This perception is heightened by America's unquestioned primacy among the powers of the infidel world.

TRAVESTIES

To most Americans, the declaration is a travesty, a gross distortion of the nature and purpose of the American presence in Arabia. They should also know that for many—perhaps most—Muslims, the declaration is an equally grotesque travesty of the nature of Islam and even of its doctrine of jihad. The Quran speaks of peace as well as of war. The hundreds of thousands of traditions and sayings attributed with varying reliability to the Prophet, interpreted in various ways by the *ulema,* offer a wide range of guidance. The militant and violent interpretation is one among many. The standard juristic treatises on *sharia* normally contain a chapter on jihad, understood in the military sense as regular warfare against infidels and apostates. But these treatises prescribe correct behavior and respect for the rules of war in such matters as the opening and termination of hostilities and the treatment of noncombatants and prisoners, not to speak of diplomatic envoys. The jurists also discuss—and sometimes differ on—the actual conduct of war. Some permit, some restrict, and some disapprove of the use of mangonels, poisoned arrows, and the poisoning of enemy water supplies—the missile and chemical warfare of the Middle Ages—out of concern for the indiscriminate casualties that these weapons inflict. At no point do the basic texts of Islam enjoin terrorism and murder. At no point do they even consider the random slaughter of uninvolved bystanders.

Nevertheless, some Muslims are ready to approve, and a few of them to apply, the declaration's extreme interpretation of their religion. Terrorism requires only a few. Obviously, the West must defend itself by whatever means will be effective. But in devising strategies to fight the terrorists, it would surely be useful to understand the forces that drive them.

Will Indonesia Survive?

Donald K. Emmerson

THE CENTER CAN HOLD

ANYONE SKIMMING recent Western reporting on Indonesia could be forgiven for assuming that the world's fourth most populous country is on the verge of disintegration. The recent secession of East Timor is unlikely to cause a chain reaction, however. The geographic and cultural patchwork of Indonesia may shrink, but it is not about to unravel.

A vast archipelago through whose waterways pass two-fifths of world shipping, Indonesia has recently undergone a series of political reforms that could eventually lead it to become that rare thing, an Islamic democracy. Its size, location, and natural resources make it a potentially formidable obstacle to any Chinese attempt to gain hegemony over Southeast Asia. The scale and diversity of the Indonesian economy enhance its importance for the larger region and make urgent its resurrection from the Asian financial crisis. Whether Indonesia will survive in something resembling its present form is thus a topic of concern well beyond the South Pacific.

Since its economy began to fail in 1997, Indonesia has witnessed several thousand deaths from political violence. This number will mount as unrest continues. But although the toll is tragic, it is not enough to destabilize a country of some 216 million people. And although separatist movements have gained ground in several outlying provinces, they do not yet command enough resources or support to impose their will on the government. The country's periphery is restive, but the provinces remain Jakarta's to lose.

DONALD K. EMMERSON is Senior Fellow at Stanford University's Asia-Pacific Research Center.

THE YEAR OF LIVING DANGEROUSLY

MANY OBSERVERS who forecast Indonesia's disintegration see East Timor as both omen and model. Indonesia's 1975–76 invasion and annexation of the eastern half of the island of Timor was finally reversed in 1999. The East Timorese voted overwhelmingly for separation from Indonesia in U.N.-supervised balloting last August, and Jakarta ratified the divorce the following month. The U.N. Transitional Authority in East Timor (UNTAET) has been charged with preparing the territory for independence.

But East Timor is a very small place—not much more than half a million people on fewer than 15,000 square kilometers of land. Excising that territory from the vast eastern underbelly of a country that is 1.9 million square kilometers large has left but a tiny scar. Indonesia has not only survived the surgery but emerged with its prospective health improved.

To be sure, the operation was botched. On September 4, the U.N. announced the results of the referendum: Jakarta had lost by a four-to-one margin. Violent reprisals by government supporters quickly followed, destroying an estimated 70 percent of East Timor's urban infrastructure. Hundreds of pro-independence East Timorese were killed, and hundreds of thousands more were intimidated into fleeing to western Timor. The Indonesian army's role in the violence ran a short gamut from acquiescence to connivance.

Whether or not the government recognized it as such, however, the loss of East Timor was actually a net gain for Indonesia as a whole, because it could only help sustain the latter's two fragile recoveries—from authoritarian rule and from economic recession. Between mid-1997 and mid-1998, Indonesia's per capita GDP shrank by 16.2 percent. Jakarta could ill afford to continue its two-decades-long repression of the East Timorese. However bloody and belated the separation was, relinquishing the territory removed an impediment to crucial political and financial support from foreign donors and lenders sensitive to human rights.

Indonesians who opposed giving up East Timor feared a "domino effect" in which other provinces would follow East Timor out the door. Such a move would set an example for other regions, they warned.

Jakarta needed to stand fast to avoid an exodus that would destroy the country. Granted, such an exodus could still occur. But six months after the People's Consultative Assembly in Jakarta canceled East Timor's provincial status, the rest of Indonesia remains intact—troubled (in some places, violently so), but still one country.

Why? Compared to Indonesia's other provinces, East Timor is unique. A Portuguese colony for nearly 500 years, it was never part of the Dutch East Indies, the entity that eventually became Indonesia. Nine out of ten East Timorese are Catholic, whereas nine of ten Indonesians are Muslim. In 1975, a change of regime in Lisbon triggered the beginning of the end of the Portuguese empire. Free from Portugal's control, political rivalries in East Timor spiraled into civil war. One cannot say how successfully the East Timorese might have managed their independence had they been left alone, but it can hardly be said that the Indonesian invasion of December 1975 rescued the East Timorese from themselves. It did make it clear that Suharto, then Indonesia's president, and his fellow generals had decided to smash the partition that had long kept separate the two halves of Timor. The United Nations never accepted East Timor's absorption into Indonesia. Washington gave only de facto acquiescence, without approving of Suharto's methods. To the extent that nationhood is the product of a shared past, therefore, Indonesia is more Indonesian without East Timor than with it.

WHO'S NEXT?

MORE THAN 3,000 kilometers northwest of East Timor lies the province of Aceh (pronounced "Atch-eh"), which is widely held to be the next most plausible candidate for independence. But if Aceh does leave Indonesia—more accurately, if it is permitted to do so—such an outcome will flow not from any East Timor precedent but from distinctive local conditions and Aceh's interactions with Jakarta.

The Acehnese differ from the East Timorese in nearly every respect. Both encountered the Portuguese early in the sixteenth century, but Aceh did so as an expanding sultanate that refused to succumb to colonial rule. No part of the archipelago that became the Dutch East Indies took longer for the Dutch to pacify.

Centuries before the Europeans' arrival, Aceh's location on the northwestern end of the island of Sumatra exposed it to Islamicization by Muslim traders. Acehnese sometimes call their homeland "the front porch of Mecca," due to its relative proximity to Saudi Arabia. Aceh's population is about 97 percent Muslim, a figure that may actually have risen recently as non-Muslims, fearing turmoil, have fled.

Aceh's natural wealth is also distinctive. Indonesia is the world's leading exporter of liquefied natural gas (LNG), and two-fifths of the country's LNG exports originate on Aceh's northern coast. In contrast, although UNTAET has signed an agreement with Australia to develop petroleum resources beneath the Timor Sea on behalf of the future sovereign state of East Timor, the new nation's share of the eventual annual revenues is expected to amount to only a few million dollars.

As for industry, Aceh's was much more advanced even before the torching and looting of East Timor's infrastructure in 1999.

Aceh's autonomous identity as an Islamic state and its natural resources do make secession more plausible. No regionalist leader articulates a harder anti-Jakarta line than Tengku Hasan M. di Tiro, the titular head of the Free Aceh Movement (abbreviated GAM in Indonesian). Di Tiro avows his fealty to Aceh's past and enmity toward the "imperialist" Javanese (who account for about half of Indonesia's population and have disproportionately dominated its institutions). Seemingly obsessed by history, di Tiro refers frequently to the long Acehnese struggle against the Dutch and then the Javanese. He considers himself a head of state—the 41st ruler of Aceh since 1500. The 34th through 40th, he notes, all died in the struggle against the Dutch, but he detests the Javanese more than the Europeans whom they replaced. More brutally and duplicitously than their predecessors, he insists, the Javanese repressed and exploited the real Acehnese nation in the name of an imaginary one. "I myself," he told me, "am older than this so-called Indonesia." (Indonesia's first president, Sukarno, declared the country's independence in 1945, when di Tiro was 15.) When asked what sort of government an independent Aceh might have under his leadership, he referred to an Anglo-Acehnese commercial treaty signed in 1603. He also cited Aceh's natural-gas reserves as proof of the viability of its independence.

Despite di Tiro's confidence, Aceh's exit from Indonesia is hardly inevitable. From 1968 to 1998, when he finally resigned, Suharto's authoritarian "New Order" transformed the economy and society of the entire country, including Aceh. By erecting an industrial enclave near Lhokseumawe, the province's second-largest city, Jakarta unwittingly stimulated GAM recruitment. Rural Acehnese resented the disparity in wealth between themselves and the Javanese brought in to staff the modern complex, and disputes broke out over land rights and pollution. Above all, the Acehnese objected to having "their" valuable resources siphoned off to Jakarta. But the answer to these grievances need not be independence. Jakarta could rechannel revenues back to a truly autonomous Aceh, possibly inside a federalized Indonesia. So the natural wealth that could make Aceh's independence more viable could also make the matter more negotiable—if Indonesia's political center is willing to ease its grip on the periphery.

Economic growth during the "New Order" diversified the Acehnese. A relatively secular and technocratic elite grew up around the university in the provincial capital, Banda Aceh. Migrants left for Java to pursue studies or careers. Di Tiro's name still garners respect in Aceh, but during his decades-long exile in Sweden, parts of Acehnese society passed him by. Inside the province, nongovernmental organizations have sprung up to represent social groups—students, women, entrepreneurs—with an interest in peace and justice as well as sovereignty. Educated, professional, and commercial Acehnese abhor the Indonesian army, which has abused citizens with such impunity for so long. But they are also impatient with GAM's intransigence and violence.

Nor will religious issues necessarily lead to secession. The Acehnese are devout Muslims, but the overwhelming majority of other Indonesians are Muslim, too. This should mitigate in Aceh the sense of alienation that has contributed to unrest among religious minorities elsewhere in Southeast Asia.

THE OUTSIDERS

AFTER ACEH, the province many observers consider most likely to secede is Papua—formerly known as Irian Jaya, but renamed by Jakarta in a symbolic concession to local identity. Half as populous as Aceh, Papua sprawls over the easternmost end of Indonesia, covering the western half of the island it shares with Papua New Guinea. The province's two million inhabitants are spread across a territory more than seven times larger than Aceh and nearly 3,500 kilometers away. Some three-fifths of Papua's population is Protestant, but the potential for political solidarity is limited by the diversity of a dispersed population. In February, the leaders of 11 Papuan Protestant denominations demanded justice but disavowed violence, and remained neutral on independence.

Many inhabitants of other islands (notably Java) have migrated into Papua to exploit its local resources. This has complicated ethnic Papuans' ability to claim that their interests and those of the territory are one and the same. Unlike the Acehnese, ethnic Papuans speak hundreds of distinct languages, and the province's mountainous terrain further limits the ability of the sovereignty-seeking Free Papua Organization to mobilize a united front against Jakarta.

Like Aceh, Papua is rich in natural wealth, but unlike Aceh, its economy and infrastructure lag far behind those of Indonesia proper. Here again, the fruits of local resources are tasted mainly in Java, and the gulf between productive enclaves and backward hinterlands motivates resentment and secessionism. The rift in wealth and status is even greater in Papua than in Aceh and thus is potentially more destabilizing. But the sheer size of the gap in Papua also magnifies the local allure of Jakarta's attempts to bridge it, thereby potentially helping Jakarta's agents co-opt and divide pro-independence elements.

Aside from Aceh and Papua, other provinces on the lengthening list of potential defectors include Riau and East Kalimantan. All four of these peripheral regions combine natural wealth with small populations to generate per capita incomes far above the national average. This lets local elites believe that their homelands can make it on their own, but it also enables Jakarta to elicit local support by returning to these provinces some of the substantial revenues now taken from them.

Central authorities rightly worry about losing income from oil and gas reserves in Aceh, Riau, and East Kalimantan. But the restructuring of Indonesia's economy toward manufacturing and services has greatly reduced the proportional contributions of oil and gas to national revenue. By 1996, such receipts accounted for only 21 percent of central government income. Compared with the outer islands, Java's larger population, better infrastructure, and more diversified economy have made it the most important origin of national revenue.

Indonesia's restive periphery is still Jakarta's to lose.

The havoc done to Indonesia's economy by the East Asian financial crisis in 1997–98 steeply increased Jakarta's need for income. Indonesia's public obligations now equal its GDP, and some three-fifths of its national budget is earmarked to servicing this massive debt. But if the current economic recovery can be sustained, the urgency will decline. So, too, will the efficiency of currently exploited hydrocarbon fields, including the shrinking reservoir of gas that has bolstered the economic hopes of the Acehnese.

In Riau and East Kalimantan, pro-independence moves and views have thus far been relatively mild. The prospect of autonomy within Indonesia is much more popular in these places than in Aceh.

Horrific violence in a fifth province, the outer island of Maluku, has led observers to warn that it too might break away. But the waves of killing and destruction there have not been directed against Jakarta. They stem mainly from the collapse of a delicate balance of economic and political power between Muslims and Christians. In Maluku, resentments have been fierce, but they have been aimed not so much "vertically" (against national authority) as "horizontally," in deadly, escalating exchanges between local communities. People in Maluku had many reasons to be disappointed with faraway central authorities, but one chief grievance was in principle entirely resolvable: Jakarta's failure to intervene impartially and effectively to help end the violence.

ENTER GUS DUR

WHAT ALL THESE FACTS imply is that the fate of Indonesia's troubled periphery remains in the hands of Jakarta. By late 1999, in contrast, many analysts still believed that part of the periphery was about to leave. They were especially perturbed by an incautious remark made in November by Indonesia's new leader, Abdurrahman Wahid. Wahid had been elected president in October by the People's Consultative Assembly—itself largely a product of the country's democratic national election five months earlier, the first such contest in 44 years.

After East Timor's vote for separation, Wahid said it would be unfair not to let Aceh have a referendum, too. Wahid's comment shocked people by seeming to endorse the domino theory. If Jakarta felt obliged to treat all the provinces similarly, whatever one of them gained would have to be granted to the others. Consistency would scuttle the country even if diversity did not. But this fear proved groundless. Not even the liberally minded Wahid—let alone other Indonesian leaders—was prepared to apply the East Timor precedent to the rest of Indonesia. Wahid soon explained that in the referendum that he envisioned, the Acehnese would be allowed to decide only whether to apply Islamic laws inside their province, not whether to withdraw from the republic.

In the few months since his presidency began, Wahid (better known by his nickname, Gus Dur) has often made off-the-cuff comments that have required backtracking and clarification. He "has been very skillful in solving problems created by himself," wryly noted one Indonesian newspaper. Assembly Chair Amien Rais, a possible successor to Wahid, has said that for Indonesians, "there are three mysteries in life: when they are going to die, the weather, and what their president is going to say or do next."

The more Wahid changes his mind—or at least his words—the less Indonesians will believe anything he says. So his presidency could self-destruct, and disarray in Jakarta might then stoke separatism in the regions. But Wahid's inconsistency can also be an asset. Indonesia has only recently emerged from decades of deadening autocratic consistency. Throughout his long rule, Suharto refused to give power to the regions.

In this context, many Indonesians find Wahid's policy shifts refreshing—if only because they evoke possibilities of change after stasis.

There is also more than a little method in Wahid's madness. His headline-grabbing unpredictability keeps his enemies off balance and the spotlight on himself. Media attention magnifies his influence, and he uses self-deprecatory humor to advance his views. In the end, those views reflect Gus Dur's sense of himself not as a commander but as a teacher—engaging his people in a dialogue that will move the country toward tolerance, pluralism, and democracy. In the meantime, he has begun addressing the army's intrusive and repressive habits—but he has not stopped security forces from cracking down hard on GAM in Aceh. The first policy wins him points in regions where the army is hated; the second sends a clear antisecessionist signal to the one region where such hatred may be greatest.

MAGNA JAKARTA

KEEPING the country together will require more than counterinsurgency and civilian control of the army. Jakarta will also need to meet a third challenge: decentralization. In mid-1999, new legislation shifted political and economic power from the center to the regions. But these laws still have not been put into practice, and the regions are impatient. Wahid's skills are political, not managerial, and differences between his ministers have corroded their ability to work as a team. Now, bold steps are needed. If Indonesia is to retain its present borders, it may even have to reinvent itself as a federal state.

After World War II, the Dutch experimented with federalism as a way to retain influence in the East Indies and isolate Sukarno's Java-based republic. Many Indonesians still shun the "F word" because it smacks of colonialism. Wahid nevertheless hopes to introduce much of the substance of federalism without using the name.

Wahid has kept up a punishing schedule of travel abroad, partly to solicit aid and investment but also to line up support for keeping Indonesia whole. He has tried especially hard to mobilize neighboring and Muslim states against Acehnese independence. The success of this campaign so far has enabled Jakarta to ask GAM, in effect, Why seek sovereignty if it will only isolate you?

In Southeast Asian international relations, realpolitik has traditionally trumped moralpolitik. Neighboring states dependent on the region's biggest and potentially most powerful country will think twice before risking its ire by supporting its dismemberment. One might think that China would encourage provincial defections to cut the republic—a potential rival—down to size. But China's leaders have so far been more concerned about upholding in Indonesia the principle of single-state sovereignty so crucial to how they view their own country. Accurately or not, they worry that the dominoes from an Indonesian collapse could tumble northward: Aceh or Papua today, Xinjiang or Tibet tomorrow.

Jakarta would be wrong, however, to think that foreign governments will always be allergic to secession. Washington has assured Jakarta of U.S. support for Indonesia's territorial integrity, arguing that East Timor was a special case. But the more brutal Jakarta's attempts to hold Indonesia together, the less enamored of Indonesian sovereignty Washington will become. Moralpolitik can be sidelined, but it will never go away; human rights activists and their allies in Congress will make sure of that. Wahid's minister of regional autonomy, Ryaas Rasyid, is especially sensitive to this prospect. He actually ranks Papua above Aceh as a candidate for exit. The Papuans are Christians, he reasons, and thus more likely in the long run to garner Western sympathy than the Muslim Acehnese.

Papuan history may be cited to back Rasyid up. Compared with Aceh's participation in the Indonesian Revolution, the circumstances of Papua's entry into Indonesia were more controversial—indeed, more like East Timor's. The western half of New Guinea was not added to the Republic of Indonesia until 1962–63, when diplomatic pressure and a military campaign mounted by Jakarta obliged the Netherlands to turn the territory over, so long as this was eventually shown to be an "act of free choice." In 1969, Jakarta "kept" this promise by manipulating selected tribal leaders into agreeing, without a vote, to affiliate with Indonesia. Other things being equal, this history will make it harder for Jakarta to resist giving the people of Papua a new and truly free choice between futures.

Indonesia's future in the near term depends partly on the survival of Wahid. At 59, he is comparatively young for a head of state. But although his stamina is impressive, he suffers from high blood pressure, diabetes, and the aftereffects of two strokes. He is blind in one eye and has only 20 percent vision in the other. Wahid's presidency is scheduled to run to 2004, but if he becomes incapacitated, Vice President Megawati Sukarnoputri is slated to replace him. She lacks Wahid's political skills, however, as well as his Muslim credentials and possibly his willingness to experiment with federalism by another name. Her chief rival, Assembly Chair Rais, is a committed Muslim who clearly favors decentralization. But just as Sukarnoputri's presidency would worry some Muslim politicians, Rais' would disturb many non-Muslim leaders.

Indonesia, then, will survive. Aceh and Papua may not remain inside it, but their farewells, if they happen, are unlikely to set in motion a process that reduces the republic to the island of Java. Adaptations to differing localities and demands can still usefully be made, even at some cost in consistency. Barring another economic collapse, co-optation by Jakarta can be effective. Revenues from resources can be shared. Decentralization can be adopted. A pseudo-federal system can be tried. Centripetal diplomacy can work. But these "cans" cannot be turned into "wills" without sustained, focused, and adroit behavior by a central government that is weak, divided, and embattled on many fronts at once.

Calling All Regio-Cops

Peacekeeping's Hybrid Future

Michael Hirsh

On September 6, an angry crowd stormed a U.N. relief office in West Timor. The mob sacked the building and, in a sickening echo of Mogadishu in 1993, burned the bodies of three U.N. workers in the streets. The U.N. quickly evacuated its remaining personnel from the Indonesian province, casting a pall on its unsteady mission across the border in the newly independent East Timor.

The disaster underscored an independent report that the U.N. had released just a few weeks before. Published at a time when, in Sierra Leone, hundreds of peacekeepers were taking turns being held hostage—the most recent victims being British troops who went in to rescue their blue-helmeted predecessors—the paper was a call to arms that harshly criticized the U.N.'s peacekeeping efforts and laid out a prescription for more robust forces, command, and control.

These events and the U.N. report reinvigorated a debate that has become all too familiar. The debate revolves around several key questions: Can U.N. peacekeeping be made to work at long last, or are such efforts doomed to failure? Are international norms effective, or is raw military might the only thing that can stop the villainous Foday Sankohs of the world? Is humanitarian intervention impractical, or is there some way of balancing both sovereign rights and global values? Such questions have absorbed academics and the international punditocracy for much of the last decade, ever since the tidy Cold War world of interstate conflicts—in which the U.N. played a simple, uncontroversial role as a buffer along cease-fire lines and borders (as in Cyprus and the Middle East)—descended into today's maelstrom of ethnic, tribal, and religious bloodshed.

This debate over humanitarian intervention is an important and well-intentioned one. It is also, for the most part, a phony debate. The discussion, at least as it has been framed in recent years, offers up false choices. For most of the post–Cold War period, arguments about a new world order have centered on whether either the United States or the United Nations, acting separately or in concert, could become some form of globo-cop. But ten years after the fall of the Soviet

---

MICHAEL HIRSH is *Newsweek*'s Chief Diplomatic Correspondent.

Union, it is high time for the world to recognize that neither option will come to pass. Washington does not have the will for it, and the U.N. (thanks largely to American stinginess) does not have the way.

Out of this vacuum, however, a new system is emerging on the ground, crisis by crisis. Call it the rule of the regio-cops. It is a hybrid system, dependent on both U.N. legitimation and local muscle. To work, the new system needs regional powers and organizations to do the dirty work of peacekeeping and peacemaking. But such regional forces are increasingly being trained and pressured to act in accordance with U.N. norms, and typically go in under the auspices of Security Council resolutions.

This was the model followed for East Timor in September 1999, when President Bill Clinton happily accepted Australia's offer to send in combat troops to stop Indonesia's murderous militias—even as the U.S. president took the lead in organizing a multinational response and orchestrating a U.N. resolution. It was the approach in Kosovo, too. The United States insisted on using NATO to drive out Slobodan Milŏsević—mindful of how U.N. troops had abjectly failed to stop earlier atrocities in Bosnia—but ultimately acted under the U.N. flag.

Now the pattern is spreading, gingerly, to western Africa. This past summer, when Clinton announced he was sending U.S. military trainers to Nigeria, it was an implicit recognition not just of the democratic government's newfound legitimacy, but of the fact that, as the region's major power, Nigeria must play the key role in stopping the atrocities in Sierra Leone—no matter how brutally Nigeria's troops may have acted there before.

ON THE CHEAP

Will this pattern spread further? Should it? To answer this, some hard facts must be faced. The current dispute over peacemaking usually centers on whether U.N. resources should be beefed up to deal with certain situations—typically civil conflicts that hover precariously between peace and outright war—into which U.N Secretary-General Kofi Annan has boldly pushed the world body. The report of last summer's U.N. peacekeeping commission chaired by Lakhdar Brahimi, sharply analyzes the current system's flaws and lays out a corrective plan. At the U.N. Millennium Assembly in New York in September, leader after leader took the rostrum to give explicit or implicit support to the Brahimi prescriptions. Among those leaders was President Clinton, who called for a greater U.N. role in humanitarian interventions.

But to think that the Brahimi panel's advice will be carried out, now or ever, is to strain common sense to the breaking point. Demands for a more robust U.N. force, including combat-ready "standby" units, long predate the fall of communism—and there is little reason to think they will succeed now where they have failed in the past. While the new peacekeeping recommendations (which would cost an estimated $200 million a year to implement) were being touted in New York, a skinflint U.S. Congress in Washington, D.C., was trying to cut even more from the U.N.'s present peacekeeping budget. At one point, members of Congress actually tried to entirely eliminate African peacekeeping in order to meet budget caps—this despite the efforts of Richard Holbrooke, Washington's U.N. ambassador, to give Africa a higher profile in U.S. national security considerations than ever before.

Hence the absurdity of Clinton's exhorting the U.N. to prepare for more intervention when he has failed to deliver on his four-year-old promise to pay most of Washington's back dues. According to U.N. budget chief Joseph Connor, the United States is responsible for more than half of the world's $3.24 billion total in U.N. arrears. "The United States said, 'Show reform and we will pay,'" Connor complained during the Millennium Assembly. "We showed reform. [The money's] not there." With the United States still refusing to pay, other nations, including long-compliant members such as Japan, are increasingly reluctant to pick up the tab.

And hence one should be realistic about the prospects for U.N. peacekeeping. The United States, as the world's sole superpower, has a greater stake in a peaceful global system than any other country. If Washington is not going to do more for the U.N. now—at a time of unprecedented U.S. prosperity and a record budget surplus, and at a moment when not a single American soldier risks wearing a U.N. blue helmet anywhere in the world—it is unlikely to any time soon. Nor is it likely that Washington will prove any more willing to take on a regular role as the U.N.'s "subcontractor"—as it has only twice before, in Korea and Kuwait, when it mustered multinational forces under the U.N. banner. This is especially true after Kosovo, which set a zero-casualty threshold for U.S.-led humanitarian intervention.

RUDDERLESS

Yet this does not mean that the impulse for humanitarian intervention is going to wither away along with the U.N. budget. Whether Washington likes it or not, interventions are here to stay. They will go on in their haphazard way, with the biggest headlines and the most horrific TV footage typically drawing the biggest efforts, even as academics and experts parse various "rules" for when America and other major powers should jump in—as if such fastidious guidelines carried any weight against the "CNN effect."

Old-fashioned proponents of realpolitik who reject the quixotism of humanitarian intervention—or who, like the writer Edward Luttwak, simply advise us to await the peace that comes once combatants have exhausted their bloodlust—only betray their remoteness from and ignorance of the pressures put on elected officials in the era of "superempowered" democracy (which usually means a superempowered media). It may well be, as Luttwak argues, that humanitarian interventions "artificially freeze conflict." But in a globalized world dominated by Western mores, people do not really care about that. They simply do not want to see slaughter on their TV screens. Egged on by the ever-multiplying hordes of pundits, they will usually demand that their governments do something about it—usually something fast and easy. We live in a world defined by Wilsonian idealism, as even Henry Kissinger has grudgingly admitted. *The New Republic*'s Leon Wieseltier, writing during the Kosovo war, solemnly summed up the popular sentiment: any "place in which innocent men, women, and children are being expelled and exterminated is an important place. It is a place that asks about the philosophy by which we claim to live."

So intervention will continue. But if we stick to the present system, this intervention is doomed to remain amateurish, late, and woefully under-resourced, as the experiences in Bosnia, Kosovo, and Sierra Leone have shown. A Wilsonian world this may be, but it is a miserly and self-absorbed Wilsonianism. Just as the death of the nation-state has been greatly exaggerated, so has the idea that the needs of the "international community" will ever trump national interests. Americans today may no longer have a clear idea of what their national interests are, but one interest of which they are quite sure is that their sons and daughters never again die in battle.

If the United States will not lead the charge for the U.N., no one else is likely to fill the vacuum. Indeed, despite the aggressively pro-U.N. rhetoric of British Prime Minister Tony Blair and other Western leaders, U.N. peacekeeping today has been largely sloughed onto the developing world. As the Brahimi report notes,

> In contrast to the long tradition of developed countries providing the bulk of the troops for U.N. peacekeeping operations during the Organization's first 50 years, in the last few years 77 percent of the troops in formed military units ... were contributed by developing countries.

OUT OF THE BOX

The report paints a bleak picture. But there may yet be a way out of this box—if the terms of the debate are drastically altered to account for regional devolution. The emergence of U.N.-sanctioned regio-cops changes many things. For one, it may allow us to finally leave behind the interminable debate between proponents of international norms and institutions (like the U.N.) and those who push might-makes-right realism. Under the new system, without the imprimatur of a U.N. Security Council resolution, intervention by regional powers will become a mere invasion—however honorably motivated—and carry with it the threat of regional hegemony. It will be unwelcome to the locals and lay the seeds for future conflict.

On the other hand, without a force or coalition of forces representing regional military muscle, a perpetually cash-strapped U.N. is certain to continue to lose credibility, as it did in Bosnia, East Timor, and Sierra Leone before regional powers stepped in. Current events have forced realpoliticians and liberal internationalists, so long at odds, into bed together. One mindset has, in many situations, become impossible without the other.

This suggests what the most important future role for the U.N. might become—a legitimizer for local forces. To many nations, today's Security Council may seem more like a domineering Star Chamber than a fount of international jurisprudence. The council's image would certainly benefit if other major powers such as Germany and Japan were made permanent members, thus ridding it of its World War II–era mustiness. But flawed or not, the Security Council still has unique potential. It is the only effective tribunal and repository for international case law for dealing with ethnic cleansing and other humanitarian horrors. As such, it must continue to act as the arbiter of interventions.

The use of U.N.-approved regional peacekeepers will help solve another critical problem: how to keep humanitarian intervention aligned with national interest. Australia, watching the chaos in Timor just across the sea and perhaps fearing an onslaught of boat people, was only too eager to intervene for free. Others in similar situations may not behave as uprightly as did the Australians, but there are hopeful signs. Whereas in the past many regional players took advantage of a kind of geopolitical schadenfreude—exploiting the weakness of their neighbors at war—with their national economies becoming increasingly regionalized, few governments now want to risk the economic dislocation and refugee flows that are the major byproducts of nearby conflict. Hence the growing strength of regional organizations across the globe, from the Regional Forum of the Association of Southeast Asian Nations (ASEAN) to the once-toothless Organization of American States (OAS). Many of these groups began as economic bodies but have since developed security arms.

And regionalism addresses still another problem that has long bedeviled U.N. peacekeeping: how to command and control polyglot troops who often, in Babel-type confusion, follow different military customs and work at cross-purposes. Finally, U.S. presidents and other major-power leaders who now have trouble prying U.N. funds from their legislatures could, in the future, disguise money for regionalism as bilateral aid.

NOW THE BAD NEWS

Of course, there are plenty of places where U.N.-approved regional solutions would prove impossible, or problematic at best. The Security Council's permanent five members, with their sacrosanct vetoes, are obviously immune. Nor do local solutions always make things easier. For what regional power could intervene between India and Pakistan? China? Afghanistan? There is no one nation trusted enough to play the part. Meanwhile, the newly cooperative Nigeria, freed from its rogue past, could conceivably become the U.N.-legitimized regio-cop of western Africa. But no one in the east of the continent wants the recalcitrant Ethiopians or the Kenyans, the dominant powers of that region, moving in to solve their problems any time soon. As for central Africa, the regional powers there are already doing battle in the Democratic Republic of the Congo. And in South America, Chile, Argentina, and Brazil co-exist in simmering mistrust of each other's militaries. All these situations show that the need remains for a strong peacekeeping capacity within the U.N. as well. And unlike U.N. troops, regional powers rarely stay committed to peacekeeping for long periods—the Australians, for instance, had to introduce a special tax to fund their East Timor adventure and left after just five months on the ground.

But there are regional paths out of many of these nettles—most of them depending on U.S. aid, support for regional organizations and, mainly, the kind of long-term assiduousness that has been lacking in the Clinton administration's foreign policy. Washington has pushed Buenos Aires, for instance, to develop a peacekeeping role (and gave Argentina a small role in the Haiti intervention). But the Pentagon could make its extensive joint military exercises in Latin America far more contingent on regional cooperation under the auspices of the still-teething OAS—which ably preempted a war between Ecuador and Peru in the mid-1990s and recently took Peruvian President Alberto Fujimori to task for election fraud. In Southeast Asia, it is conceivable that the ASEAN Regional Forum could gain more bite with greater Chinese participation and, if Beijing behaves itself, eventually take up the U.N. flag in Cambodia.

Overall, then, there seem to be more cases where regionalism would work than where it would not. Last year, a National Intelligence Council study identified 23 countries with ongoing humanitarian emergencies and cited 9 others that were likely to develop crises. Of those 32 cases, the vast majority could benefit from regional peacekeeping or peace enforcement solutions—with some some key exceptions, such as India, Pakistan, Russia, and possibly Nigeria itself. Moreover, in some places, regionalism has already become a tradition. The United States has long acted as a regio-cop south of its border, most recently in Haiti. And Saudi Arabia played such a role in the Gulf War, making the U.S.-led intervention palatable among the Arab world (if not to Osama bin Laden).

Nowhere has the new regional approach to peacemaking and peacekeeping been better demonstrated than in Kosovo. After the failures of Bosnia, the United States went into the Kosovo crisis with a bone in its teeth, brazenly determined to run the campaign through NATO alone. The U.N.—at first—was given no role at all. The Russians and their protests were barely tolerated and treated to dismissive hand-holding diplomacy. "We're just trying to make them think they have a part," said a U.S. official during the war.

All this had changed by the end of the 78-day NATO bombing campaign, however. Milŏsević had stood firmer than anyone had expected, and Clinton, by early June, faced the politically nightmarish prospect of ordering a ground invasion. Washington needed Moscow's help; to get Moscow on board, it needed the United Nations. Backed by a Security Council resolution and a U.N.-sanctioned peacekeeping force, the Russians proved crucial to finally forcing Milŏsević to cave in. NATO, the mightiest regio-cop in history, had to resort to U.N. legitimation to get what it wanted.

THE WAY OF THE GUN

Ironically, much of this "new" vision of peacekeeping is provided for in the U.N. Charter (in the long-ignored Chapter 8). But few observers have connected the dots between that section and the more commonly used Chapter 7, which dictates responses to threats to the peace. And regionalism gets a mere paragraph in the 70-page Brahimi report. Even such astute observers as Stanley Hoffmann, who nimbly took a middle road between the excesses of both traditional realism and liberal internationalism in his important 1998 work *World Disorders*, have tended to overlook the potential of the hybrid approach. In the book, Hoffmann concedes that the Security Council is "the main source of authority" when it comes to global legitimacy. But he plays down the potential link between U.N. power and regionalism, dismissing regional organizations as "too often embroiled in or neutralized by disputes among or within states of the region, or else lacking in means of enforcement."

That is still sometimes true. Improving matters further will depend on the initiative of the nation that will undoubtedly continue to dominate the twenty-first century: the United States. Indeed, Clinton administration officials insist that they have long seen regional peacekeeping as their paradigm, pointing to such small-bore efforts as the African Crisis Response Initiative.

But their scattershot approach has missed many opportunities. Had Clinton recognized the possibilities of regional action earlier, for instance, he might have exploited the offers of Nigeria, Tanzania, Ghana, and others to send peacekeepers to Rwanda in the early stages of the 1994 genocide. In the end—as James Miskel of the U.S. Naval War College and others have noted—those troops stayed home because they lacked transport and other equipment. And today the U.S. president considers his failure to act in Rwanda one of his deepest regrets.

Given the alternatives, why has the regional option been so marginalized? One answer is that moving to regionalism is, structurally, a steep uphill climb. The entire U.S. government is still built around bilateral relations. U.S. ambassadors to nations are far more powerful than their counterparts to regional organizations; within the State Department, weak desk officers run most regional policy. And decision-making tends to follow the organizational structure. Another reason is that few in Washington care to face up to the possibility that they may have to act less unilaterally and become more indulgent of others' agendas. As for the U.N., it is loath to sideline its own forces.

And regionalism will not look as pretty as U.N. initiatives. Any order the Nigerians now bring to Sierra Leone, for example, is bound to be more rough-edged than that promised (though never delivered) by the U.N.-sponsored Lomé Accord. The last time the Nigerians intervened in that conflict, they occupied Freetown with 10,000 troops while ceding the rebels free run of the countryside—and the diamond trade. But whatever their methods, Nigerians did manage to stop the killing and the limb-hacking. As one Pentagon planner put it tersely, "To pursue regionalism, the United States really has to have a tolerance of regional objectives"—and, he could have added, of regional methods. Still, the United States and the United Nations could make their support conditional on regional actors' observing international norms of behavior.

A system of U.N.-sponsored regio-cops, then, will be far from ideal. It is a messy, often inconsistent muddle-through solution with many risks. But in an environment of astringent alternatives—a determinedly minimal U.S. role and a grossly underfunded and undersupported U.N.—there may be no other practicable way for the international community to stop the atrocities it no longer seems able to stomach.

Rwanda in Retrospect

Alan J. Kuperman

A HARD LOOK AT INTERVENTION

SEVERAL YEARS after mass killings in Bosnia, Somalia, and Rwanda, the United States is still searching for a comprehensive policy to address deadly communal conflicts. Among Washington policymakers and pundits, only two basic principles have achieved some consensus. First, U.S. ground troops generally should not be used in humanitarian interventions during ongoing civil wars. Second, an exception should be made for cases of genocide, especially where intervention can succeed at low cost. Support for intervention to stop genocide is voiced across most of the political spectrum.

Despite this amorphous consensus that the United States can and should do more when the next genocide occurs, there has been little hard thinking about just what that would entail or accomplish. A close examination of what a realistic U.S. military intervention could have achieved in the last clear case of genocide this decade, Rwanda, finds insupportable the oft-repeated claim that 5,000 troops deployed at the outset of the killing in April 1994 could have prevented the genocide. This claim was originally made by the U.N.'s commanding general in Rwanda during the genocide and has since been endorsed by members of Congress, human rights groups, and a distinguished panel of the Carnegie Commission on Preventing Deadly Conflict. Although some lives could have been saved by intervention of any size at any point during the genocide, the hard truth is that even a large force deployed immediately upon

---

ALAN J. KUPERMAN is MacArthur Transnational Security Fellow at MIT's Center for International Studies and Fellow of the Institute for the Study of World Politics.

reports of attempted genocide would not have been able to save even half the ultimate victims.

PRELUDE TO GENOCIDE

RWANDAN POLITICS were traditionally dominated by the Tutsi, a group that once made up 17 percent of the population. Virtually all the rest of the population was Hutu, and less than one percent were aboriginal Twa. All three groups lived intermingled throughout the country. During the transition to independence starting in 1959, however, the Hutu seized control in a violent struggle that spurred the exodus of about half the Tutsi population to neighboring states.

The Hutu themselves were divided into two regional groups. The majority lived in the central and southern part of the country and supported the PARMEHUTU (Parti du mouvement et de l'émancipation des Bahutu), which assumed power upon independence, while a minority lived in the northwest, historically a separate region. During the first decade of independence, Tutsi refugees invaded Rwanda repeatedly, seeking a return to power. The ruling Hutu responded by massacring domestic Tutsi. In 1973, a northwestern Hutu officer, Juvénal Habyarimana, led a coup that shifted political power to his region. Northwestern Hutu came to dominate Rwanda's political, military, and economic life, engendering resentment from other Hutu as well as from the Tutsi. But large-scale violence against domestic Tutsi largely disappeared for 15 years in the absence of any further attempted invasions by refugees.

Stability began to unravel in October 1990, when an expatriate rebel force composed mainly of Uganda-based Tutsi refugees, the Rwandan Patriotic Army (RPA), invaded northern Rwanda. The RPA and its political arm, the Rwandan Patriotic Front (RPF), were led by battle-tested soldiers who had fought with the Ugandan guerrilla Yoweri Museveni to overthrow Uganda's government in 1986 before turning their efforts toward home. By early 1993, the rebels had made substantial inroads against the Hutu-dominated Rwandan Armed Forces (or FAR, in the French acronym). This military advance, combined with diplomatic pressure from the international community, compelled Habyarimana to agree to share power in the Arusha accords of August 1993.

The peacekeepers of the U.N. Assistance Mission for Rwanda (UNAMIR) then arrived, but for eight months the Rwandan leader obstructed and tried to modify the power-sharing provisions. The extremist wing of his northwestern Hutu clique viewed the accords as abject surrender to the Tutsi, who they feared would seize the spoils of rule and seek retribution. Habyarimana attempted to retain power by co-opting the opposition Hutu through bribery and appeals to solidarity against the Tutsi, and he succeeded in splitting off radical factions from the main opposition parties. But he and the extremists also developed a forceful option—training militias, broadcasting anti-Tutsi hate radio, and plotting to kill moderate Hutu leaders and Tutsi civilians. On April 6, 1994, as Habyarimana appeared to be acquiescing to international pressure to implement the accords, his plane was mysteriously shot down. The genocide plan was put in motion.

The most remarkable aspect of the genocide was its speed.

In most areas of Rwanda, violence began on the following day. The government radio station and the extremists' counterpart—Radio-Télévision Libre des Mille Collines—urged the Hutu to take vengeance against the Tutsi for their alleged murder of the president. Led by militias, Hutu began to attack the homes of neighboring Tutsi, attempting to rob, rape, and murder them, and often setting fire to their homes. This initial step did not eliminate a high proportion of Tutsi, however, because their attackers were generally poorly armed. The vast majority of Tutsi fled their homes and sought refuge in central gathering places—churches, schools, hospitals, athletic fields, stadiums, and other accessible spaces. Tutsi often passed through more than one such site to gather in larger concentrations, either voluntarily or at government direction. Within a few days, most of Rwanda's Tutsi had congregated at such centralized sites throughout the country, in groups ranging from a few hundred to tens of thousands.

At first, the assembled Tutsi gained a defensive advantage. The surrounding crowds of militia-led Hutu were generally armed only with swords, spears, and machetes—or with the traditional *masu*, a large club studded with nails. By using walls and buildings for defense,

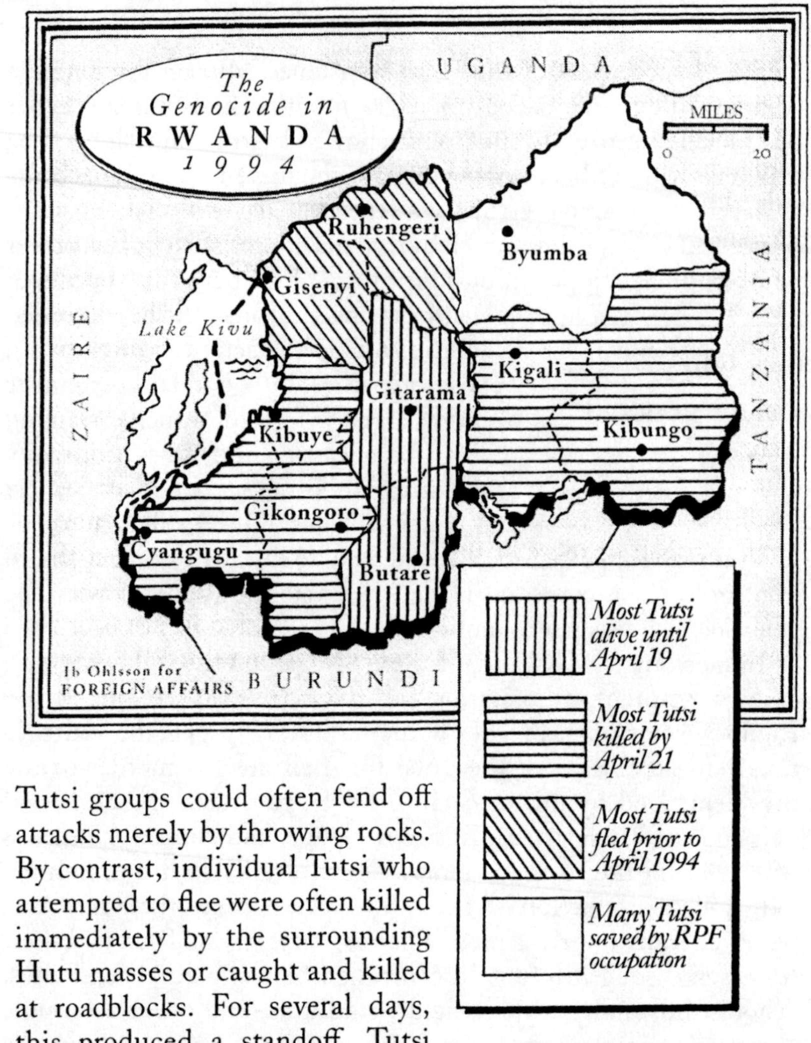

Tutsi groups could often fend off attacks merely by throwing rocks. By contrast, individual Tutsi who attempted to flee were often killed immediately by the surrounding Hutu masses or caught and killed at roadblocks. For several days, this produced a standoff. Tutsi living conditions were deteriorating and supplies were dwindling, but most Hutu were unwilling to risk casualties by attacking.

This situation changed in most of Rwanda within a week, by about April 13, when better-armed Hutu reinforcements—composed of members of the regular army, the reserves, the Presidential Guard (PG), or the national police—began arriving at the Tutsi gathering sites. Although these forces were few in number at each site, they were armed with rifles, grenades, or machine guns, which tilted the balance of force. They would typically toss a few grenades on the Tutsi and follow with light-arms fire. Survivors who attempted to flee were usually mowed down by gunfire or caught and killed by the surrounding mob. Militia-led Hutu would then enter the site, hacking to death those still alive. Some Tutsi escaped in the initial mayhem or avoided death by hiding beneath their dead compatriots, but many were later caught at roadblocks and killed on the spot or taken to other central sites to face a similar ordeal. A few lucky Tutsi survived by hiding in places such as pit latrines or the homes of sympathetic Hutu, living to tell their harrowing tales.

Perhaps the most remarkable aspect of the genocide was its speed. According to survivor testimonies gathered by African Rights and Human Rights Watch, the majority of Tutsi gathering sites were attacked and destroyed before April 21, only 14 days into the genocide. Given that half or more of the ultimate Tutsi victims died at these sites, the unavoidable conclusion is that a large portion of Rwanda's Tutsi had been killed by April 21—perhaps 250,000 in just over two weeks. That would be the fastest genocide rate in recorded history.

Despite this generally rapid pace, two factors constrained the speed and extent of the killing in Rwanda. First, Hutu extremists generally avoided large-scale massacres when international observers were present—as part of a comprehensive strategy to hide the genocide from both the outside world and Rwanda's remaining Tutsi until it could be completed. Wherever Tutsi were congregated under the watch of outside observers, the extremists favored an alternate strategy of slow, stealthy annihilation: Hutu leaders would arrive each day at such sites with a list of up to several dozen names, usually starting with the Tutsi political elite. These Tutsi would be removed under a false pretense such as interrogation before being taken to a remote location and executed. This occurred at several places across Rwanda: Kamarampaka Stadium and the Nyarushishi camp in Cyangugu prefecture, where Red Cross aid workers were present; the Kabgayi Archbishopric in Gitarama, under the watchful eyes of the pope's subordinates; Amahoro stadium in Kigali, where U.N. troops stood guard; and smaller sites in Kigali such as the St. Famille and St. Paul's churches. At such sites, the slower pace of killing meant that the vast majority of Tutsi there were still alive at the end of April, and a good number survived the entire ordeal.

Second, the killing varied among Rwanda's ten original prefectures. Byumba prefecture in the north was the base of the Tutsi-led rebels, who generally prevented large-scale massacres of Tutsi there. The two prefectures most dominated by Hutu extremists, Gisenyi and Ruhengeri in the northwest, also suffered relatively little killing because much of their Tutsi populations had fled prior to the genocide in response to earlier threats and harassment.

Two prefectures with high Tutsi populations and strong Hutu opposition movements also initially managed to avoid the genocide. Butare prefecture in the south was governed by a Tutsi prefect who managed to keep matters relatively calm until he was removed from office on April 18. Widespread killing then began with a vengeance, and tens of thousands of Tutsi perished in the next few days. Similarly, Gitarama prefecture, the heart of central Rwandan Hutu opposition to the northwestern Hutu regime, generally resisted implementing the genocide until government forces arrived to spur them on. Large-scale killing commenced there about April 21. Finally, the nature of killing in the capital, Kigali, also differed significantly from that in the rest of the country. During the first two days, a highly organized and thorough assassination campaign was carried out there against opposition politicians and prominent liberals such as human rights advocates. Unlike elsewhere, many of Kigali's initial victims of Hutu extremism were fellow Hutu.

Civil war also erupted in Kigali almost immediately. On April 7, an RPA battalion that had been stationed in the capital since December 1993 under the Arusha accords demanded a halt to atrocities against civilians—and then clashed with government forces when its demand was ignored. With the president and the moderate opposition dead, war breaking out in Kigali, and radio broadcasts urging Hutu to kill their neighbors, the capital descended into chaos. Corpses began to pile up, totaling as many as 20,000 during the first week. Unlike in the countryside, however, Tutsi had a decent chance of gaining some refuge by reaching a central gathering site where foreigners stood guard. Although the extremists could not hide the chaos and violence in the capital, they generally avoided wholesale massacres before such witnesses in hopes of averting foreign military intervention.

ESTIMATED PACE OF GENOCIDE IN RWANDA
APRIL – JULY 1994

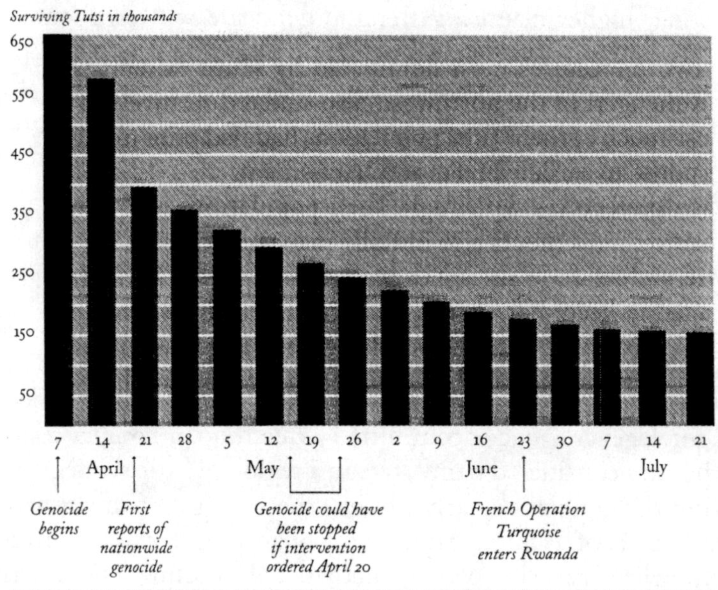

By late April, only three weeks after the president's plane crash, almost all the large massacres were finished. The rebels themselves acknowledged on April 29 that "the genocide is almost completed." Human Rights Watch concurs that "in general, the worst massacres had finished by the end of April." By that time, it notes, "perhaps half of the Tutsi population of Rwanda"—some two-thirds of the ultimate Tutsi victims—already had been exterminated. Killing of the remaining Tutsi continued at a slower pace for another two and a half months until halted by the rebels' military victory and a belated French-led intervention.

Precise Tutsi death totals are difficult to determine because of several factors, including the inability to distinguish Tutsi from Hutu corpses. But estimates can be made by subtracting the number of Tutsi survivors from the number living in Rwanda immediately prior to the genocide. Estimated 1994 population figures, which are extrapolated from the 1991 census and account for annual population growth of three percent, indicate that Rwanda's pre-genocide population included approximately 650,000 Tutsi. There is no evidence for other, higher claims.[1] After the genocide and civil war, some 150,000 Tutsi survivors were identified by aid organizations. Thus an estimated 500,000 Rwandan Tutsi were killed, more than three-quarters of their population. The number of Hutu killed during the genocide and civil war is even less certain, with estimates ranging from 10,000 to well over 100,000.

THE KNOWLEDGE GAP

ALTHOUGH U.S. intelligence reports from the period of the genocide remain classified, they probably mirrored those of the international news media, human rights organizations, and the U.N.—because U.S. intelligence agencies committed virtually no in-country resources to what was considered a tiny state in a region of little strategic value. During the genocide's early phases, the U.S. government actually received most of its information from nongovernmental organizations. A comprehensive review of such international reporting—by American, British, French, Belgian, and Rwandan media, leading human rights groups, and U.N. officials—strongly suggests that President Clinton could not have known that a nationwide genocide was under way in Rwanda until about April 20.

This conclusion is based on five aspects of the reporting during the first two weeks. First, violence was initially depicted in the context of a two-sided civil war—one that the Tutsi were winning—rather than a one-sided genocide against the Tutsi. On April 13, the Western press accurately reported that Rwanda's Hutu interim government had fled the capital for refuge in Gitarama and that "the fall of Kigali seems imminent" (Paris Radio France International). When Western troops arrived to evacuate foreign nationals, the Tutsi rebels did not

[1] Some accounts claim that one million Tutsi lived in Rwanda before the genocide, making up 12 percent of the population, which would correspond with the estimate of 850,000 killed. But historical demographic data suggest otherwise. In 1956, a Belgian census counted almost 17 percent of the population as Tutsi, but half of those fled or died in the violence that accompanied independence. The remaining 9 percent subsequently had a lower fertility rate than the Hutu, reducing the Tutsi population to the 8 percent reported in the 1991 census.

seek assistance but rather demanded that the troops depart immediately so as not to interfere with their imminent victory. The Canadian commander of the U.N. peacekeepers in Rwanda, General Romeo Dallaire, also identified the problem as mutual violence, stating on April 15 that "if we see another three weeks of being cooped up and seeing them pound each other" (*The Guardian*), the U.N. presence would be reassessed. In addition, until April 18 both the government and the rebels stated publicly that the FAR was not participating in massacres. (The government was engaged in a cover-up, and the rebels initially avoided implicating the FAR in the vain hope of winning its allegiance against the extremist Hutu.)

Second, the violence was reported to be waning when it actually was accelerating. Just four days in, on April 11, *The New York Times* reported that fighting had "diminished in intensity" and *Le Monde* wrote three days later that "a strange calm reigns in downtown" Kigali. The commander of Belgian peacekeepers stated that "the fighting has died down somewhat, one could say that it has all but stopped" (Paris Radio France International). On April 17, Dallaire told the BBC that except for an isolated pocket in the north, "the rest of the line is essentially quite quiet." Only on April 18 did a Belgian radio station question this consensus, explaining that the decline in reports of violence was because "most foreigners have left, including journalists."

Third, most early death counts were gross underestimates and never suggested genocidal proportions. Three days into the killing, on April 10, *The New York Times* quoted varying estimates of 8,000 or "tens of thousands" dead. But during the second week, media estimates did not rise at all. On April 18, the *Times* still reported only 20,000 deaths, underestimating the actual carnage at that point by about tenfold. The true scope of the killing emerged only on April 20, when Human Rights Watch estimated that "as many as 100,000 people may have died to date," followed the next day by a Red Cross estimate of perhaps "hundreds of thousands."

Fourth, the initial focus of international reporting was almost exclusively on Kigali, a relatively small city, and thus failed to indicate the broader scope of violence—a consequence both of Hutu concealment efforts and of the Western evacuation of expatriates and reporters from the countryside. Although a few early reports of rural violence did trickle out to the West, these indicated military combat, mutual ethnic violence, or criminal looting rather than an extermination campaign. An RPF official told the BBC on April 12 only that "we want to stop the senseless killing that is going on in Kigali." The first international report of a large-scale massacre outside the capital did not emerge until April 16. As late as April 20, U.N. Secretary-General Boutros Boutros-Ghali still described the killings as "mainly in Kigali." This initial obsession with the capital, which contained only four percent of Rwanda's population, obscured the national scope of violence and thus its genocidal intent.

The rebels' own radio station did not report the nationwide scope of the violence until April 19. American newspapers failed to give any such indication until April 22, when they belatedly reported that fighting bands had reduced "much of the country to chaos" (*The New York Times*). Many foreign observers still could not conceive that a genocide was under way. On April 23, *The Washington Post* pondered why only 20,000 refugees had crossed the border—even though half a million Tutsi had fled their homes—and reported that aid workers had concluded that "most of the borders have been sealed by the Rwandan Army." Only on April 25 did *The New York Times* solve the riddle, reporting that violence had "widened into what appears to be a methodical killing of Tutsi across the countryside." The missing refugees "either have been killed or are trying to hide."

Fifth, no credible and knowledgeable observers, including human rights groups, raised the prospect that genocide was occurring until the end of the second week. In opinion articles published on April 14 and 17, Human Rights Watch gave no hint of an attempted nationwide genocide. The rebels did not use the term until April 17. Human Rights Watch finally raised the prospect in an April 19 letter to the U.N. Security Council. Other international observers remained considerably more cautious. The pope first used the word "genocide" on April 27. The U.S. Committee for Refugees waited until May 2 to urge the Clinton administration to make such a determination. Only on May 4 did Boutros-Ghali finally declare a "real genocide." Thus the earliest President Clinton credibly could have made a determination of attempted genocide was about April 20, 1994—two weeks into the violence.

THE MILITARY SCENE

At the time of Habyarimana's death, Rwanda hosted three military forces—those of the government, the rebels, and the United Nations. Government forces totaled about 40,000, including the army, the national police, and 1,500 PG troops. But except for the PG and a few other elite battalions, this force was largely hollow, having expanded sixfold in three years responding to the rebel threat. Another 15,000 to 30,000 Hutu were scattered around the country in militias, but many apparently did not possess firearms or ammunition. Rebel arms were more primitive than the FAR's and included few motorized vehicles and no aircraft.

UNAMIR had about 2,500 peacekeepers, most either in Kigali or in the north near the demilitarized zone. Their presence was subject to the consent of the Rwandan government. Rules of engagement were somewhat ambiguous but were generally interpreted to bar the use of force except in self-defense or in joint operations with Rwandan national police.

On the first day of violence, the PG executed ten Belgian peacekeepers who were attempting to protect Rwanda's opposition prime minister. These deaths and the emerging chaos in Kigali prompted Western governments to evacuate their nationals. European troops began arriving on April 9 and evacuated several thousand Westerners before departing on April 13. On April 10, Dallaire also requested 5,000 more U.N. troops to halt what he perceived to be mutual killing confined to the capital. Instead, Belgium announced on April 14 that it would be withdrawing its UNAMIR battalion, which triggered unease among the other troop-contributors and led the U.N. Security Council a week later to cut authorized troop levels to a skeleton crew of 270.

Rebel forces, estimated at 20,000, had been constrained by the Arusha accords to a small area of northern Rwanda; the exception was one authorized Kigali battalion, which the RPF had reinforced clandestinely to about 1,000 troops. When the civil war was renewed on April 7, the northern-based rebels set out to help the stranded battalion in the capital and engage FAR troops elsewhere, making quick progress down Rwanda's entire eastern flank by late April. Thereafter, the war had two stationary fronts, in Kigali and Ruhengeri, until the end of June, as well as a broad mobile front moving westward through southern Rwanda. In just three months, the rebels captured most of the country—Gitarama on June 9, Kigali on July 4, Butare on July 5, Ruhengeri on July 14, and Gisenyi on July 17—before finally declaring a cease-fire on July 18.

As reports of genocide reached the outside world starting in late April, public outcry spurred the United Nations to reauthorize a beefed-up "UNAMIR II" on May 17. During the following month, however, the U.N. was unable to obtain any substantial contributions of troops and equipment. As a result, on June 22 the Security Council authorized France to lead its own intervention, Operation Turquoise, by which time most Tutsi were already long dead.

POTENTIAL U.S. INTERVENTIONS

IN RETROSPECT, three levels of potential U.S. military intervention warrant analysis: maximum, moderate, and minimal. None would have entailed full-blown nationwide policing or long-term nation-building by American troops. Based on historical experience, full-blown policing would have required some 80,000 to 160,000 personnel—that is, ten to twenty troops per thousand of population—an amount far more than logistically or politically feasible. Nation-building would have been left to a follow-on multinational force, presumably under U.N. authorization.

Maximum intervention would have used all feasible force to halt large-scale killing and military conflict throughout Rwanda. Moderate intervention would have sought to halt some large-scale killing without deploying troops to areas of ongoing civil war, in order to reduce U.S. casualties. Minimal intervention would have relied on air power alone.

A maximum intervention would have required deployment of a force roughly the size of one U.S. division—three brigades and supporting units, comprising about 15,000 troops and their equipment—with rules of engagement permitting the use of deadly force to protect endangered Rwandans. After establishing a base of operations at Kigali airport, the force would have focused on three primary goals: halting armed combat and interposing itself between FAR and RPF forces on the two stationary fronts of the civil war; establishing order

THREE POSSIBLE INTERVENTIONS

	Force size	*Airlift in days*	*Tutsi saved*	*Percentage of death toll*
Maximum	Division 13,500 troops; 27,000 tons	40	125,000	25
Moderate	Reinforced Brigade 6,000 troops; 10,000 tons	21	100,000	20
Minimum	Air Assault Brigade 2,500 troops (outside Rwanda); 4,500 tons	14	75,000	15

in the capital; and finally fanning out to halt large-scale genocidal killing in the countryside. None of these tasks would have been especially difficult or dangerous for properly configured and supported American troops once they were in Rwanda. But transporting such a force 10,000 miles to a landlocked country with limited airfields would have been considerably slower than some retrospective appraisals have suggested.

The first brigade to arrive would have been responsible for Kigali: coercing the FAR and RPF to halt hostilities, interposing itself between them, and policing the capital. The second brigade would have deployed one battalion in the north to halt the civil war in Ruhengeri and another as a rapid-reaction force in case American troops drew fire. The third brigade, supplemented by a battalion of the second brigade, would have been devoted to halting the killing in the countryside. Such an effort would have required roughly 2,000 troops to halt the war in Kigali, 3,000 to police Kigali, 1,000 to stop the fighting in the north, 1,500 for a rapid-reaction force, and 6,000 to stop the genocide outside Kigali—a total of about 13,500 troops, in addition to support personnel.

The time required to deploy such a force would have depended mainly on its weight. A division-size task force built around one brigade each from the 101st Air Assault, 82nd Airborne, and a light army division can be approximated as the average of those divisions—26,550 tons, including 200 helicopters and 13,500 personnel. (The Marines could also have substituted for the one of the brigades.)

Because Rwanda is a landlocked country in Central Africa, and because speed is critical in stopping a genocide, the entire force would have been airlifted. The rate of airlift would have been constrained by factors such as the delay in loading planes at U.S. bases, excessive demand for air refueling, fuel shortages in Central Africa, and the limited airfield capacity in Kigali and at the potential staging base at Entebbe in neighboring Uganda. At an optimistic rate of 800 tons daily, the task force would have required 33 days to airlift. Personnel, which are much quicker to transport than their cargo, could have been sent first—but it would have been imprudent to deploy them into the field without sufficient equipment and logistics. Several additional days would also have been required for the delay between the deployment order and start of airlift, for the gradual increase in the capacity of theater airfields unaccustomed to such traffic, and for travel to and unloading at the theater. In addition, the rate of force deployment might have been slowed by the need to use limited airlift capacity for food, medicine, and spare parts to sustain the first troops to arrive. Thus the entire force could not have closed in the theater until about 40 days after the president's order.

Hutu ringleaders spread false reports of an impending Western intervention to help speed the killings.

Advance units, however, could have begun operations much sooner. Approximately four days after the order, a battalion or two of Army Rangers could have parachuted in and seized Kigali airport at night. Follow-on troops could have expanded outward from the airfield to establish a secure operating base. Within about two weeks, sufficient troops and equipment could have arrived to halt the fighting, form a buffer between the FAR and the RPF in Kigali and northwest Rwanda, and fully police the capital. Only later, however, could the intervention force have turned in earnest to stopping the genocide in the countryside as helicopters, vehicles, and troops arrived.

Some observers have suggested that the genocide would have ceased spontaneously throughout Rwanda upon the arrival of Western enforcement troops in Kigali—or possibly even earlier, upon the mere announcement of a deployment. They claim that the extremists would have halted killing in hopes of avoiding punishment. But these

Hutu were already guilty of genocide and could not have imagined that stopping midway would gain them absolution. More likely, the announcement of Western intervention would have accelerated the killing as extremists tried to finish the job and eliminate witnesses while they had a chance. Such was the trend ahead of the RPA advance, as Hutu militias attempted to wipe out remaining Tutsi before the rebels arrived. During the genocide, the ringleaders even trumpeted false reports of an impending Western intervention to help motivate Hutu to complete the killings. Although the Hutu generally held back from mass killing at sites guarded by foreigners to avoid provoking Western intervention, they would have lost this incentive for restraint had such an intervention been announced.

A major intervention would have saved 275,000 Tutsi, compared to the 150,000 who actually survived.

The 6,000 U.S. troops deployed to the countryside would have been insufficient to establish a full police presence, but they could have found and protected significant concentrations of threatened Rwandans. Ideally, helicopter reconnaissance could have identified vulnerable or hostile groups from the air and then directed rapid response forces to disperse hostile factions and secure the sites. Alternately, ground troops could have radiated out from Kigali in a methodical occupation of the countryside. Displaced Rwandans could have been gathered gradually into perhaps 20 large camps for their protection.

Depending on the search method, large-scale genocide could have been stopped during the fourth or fifth week after the deployment order, by May 15 to May 25. Interestingly enough, this would have been before the task force's airlift had been completed. Based on the genocide's progression, such an intervention would have saved about 275,000 Tutsi, instead of the 150,000 who actually survived. Maximum credible intervention thus could not have prevented the genocide, as is sometimes claimed, but it could have spared about 125,000 Tutsi from death, some 25 percent of the ultimate toll.

A more modest intervention would have refrained from deploying U.S. troops to any area in Rwanda in which FAR and RPA troops were actively fighting. In late April, this would have limited U.S. troops to a zone consisting of six prefectures in the south and west of Rwanda. A single reinforced brigade would have sufficed given the reduced territory, population, and threat of potential adversaries. Ideally, the ready brigade of the 101st Air Assault Division would have been designated and supplemented by two additional light-infantry battalions, supporting units for peace operations, and additional helicopters and motorized vehicles: a force of 6,000 personnel, weighing about 10,000 tons.

For such an action, three main objectives would have been set: first, to deter and prevent entry of organized military forces into the above-mentioned zone; second, to halt large-scale genocide there; and third, to prepare for a handoff to a U.N. force. Strategic airlift would not have relied on Kigali airport, which was still a battleground in the civil war, but rather on neighboring Bujumbura in Burundi and Entebbe in Uganda—which would have further constrained the deployment rates. Still, facing little military threat in the zone, these troops probably could have stopped large-scale genocide there within three weeks after the deployment order, by May 11, 1994. About 200,000 Tutsi from the zone could have survived, as opposed to about 100,000 from this part of Rwanda who actually did. Elsewhere in Rwanda, genocide would have continued until stopped by the RPA, as occurred, leaving only 50,000 survivors outside the zone of intervention. Moderate intervention thus could have spared about 100,000 Tutsi from death, or 20 percent of the ultimate toll. Surprisingly, moderate intervention in this case would have saved almost as many lives as the maximum alternative, because by avoiding combat areas the interveners could have turned sooner to counter genocide in the zone where most Tutsi lived.

The third alternative, a minimal intervention, would have attempted to mitigate the genocide without introducing U.S. ground troops into Rwanda, relying on airpower alone from bases in neighboring countries. For example, the United States could have threatened to bomb the extremist ringleaders and the FAR's military assets unless the killing was halted—and then followed through if necessary. But if the threat alone failed to coerce, U.S. pilots would have had difficulty locating the ringleaders or hitting FAR positions without killing rebels as well. Even if air coercion had succeeded in Rwanda, a follow-on ground force would have been needed to keep the peace. Alternatively, the

United States could have pursued airborne policing, which would have attempted to interdict physically and intimidate psychologically the perpetrators of the genocide throughout Rwanda. Significant numbers of U.S. attack helicopters and fixed-wing aircraft could have patrolled Rwanda daily from bases in neighboring countries. If armed factions threatening large groups of civilians were spotted, air-to-ground fire could have dispersed the assailants, at least temporarily. Such air patrols would have continued until deployment of non-American ground troops or until the RPF won the civil war. But airborne policing could not have prevented smaller acts of violence in the meantime.

Another minimal approach would have been to help the Rwandan Tutsi escape to refugee camps in bordering states—Burundi, Tanzania, Uganda, or Zaire—by using helicopter patrols to ensure safe passage. Rwanda has only about 600 miles of paved roads. Assuming a team of 20 helicopters with standard maintenance needs, five helicopters could have been kept aloft at a time, with each responsible for 120 miles of roadway. If these helicopters flew at a ground speed of 120 miles per hour, each section of roadway could have been patrolled approximately every hour. Airborne broadcasts and leaflets would have directed the Tutsi to the exit routes. Air-to-ground fire would have broken up roadblocks and dispersed armed gangs to ensure the free flow of refugees. But this strategy could not have saved those Tutsi unable to reach major roads and would have caused a major refugee crisis.

Each of the airpower options would have had drawbacks, including the risk of losing airborne personnel to anti-aircraft fire, but each also had the potential to save tens of thousands of Tutsi. Coercion might have stopped the genocide quickly, potentially facilitating a cease-fire in the civil war. Airborne policing could have allowed more Tutsi to be saved by France's Operation Turquoise or a similar follow-up deployment. Free passage also would have kept more Tutsi alive, albeit as refugees, and they might have returned home quickly after the RPF's victory. About 300,000 Tutsi still were alive in late April 1994, of whom about 150,000 subsequently perished. If minimum intervention had been able to avert half these later killings, it could have spared about 75,000 Tutsi from death, or 15 percent of the genocide's ultimate toll.

A WESTERN FAILURE OF WILL?

MANY OBSERVERS have claimed that timely intervention would have prevented the genocide. Some even asserted at first that UNAMIR itself could have done so, although most now acknowledge that the peacekeepers lacked sufficient arms, equipment, and supplies. Conventional wisdom still holds that 5,000 well-armed reinforcements could have prevented the genocide had they been deployed promptly when the killing began—and that the West's failure to stop the slaughter resulted exclusively from a lack of will. Rigorous scrutiny of six prominent variations of this assertion, however, finds all but one dubious.

Human Rights Watch makes the boldest claim: Diplomatic intervention could have averted the genocide without additional military deployment. These advocates contend that a threat from the international community to halt aid to any Rwandan government that committed genocide would have emboldened Hutu moderates to face down the extremists and extinguish violence. As proof, they note that moderate FAR officers appealed for support from Western embassies during the first days of violence, and that the intensity of massacres waned after the West intensified its condemnations in late April.

However, this argument ignores the fact that virtually all of Rwanda's elite military units were controlled by extremist Hutu, led by Colonel Theoneste Bagosora. These forces demonstrated their power and ruthlessness by killing Rwanda's top political moderates during the first two days of violence. By contrast, moderate Hutu officers had virtually no troops at their disposal. The moderates avoided challenging the extremists not because of a lack of Western rhetorical support but because of mortal fear for themselves and their families. This fear was justified given that the extremists stamped out any nascent opposition throughout the genocide—coercing and bribing moderate politicians, removing them from office or killing them if they did not yield, shipping moderate soldiers to the battlefront, and executing civilian opponents of genocide as "accomplices" of the rebels. The decline in massacres in late April is explained simply by the dwindling number of Tutsi still alive. International condemnation did little except compel extremists to try harder to hide the killing and disguise their rhetoric. Even these superficial gestures were directed mainly at persuading France to renew its military support for the anti-Tutsi war—hardly an indication of moderation.

The only way that the army's Hutu moderates could have reduced the killing of Tutsi civilians would have been to join forces with the Tutsi rebels to defeat the Hutu extremists. This was militarily feasible, given that the Tutsi rebels alone defeated both the FAR and the Hutu militias in just three months—but it was politically implausible. By April, Rwanda had already been severely polarized along ethnic lines by four years of civil war, the calculated efforts of propagandists, and the October 1993 massacre of Hutu by Tutsi in neighboring Burundi. Even moderate Hutu politicians once allied with the rebels had come to fear Tutsi hegemony. Although the moderate Hutu officers sincerely favored a cease-fire and a halt to the genocide, they could not realistically have defected to the Tutsi rebels—at least until the FAR's defeat became imminent.

U.N. peacekeepers were vulnerable to violent retaliation.

The second claim is that 5,000 U.N. troops deployed immediately upon the outbreak of violence could have prevented the genocide. But this assertion is problematic on three grounds. It assumes such troops could have been deployed virtually overnight. In reality, even a U.S. light-infantry ready brigade would have required about a week after receiving orders to begin significant operations in the theater and several more days for all its equipment to arrive. Further delays would have resulted from reinforcing the brigade with heavy armor or helicopters, or from assembling a multinational force. Even if ordered on April 10, as requested at the time by Dallaire, reinforcements probably could not have begun major operations to stop genocide much before April 20. Moreover, it is unrealistic to argue that urgent intervention should have been launched on April 10—given that the international community did not realize genocide was under way until at least ten days later.

Intervention advocates, such as the Carnegie Commission, also erroneously characterize the progression of the genocide. The commission claims that there was a "window of opportunity ... from about April 7 to April 21" when intervention "could have stemmed the violence in and around the capital [and] prevented its spread to the countryside." In reality, killing started almost immediately in most of

Rwanda, and by April 21, the last day of this purported "window," half the ultimate Tutsi victims already were dead. Even if reinforcements had arrived overnight in Kigali, Dallaire was unaware of genocide outside the capital and thus would not have deployed troops to the countryside in time to prevent the massacres.

Furthermore, 5,000 troops would have been insufficient to stop genocide without running risks of failure or high casualties. Only 1,000 troops would have been available for policing Kigali—some three troops per thousand residents, which is grossly inadequate for a city in the throes of genocide. In the countryside, U.S. commanders would have faced a stark choice: either concentrate forces for effective action, leaving most of the country engulfed in killing; or spread forces thin, leaving troops vulnerable to attack. To avoid such painful choices in the past, U.S. military planners have insisted on deploying more than 20,000 troops for interventions in the Dominican Republic, Panama, and Haiti—all countries with populations smaller than Rwanda's.

A third claim is that U.N. headquarters had three months' advance notice of genocide and could have averted the killing simply by authorizing raids on weapons caches. Critics cite the so-called genocide fax—a January 11, 1994, cable from Dallaire to U.N. headquarters in New York that conveyed a Hutu informant's warning that extremists were planning to provoke civil war, kill Belgian peacekeepers to spur their withdrawal, and slaughter the Tutsi with an *Interahamwe* militia of 1,700 troops that the informant was training. The cable also reported an arms cache containing at least 135 weapons, which Dallaire wanted to seize within 36 hours.

Dallaire, however, raised doubts about the informant's credibility in this cable, stating that he had "certain reservations on the suddenness of the change of heart of the informant.... Possibility of a trap not fully excluded, as this may be a set-up." Raising further doubt, the cable was the first and last from Dallaire containing such accusations, according to U.N. officials. Erroneous warnings of coups and assassinations are not uncommon during civil wars. U.N. officials were prudent to direct Dallaire to confirm the allegations with Habyarimana himself, based on the informant's belief that "the president does not have full control over all elements of his old party/faction." Dallaire never reported any confirmation of the plot.

Even if the U.N. had acquiesced to Dallaire in January 1994, it is unlikely the weapons cache could have been seized or that doing so would have prevented the genocide. The U.N. actually did reverse itself barely three weeks later, on February 4, 1994, granting Dallaire authorization to raid weapons depots. But his forces failed in every attempt, even after an informant identified three new caches on February 7. By mid-March, six weeks after receiving authorization, the peacekeepers had captured only a paltry total of 16 weapons and 100 grenades; their rules required cooperating with Rwandan police, who tipped off the extremists. If the U.N. had permitted Dallaire to act without consulting local authorities, Kigali could have responded under Chapter VI of the U.N. Charter (which governs consensual peacekeeping operations) by simply expelling the force. The peacekeepers also were vulnerable to violent retaliation, as they were dispersed and still lacked armored personnel carriers at the time. In addition, Dallaire's cable identified a cache of only 135 weapons—a tiny fraction of the 20,000 rifles and 500,000 machetes imported by the government over the preceding two years. Even had Dallaire managed to seize this cache without prompting expulsion or retaliation, he could not have derailed the wider genocide plot without significant reinforcements.

A fourth claim holds that quickly jamming or destroying Hutu radio transmitters when the violence broke out could have prevented the genocide. A Belgian peacekeeper who monitored broadcasts testified, "I am convinced that, if we had managed to liquidate [Radio Mille Collines], we could perhaps have avoided, or in any case limited, the genocide." A human rights advocate characterized the jamming as "the one action that, in retrospect, might have done the most to save Rwandan lives." But radio broadcasts were not essential to perpetuating or directing the killing. By April, Rwandans had been sharply polarized along ethnic lines by civil war, propaganda, and recent massacres in Burundi. Habyarimana's assassination was a sufficient trigger for many extremist Hutu to begin killing. Moderate Hutu were usually swayed not by radio broadcasts but by threats and physical intimidation from extremist authorities. Furthermore, orchestration of the genocide relied not merely on radio broadcasts but on the government's separate military communications network. Silencing the radio might have had most impact prior to the genocide, when broadcasts were fostering polarization, but such action would have been rejected at the time as a violation of sovereignty. Even if hate radio had been preventively extinguished, the extremists possessed and used other means to foster hatred.

The fifth variant of the intervention argument is that the Western forces sent to evacuate foreign nationals during the first week could have restored order in Kigali—and thereby prevented the genocide had they merely been given the orders to do so. Just four days after Habyarimana's assassination, some 1,000 lightly armed Western evacuation troops, mainly French and Belgian soldiers, had arrived in Kigali, where Belgium's 400-troop UNAMIR contingent was already stationed. Another 1,100 reserves were less than two hours away by air. But it is doubtful that this small force, lacking the right equipment or logistical support, could have quickly quashed violence in the capital—or that doing so would have stopped the genocide elsewhere. The Western evacuators had to commit half their force to guarding the airport at the town's outskirts and a few key assembly points, leaving few available for combat. In addition, coordinated action would have been inhibited by the widespread perception that France and Belgium sympathized with opposite sides in the civil war. Moreover, Kigali was defended by 2,000 elite Rwandan army troops and several thousand regulars equipped with heavy weapons, another 2,000 armed fighters of the Hutu militia, and 1,000 national police. Also located there were more than 1,000 Tutsi rebels who had access to surface-to-air missiles and had explicitly threatened to attack the evacuators if they extended their mission. Even if the small Western force had somehow halted the violence in Kigali, it lacked the equipment and logistics to deploy troops quickly to the countryside. Rural killing probably would have continued unless the ringleaders were captured and coerced to call off the slaughter. Such a search would not have been a quick or simple matter for any force, as demonstrated by the failed search for the Somali warlord Mohamed Farah Aidid by U.S. troops in 1993. Ill-equipped evacuation troops could have wasted weeks looking for the ringleaders while genocide continued at a torrid pace in the countryside, where 95 percent of Rwandans lived.

More U.N. forces deployed prior to the genocide with a robust mandate could have deterred the killing.

The sixth claim is most realistic: Had UNAMIR been reinforced several months prior to the outbreak of violence, as Belgium urged at the time, genocide might have been averted. More troops with the proper equipment, a broad mandate, and robust rules of engagement could have deterred the outbreak of killing or at least snuffed it out early. Such reinforcement would have required about 3,500 additional high-quality troops in Kigali, armored personnel carriers, helicopters, adequate logistics, and the authorization to use force to seize weapons and ensure security without consulting Rwandan police. This would have been the 5,000-troop force that Dallaire envisioned—but one deployed prior to the genocide.

Under the U.N.'s peacekeeping rules, Rwanda's government would have had to consent to such a change—and probably would have. Prior to the genocide, its cabinet still was dominated by the Hutu opposition moderates who had negotiated the Arusha accords, which called for a neutral international force to "guarantee [the] overall security of the country." The U.N. Security Council had watered down implementation of this provision, authorizing UNAMIR only to "contribute to the security of the city of Kigali." As tensions mounted in early 1994, the Rwandan government again asked the U.N. to dismantle armed groups, but the peacekeepers were too weak. Belgium pleaded for reinforcements and a new mandate from the Security Council in January and February 1994 on the grounds that UNAMIR could not maintain order. But the United States and Britain blocked this initiative before it could even reach a vote, citing the costs of more troops and the danger that expanding the mission could endanger peacekeepers—as had occurred in Somalia the previous October.

The Rwandan government, however, almost certainly would have welcomed a reinforcement of UNAMIR prior to the genocide. Five thousand troops in the capital would have meant 16 troops for every thousand Rwandans, a ratio historically sufficient to quell severe civil disorders. Such a force might well have deterred the genocide plot. Failing that, well-equipped peacekeepers could have protected moderate Hutu leaders and Tutsi in the capital and captured some of the extremists during the first days of violence, thereby diminishing the chance of large-scale massacres in the countryside.

Indeed, such early reinforcement of UNAMIR is the only proposed action that would have had a good chance of averting the genocide.

LESSONS

THE MOST OBVIOUS LESSON of Rwanda's tragedy is that intervention is no substitute for prevention. Although the 1994 genocide represents a particularly tough case for intervention in some respects—such as its rapid killing and inaccessible location—it would have been a relatively easy mission in other respects, including the limited strength of potential opponents. Yet even an ideal intervention in Rwanda would have left hundreds of thousands of Tutsi dead. To avert such violence over the long term, there is no alternative to the time-consuming business of diplomacy and negotiation. Tragically, international diplomatic efforts in Rwanda prior to the genocide were ill conceived and counterproductive.

Whether pursuing prevention or intervention, policymakers must use their imagination to better anticipate the behavior of foreign actors. In Rwanda, Western officials failed to foresee the genocide, despite numerous warning signs, in part because the act was so immoral that it was difficult to picture. Increased awareness of such risks demands that any peacekeeping force deployed preventively to a fragile area be adequately sized and equipped to stop incipient violence—rather than be sent as a lightly armed tripwire that serves mainly to foster a false sense of security. If the West is unwilling to deploy such robust forces in advance, it must refrain from coercive diplomacy aimed at compelling rulers to surrender power overnight. Otherwise, such rulers may feel so threatened by the prospect of losing power that they opt for genocide or ethnic cleansing instead. Western diplomacy that relies mainly on the threat of economic sanctions or bombing has provoked a tragic backlash not just in Rwanda, but also in Kosovo and East Timor over the last few years as local rulers opted to inflict massive violence rather than hand over power or territory to lifelong enemies. In each case, Western military intervention arrived too late to prevent the widespread atrocities.

Obviously, time is of the essence once large-scale attacks against civilians begin. Most such violence can be perpetrated in a matter of weeks, as was demonstrated in Rwanda, Kosovo, and East Timor. Despite this reality, domestic politics often prevents an American president from quickly launching a major intervention. Thus U.S. defense planners should be more creative in developing limited alternatives. The case of Rwanda underscores that lighter intervention options that avoid combat areas and focus mainly on stopping violence against civilians could save almost as many lives if pursued seriously and expeditiously. Rapid responses would be facilitated by the development of pre-prepared plans for known trouble spots and by better coordinating intelligence from available sources, including nongovernmental organizations.

That said, tradeoffs are inevitable if the United States hopes to increase its effectiveness in humanitarian military intervention. To deploy troops faster, additional "ultra-light" units (like the Tenth Mountain Division) would have to be created, either by converting existing heavier units intended for major contingencies or by increasing defense spending. The Pentagon's recent proposal to trim some heavy mechanized forces down to medium-weight units would not solve the problem, because they would still be too heavy for a quick airlift. Lighter units probably could save more lives abroad but would also be subject to more casualties and potential failure. Such tradeoffs should be made only after rigorous debate, which to date has been virtually absent in the United States.

Finally, no policy of humanitarian military intervention should be implemented without a sober consideration of its unintended consequences. Recent interventions, whether in Bosnia, Kosovo, or East Timor, have been motivated by the impulse to provide humanitarian aid to a party visibly suffering in an internal conflict. But intervention in those cases also resulted in the weaker sides being bolstered militarily. This pattern creates perverse incentives for weaker parties in such conflicts to reject compromise and escalate fighting because they expect foreign intervention or hope to attract it. The result is often tragedy, as intervention arrives too little or too late to protect civilians. Thus a policy of intervening to relieve humanitarian emergencies that stem from internal conflicts may actually increase the number and extent of such emergencies—a classic instance of moral hazard.

Inevitably, decisions on whether and how to intervene in specific cases will be caught up in politics. But this challenge should not deter hard thinking on when and how such intervention can be most beneficial—or detrimental. If Rwanda demonstrates nothing else, it is that thousands of lives are at stake in such decisions.

Promoting the National Interest

Condoleezza Rice

LIFE AFTER THE COLD WAR

THE UNITED STATES has found it exceedingly difficult to define its "national interest" in the absence of Soviet power. That we do not know how to think about what follows the U.S.-Soviet confrontation is clear from the continued references to the "post–Cold War period." Yet such periods of transition are important, because they offer strategic opportunities. During these fluid times, one can affect the shape of the world to come.

The enormity of the moment is obvious. The Soviet Union was more than just a traditional global competitor; it strove to lead a universal socialist alternative to markets and democracy. The Soviet Union quarantined itself and many often-unwitting captives and clients from the rigors of international capitalism. In the end, it sowed the seeds of its own destruction, becoming in isolation an economic and technological dinosaur.

But this is only part of the story. The Soviet Union's collapse coincided with another great revolution. Dramatic changes in information technology and the growth of "knowledge-based" industries altered

CONDOLEEZZA RICE is Senior Fellow at the Hoover Institution and Professor of Political Science at Stanford University. She is also foreign policy adviser to Republican presidential candidate George W. Bush.

Editors' Note: Democratic views will be published in forthcoming issues.

the very basis of economic dynamism, accelerating already noticeable trends in economic interaction that often circumvented and ignored state boundaries. As competition for capital investment has intensified, states have faced difficult choices about their internal economic, political, and social structures. As the prototype of this "new economy," the United States has seen its economic influence grow—and with it, its diplomatic influence. America has emerged as both the principal benefactor of these simultaneous revolutions and their beneficiary.

The process of outlining a new foreign policy must begin by recognizing that the United States is in a remarkable position. Powerful secular trends are moving the world toward economic openness and—more unevenly—democracy and individual liberty. Some states have one foot on the train and the other off. Some states still hope to find a way to decouple democracy and economic progress. Some hold on to old hatreds as diversions from the modernizing task at hand. But the United States and its allies are on the right side of history.

In such an environment, American policies must help further these favorable trends by maintaining a disciplined and consistent foreign policy that separates the important from the trivial. The Clinton administration has assiduously avoided implementing such an agenda. Instead, every issue has been taken on its own terms—crisis by crisis, day by day. It takes courage to set priorities because doing so is an admission that American foreign policy cannot be all things to all people—or rather, to all interest groups. The Clinton administration's approach has its advantages: If priorities and intent are not clear, they cannot be criticized. But there is a high price to pay for this approach. In a democracy as pluralistic as ours, the absence of an articulated "national interest" either produces a fertile ground for those wishing to withdraw from the world or creates a vacuum to be filled by parochial groups and transitory pressures.

THE ALTERNATIVE

AMERICAN FOREIGN POLICY in a Republican administration should refocus the United States on the national interest and the pursuit of key priorities. These tasks are

- to ensure that America's military can deter war, project power, and fight in defense of its interests if deterrence fails;

• to promote economic growth and political openness by extending free trade and a stable international monetary system to all committed to these principles, including in the western hemisphere, which has too often been neglected as a vital area of U.S. national interest;

• to renew strong and intimate relationships with allies who share American values and can thus share the burden of promoting peace, prosperity, and freedom;

• to focus U.S. energies on comprehensive relationships with the big powers, particularly Russia and China, that can and will mold the character of the international political system; and

• to deal decisively with the threat of rogue regimes and hostile powers, which is increasingly taking the forms of the potential for terrorism and the development of weapons of mass destruction (WMD).

INTERESTS AND IDEALS

POWER MATTERS, both the exercise of power by the United States and the ability of others to exercise it. Yet many in the United States are (and have always been) uncomfortable with the notions of power politics, great powers, and power balances. In an extreme form, this discomfort leads to a reflexive appeal instead to notions of international law and norms, and the belief that the support of many states—or even better, of institutions like the United Nations—is essential to the legitimate exercise of power. The "national interest" is replaced with "humanitarian interests" or the interests of "the international community." The belief that the United States is exercising power legitimately only when it is doing so on behalf of someone or something else was deeply rooted in Wilsonian thought, and there are strong echoes of it in the Clinton administration. To be sure, there is nothing wrong with doing something that benefits all humanity, but that is, in a sense, a second-order effect. America's pursuit of the national interest will create conditions that promote freedom, markets, and peace. Its pursuit of national interests after World War II led to a more prosperous and democratic world. This can happen again.

So multilateral agreements and institutions should not be ends in themselves. U.S. interests are served by having strong alliances and can be promoted within the U.N. and other multilateral organizations, as

well as through well-crafted international agreements. But the Clinton administration has often been so anxious to find multilateral solutions to problems that it has signed agreements that are not in America's interest. The Kyoto treaty is a case in point: whatever the facts on global warming, a treaty that does not include China and exempts "developing" countries from tough standards while penalizing American industry cannot possibly be in America's national interest.

Similarly, the arguments about U.S. ratification of the Comprehensive Test Ban Treaty are instructive. Since 1992, the United States has refrained unilaterally from testing nuclear weapons. It is an example to the rest of the world yet does not tie its own hands "in perpetuity" if testing becomes necessary again. But in pursuit of a "norm" against the acquisition of nuclear weapons, the United States signed a treaty that was not verifiable, did not deal with the threat of the development of nuclear weapons by rogue states, and threatened the reliability of the nuclear stockpile. Legitimate congressional concerns about the substance of the treaty were ignored during negotiations. When faced with the defeat of a bad treaty, the administration attacked the motives of its opponents—incredibly branding long-standing internationalists like Senators Richard Lugar (R-Ind.) and John Warner (R-Va.) as isolationists.

Certainly, Republican presidents have not been immune to the practice of pursuing symbolic agreements of questionable value. According to the Senate Foreign Relations Committee, some 52 conventions, agreements, and treaties still await ratification; some even date back to 1949. But the Clinton administration's attachment to largely symbolic agreements and its pursuit of, at best, illusory "norms" of international behavior have become an epidemic. That is not leadership. Neither is it isolationist to suggest that the United States has a special role in the world and should not adhere to every international convention and agreement that someone thinks to propose.

Even those comfortable with notions of the "national interest" are still queasy with a focus on power relationships and great-power politics. The reality is that a few big powers can radically affect international peace, stability, and prosperity. These states are capable of disruption on a grand scale, and their fits of anger or acts of beneficence affect hundreds of millions of people. By reason of size, geographic position, economic potential, and military strength, they are capable of influencing American welfare for good or ill. Moreover, that kind of power is usually accompanied by a sense of entitlement to play a decisive role in international politics. Great powers do not just mind their own business.

Great powers do not just mind their own business.

Some worry that this view of the world ignores the role of values, particularly human rights and the promotion of democracy. In fact, there are those who would draw a sharp line between power politics and a principled foreign policy based on values. This polarized view—you are either a realist or devoted to norms and values—may be just fine in academic debate, but it is a disaster for American foreign policy. American values are universal. People want to say what they think, worship as they wish, and elect those who govern them; the triumph of these values is most assuredly easier when the international balance of power favors those who believe in them. But sometimes that favorable balance of power takes time to achieve, both internationally and within a society. And in the meantime, it is simply not possible to ignore and isolate other powerful states that do not share those values.

The Cold War is a good example. Few would deny that the collapse of the Soviet Union profoundly transformed the picture of democracy and human rights in eastern and central Europe and the former Soviet territories. Nothing improved human rights as much as the collapse of Soviet power. Throughout the Cold War, the United States pursued a policy that promoted political liberty, using every instrument from the Voice of America to direct presidential intervention on behalf of dissidents. But it lost sight neither of the importance of the geopolitical relationship with Moscow nor of the absolute necessity of retaining robust American military power to deter an all-out military confrontation.

In the 1970s, the Soviet Union was at the height of its power—which it was more than willing to use. Given its weak economic and technological base, the victories of that period turned out to be Pyrrhic. President Reagan's challenge to Soviet power was both resolute and well timed. It included intense substantive engagements with Moscow across the entire range of issues captured in the "four-part agenda" (arms control, human rights, economic issues, and regional conflicts). The Bush administration then focused greater attention on rolling back Soviet power in central and eastern Europe. As the Soviet Union's might waned, it could no longer defend its interests and gave up peacefully (thankfully) to the West—a tremendous victory for Western power and also for human liberty.

SETTING PRIORITIES

THE UNITED STATES has many sources of power in the pursuit of its goals. The global economy demands economic liberalization, greater openness and transparency, and at the very least, access to information technology. International economic policies that leverage the advantages of the American economy and expand free trade are the decisive tools in shaping international politics. They permit us to reach out to states as varied as South Africa and India and to engage our neighbors in the western hemisphere in a shared interest in economic prosperity. The growth of entrepreneurial classes throughout the world is an asset in the promotion of human rights and individual liberty, and it should be understood and used as such. Yet peace is the first and most important condition for continued prosperity and freedom. America's military power must be secure because the United States is the only guarantor of global peace and stability. The current neglect of America's armed forces threatens its ability to maintain peace.

The Bush administration had been able to reduce defense spending somewhat at the end of the Cold War in 1991. But the Clinton administration witlessly accelerated and deepened these cuts. The results were devastating: military readiness declined, training suffered, military pay slipped 15 percent below civilian equivalents, morale plummeted, and the services cannibalized existing equipment to keep airplanes flying, ships afloat, and tanks moving. The increased difficulty in recruiting people to the armed forces or retaining them is hardly surprising.

Moreover, the administration began deploying American forces abroad at a furious pace—an average of once every nine weeks. As it cut defense spending to its lowest point as a percentage of GDP since Pearl Harbor, the administration deployed the armed forces more often than at any time in the last 50 years. Some of the deployments themselves were questionable, such as in Haiti. But more than anything it was simply unwise to multiply missions in the face of a continuing budget reduction. Means and mission were not matched, and (predictably) the already thinly stretched armed forces came close to a breaking point. When all these trends became so obvious and embarrassing that they could no longer be ignored, the administration finally requested increased defense spending. But the "death spiral," as the administration's own undersecretary of defense called it—robbing procurement and research and development simply to operate the armed forces—was already well under way. That the administration did nothing, choosing instead to live off the fruits of Reagan's military buildup, constitutes an extraordinary neglect of the fiduciary responsibilities of the commander in chief.

Now the next president will be confronted with a prolonged job of repair. Military readiness will have to take center stage, particularly those aspects that affect the living conditions of the troops—military pay, housing—and also training. New weapons will have to be procured in order to give the military the capacity to carry out today's missions. But even in its current state, the American military still enjoys a commanding technological lead and therefore has a battlefield advantage over any competitor. Thus the next president should refocus the Pentagon's priorities on building the military of the 21st century rather than continuing to build on the structure of the Cold War. U.S. technological advantages should be leveraged to build forces that are lighter and more lethal, more mobile and agile, and capable of firing accurately from long distances. In order to do this, Washington must reallocate resources, perhaps in some cases skipping a generation of technology to make leaps rather than incremental improvements in its forces.

The other major concern is a loss of focus on the mission of the armed forces. What does it mean to deter, fight, and win wars and defend the national interest? First, the American military must be able to meet decisively the emergence of any hostile military power in the Asia-Pacific region, the Middle East, the Persian Gulf, and Europe—areas in which not only our interests but also those of our key allies are at stake. America's military is the only one capable of this deterrence function, and it must not be stretched or diverted into areas that weaken these broader responsibilities. It is the role that the United States played when Saddam Hussein threatened the Persian Gulf, and it is the power needed to deter trouble on the Korean Peninsula or across the Taiwan Strait. In the latter cases, the goal is to make it inconceivable for North Korea or China to use force because American military power is a compelling factor in their equations.

If it is worth fighting for, you had better be prepared to win.

Some small-scale conflicts clearly have an impact on American strategic interests. Such was the case with Kosovo, which was in the backyard of America's most important strategic alliance: NATO. In fact, Yugoslav President Slobodan Milošević's rejection of peaceful coexistence with the Kosovar Albanians threatened to rock the area's fragile ethnic balance. Eastern Europe is a patchwork of ethnic minorities. For the most part, Hungarians and Romanians, Bulgarians and Turks, and even Ukrainians and Russians have found a way since 1991 of preventing their differences from exploding. Milošević has been the exception, and the United States had an overriding strategic interest in stopping him. There was, of course, a humanitarian disaster looming as well, but in the absence of concerns based on the interests of the alliance, the case for intervention would have been more tenuous.

The Kosovo war was conducted incompetently, in part because the administration's political goals kept shifting and in part because it was not, at the start, committed to the decisive use of military force. That President Clinton was surprised at Milošević's tenacity is, well, surprising. If there is any lesson from history, it is that small powers with everything to lose are often more stubborn than big powers, for whom the conflict is merely one among many problems. The lesson, too, is that if it is worth fighting for, you had better be prepared to win. Also, there must be a political game plan that will permit the withdrawal of our forces—something that is still completely absent in Kosovo.

But what if our values are attacked in areas that are not arguably of strategic concern? Should the United States not try to save lives in the absence of an overriding strategic rationale? The next American president should be in a position to intervene when he believes, and can make the case, that the United States is duty-bound to do so. "Humanitarian intervention" cannot be ruled out a priori. But a decision to intervene in the absence of strategic concerns should be understood for what it is. Humanitarian problems are rarely only humanitarian problems; the taking of life or withholding of food is almost always a political act. If the United States is not prepared to address the underlying political conflict and to know whose side it is on, the military may end up separating warring parties for an indefinite period. Sometimes one party (or both) can come to see the United States as the enemy. Because the military cannot, by definition, do anything decisive in these "humanitarian" crises, the chances of misreading the situation and ending up in very different circumstances are very high. This was essentially the problem of "mission creep" in Somalia.

The president must remember that the military is a special instrument. It is lethal, and it is meant to be. It is not a civilian police force. It is not a political referee. And it is most certainly not designed to build a civilian society. Military force is best used to support clear political goals, whether limited, such as expelling Saddam from Kuwait, or comprehensive, such as demanding the unconditional surrender of Japan and Germany during World War II. It is one thing to have a limited political goal and to fight decisively for it; it is quite another to apply military force incrementally, hoping to find a political solution somewhere along the way. A president entering these situations must ask whether decisive force is possible and is likely to be effective and must know how and when to get out. These are difficult criteria to meet, so U.S. intervention in these "humanitarian" crises should be, at best, exceedingly rare.

This does not mean that the United States must ignore humanitarian and civil conflicts around the world. But the military cannot be involved everywhere. Often, these tasks might be better carried out by regional actors, as modeled by the Australian-led intervention in East Timor. The U.S. might be able to lend financial, logistical, and intelligence support. Sometimes tough, competent diplomacy in the beginning can prevent the need for military force later. Using the American armed forces as the world's "911" will degrade capabilities, bog soldiers down in peacekeeping roles, and fuel concern among other great powers that the United States has decided to enforce notions of "limited sovereignty" worldwide in the name of humanitarianism. This overly broad definition of America's national interest is bound to backfire as others arrogate the same authority to themselves. Or we will find ourselves looking to the United Nations to sanction the use of American military power in these cases, implying that we will do so even when our vital interests are involved, which would also be a mistake.

DEALING WITH THE POWERFUL

ANOTHER CRUCIAL TASK for the United States is to focus on relations with other powerful states. Although the United States is fortunate to count among its friends several great powers, it is important not to take them for granted—so that there is a firm foundation when it comes time to rely on them. The challenges of China and North Korea require coordination and cooperation with Japan and South Korea. The signals that we send to our real partners are important. Never again should an American president go to Beijing for nine days and refuse to stop in Tokyo or Seoul.

There is work to do with the Europeans, too, on defining what holds the transatlantic alliance together in the absence of the Soviet threat. NATO is badly in need of attention in the wake of Kosovo and with the looming question of its further enlargement in 2002 and beyond. The door to NATO for the remaining states of eastern and central Europe should remain open, as many are actively preparing to meet the criteria for membership. But the parallel track of NATO's own evolution, its attention to the definition of its mission, and its ability to digest and then defend new members has been neglected. Moreover, the United States has an interest in shaping the European defense identity—welcoming a greater European military capability as long as it is within the context of NATO. NATO has a very full agenda. Membership in NATO will mean nothing to anyone if the organization is no longer militarily capable and if it is unclear about its mission.

For America and our allies, the most daunting task is to find the right balance in our policy toward Russia and China. Both are equally important to the future of international peace, but the challenges they pose are very different. China is a rising power; in economic terms, that should be good news, because in order to maintain its economic dynamism, China must be more integrated into the international economy. This will require increased openness and transparency and the growth of private industry. The political struggle in Beijing is over how to maintain the Communist Party's monopoly on power. Some see economic reform, growth, and a better life for the Chinese people as the key. Others see the inherent contradiction in loosening economic control and maintaining the party's political dominance. As China's economic problems multiply due to slowing growth rates, failing banks, inert state enterprises, and rising unemployment, this struggle will intensify.

Trade can open China's economy—and its politics, too.

It is in America's interest to strengthen the hands of those who seek economic integration because this will probably lead to sustained and organized pressures for political liberalization. There are no guarantees, but in scores of cases from Chile to Spain to Taiwan, the link between democracy and economic liberalization has proven powerful over the long run. Trade and economic interaction are, in fact, good—not only for America's economic growth but for its political aims as well. Human rights concerns should not move to the sidelines in the meantime. Rather, the American president should press the Chinese leadership for change. But it is wise to remember that our influence through moral arguments and commitment is still limited in the face of Beijing's pervasive political control. The big trends toward the spread of information, the access of young Chinese to American values through educational exchanges and training, and the growth of an entrepreneurial class that does not owe its livelihood to the state are, in the end, likely to have a more powerful effect on life in China.

Although some argue that the way to support human rights is to refuse trade with China, this punishes precisely those who are most likely to change the system. Put bluntly, Li Peng and the Chinese conservatives want to continue to run the economy by state fiat. Of course, there should be tight export controls on the transfer of militarily sensitive technology to China. But trade in general can open up the Chinese economy and, ultimately, its politics too. This view requires faith in the power of markets and economic freedom to drive political change, but it is a faith confirmed by experiences around the globe.

Even if there is an argument for economic interaction with Beijing, China is still a potential threat to stability in the Asia-Pacific region. Its military power is currently no match for that of the United States. But that condition is not necessarily permanent. What we do know is that China is a great power with unresolved vital interests, particularly concerning Taiwan and the South China Sea. China resents the role of the United States in the Asia-Pacific region. This means that China is not a "status quo" power but one that would like to alter Asia's balance of power in its own favor. That alone makes it a strategic competitor, not the "strategic partner" the Clinton administration once called it. Add to this China's record of cooperation with Iran and Pakistan in the proliferation of ballistic-missile technology, and the security problem is obvious. China will do what it can to enhance its position, whether by stealing nuclear secrets or by trying to intimidate Taiwan.

China's success in controlling the balance of power depends in large part on America's reaction to the challenge. The United States must deepen its cooperation with Japan and South Korea and maintain its commitment to a robust military presence in the region. It should pay closer attention to India's role in the regional balance. There is a strong tendency conceptually to connect India with Pakistan and to think only of Kashmir or the nuclear competition between the two states. But India is an element in China's calculation, and it should be in America's, too. India is not a great power yet, but it has the potential to emerge as one.

The United States also has a deep interest in the security of Taiwan. It is a model of democratic and market-oriented development, and it invests significantly in the mainland's economy. The longstanding U.S. commitment to a "one-China" policy that leaves to a future date the resolution of the relationship between Taipei and Beijing is wise. But that policy requires that neither side challenge the status quo and that Beijing, as the more powerful actor, renounce the use of force. U.S. resolve anchors this policy. The Clinton administration tilted toward Beijing, when, for instance, it used China's formulation of the "three no's" during the president's trip there. Taiwan has been looking for attention and reassurance ever since. If the United States is resolute, peace can be maintained in the Taiwan Strait until a political settlement on democratic terms is available.

Some things take time. U.S. policy toward China requires nuance and balance. It is important to promote China's internal transition through economic interaction while containing Chinese power and security ambitions. Cooperation should be pursued, but we should never be afraid to confront Beijing when our interests collide.

RUSSIAN WEAKNESS

RUSSIA PRESENTS a different challenge. It still has many of the attributes of a great power: a large population, vast territory, and military potential. But its economic weakness and problems of national identity threaten to overwhelm it. Moscow is determined to assert itself in the world and often does so in ways that are at once haphazard and threatening to American interests. The picture is complicated by Russia's own internal transition—one that the United States wants to see succeed. The old Soviet system has broken down, and some of the basic elements of democratic development are in place. People are free to say what they think, vote for whom they please, and (for the most part) worship freely. But the democratic fragments are not institutionalized—with the exception of the Communist Party, political parties are weak—and the balance of political power is so strongly in favor of the president that he often rules simply by decree. Of course, few pay attention to Boris Yelstin's decrees, and the Russian government has been mired in inaction and stagnation for at least three years. Russia's economic troubles and its high-level corruption have been widely discussed in recent months; Russia's economy is not becoming a market but is mutating into something else. Widespread barter, banks that are not banks, billions of rubles stashed abroad and in mattresses at home, and bizarre privatization schemes that have enriched the so-called reformers give Moscow's economy a medieval tinge.

The problem for U.S. policy is that the Clinton administration's embrace of Yeltsin and those who were thought to be reformers around him has failed. Yeltsin is Russia's president and clearly the

United States had to deal with the head of state. But support for democracy and economic reform became support for Yeltsin. His agenda became the American agenda. The United States certified that reform was taking place where it was not, continuing to disburse money from the International Monetary Fund in the absence of any evidence of serious change. The curious privatization methods were hailed as economic liberalization; the looting of the country's assets by powerful people either went unnoticed or was ignored. The realities in Russia simply did not accord with the administration's script about Russian economic reform. The United States should not be faulted for trying to help. But, as the Russian reformer Grigori Yavlinsky has said, the United States should have "told the truth" about what was happening.

Now we have a dual credibility problem—with Russians and with Americans. There are signs of life in the Russian economy. The financial crash of August 1998 forced import substitution, and domestic production has increased as the resilient Russian people have taken matters into their own hands. Rising oil prices have helped as well. But these are short-term fixes. There is no longer a consensus in America or Europe on what to do next with Russia. Frustrated expectations and "Russia fatigue" are direct consequences of the "happy talk" in which the Clinton administration engaged.

Russia's economic future is now in the hands of the Russians. The country is not without assets, including its natural resources and an educated population. It is up to Russia to make structural reforms, particularly concerning the rule of law and the tax codes, so that investors—foreign and domestic—will provide the capital needed for economic growth. That opportunity will arise once there is a new government in Moscow after last December's Duma elections and next June's presidential election. But the cultural changes ultimately needed to sustain a functioning civil society and a market-based economy may take a generation. Western openness to Russia's people, particularly its youth, in exchange programs and contact with the private sector and educational opportunities can help that process. It is also important to engage the leadership of Russia's diverse regions, where economic and social policies are increasingly pursued independently of Moscow.

In the meantime, U.S. policy must concentrate on the important security agenda with Russia. First, it must recognize that American security is threatened less by Russia's strength than by its weakness and incoherence. This suggests immediate attention to the safety and security of Moscow's nuclear forces and stockpile. The Nunn-Lugar program should be funded fully and pursued aggressively. (Because American contractors do most of the work, the risk of the diversion of funds is low.) Second, Washington must begin a comprehensive discussion with Moscow on the changing nuclear threat. Much has been made by Russian military officials about their increased reliance on nuclear weapons in the face of their declining conventional readiness. The Russian deterrent is more than adequate against the U.S. nuclear arsenal, and vice versa. But that fact need no longer be enshrined in a treaty that is almost 30 years old and is a relic of a profoundly adversarial relationship between the United States and the Soviet Union. The Anti-Ballistic Missile Treaty was intended to prevent the development of national missile defenses in the Cold War security environment. Today, the principal concerns are nuclear threats from the Iraqs and North Koreas of the world and the possibility of unauthorized releases as nuclear weapons spread.

American security is threatened less by Russia's strength than by its weakness and incoherence.

Moscow, in fact, lives closer to those threats than Washington does. It ought to be possible to engage the Russians in a discussion of the changed threat environment, their possible responses, and the relationship of strategic offensive-force reductions to the deployment of defenses. The United States should make clear that it prefers to move cooperatively toward a new offense-defense mix, but that it is prepared to do so unilaterally. Moscow should understand, too, that any possibilities for sharing technology or information in these areas would depend heavily on its record—problematic to date—on the proliferation of ballistic-missile and other technologies related to WMD. It would be foolish in the extreme to share defenses with Moscow if it either leaks or deliberately transfers weapons technologies to the very states against which America is defending.

Finally, the United States needs to recognize that Russia is a great power, and that we will always have interests that conflict as well as coincide. The war in Chechnya, located in the oil-rich Caucasus, is particularly dangerous. Prime Minister Vladimir Putin has used the war to stir nationalism at home while fueling his own political fortunes. The Russian military has been uncharacteristically blunt and vocal in asserting its duty to defend the integrity of the Russian Federation—an unwelcome development in civil-military relations. The long-term effect on Russia's political culture should not be underestimated. And the war has affected relations between Russia and its neighbors in the Caucasus, as the Kremlin hurls charges of harboring and abetting Chechen terrorists against states as diverse as Saudi Arabia, Georgia, and Azerbaijan. The war is a reminder of the vulnerability of the small, new states around Russia and of America's interest in their independence. If they can become stronger, they will be less tempting to Russia. But much depends on the ability of these states to reform their economies and political systems—a process, to date, whose success is mixed at best.

COPING WITH ROGUE REGIMES

AS HISTORY MARCHES toward markets and democracy, some states have been left by the side of the road. Iraq is the prototype. Saddam Hussein's regime is isolated, his conventional military power has been severely weakened, his people live in poverty and terror, and he has no useful place in international politics. He is therefore determined to develop WMD. Nothing will change until Saddam is gone, so the United States must mobilize whatever resources it can, including support from his opposition, to remove him.

The regime of Kim Jong Il is so opaque that it is difficult to know its motivations, other than that they are malign. But North Korea also lives outside of the international system. Like East Germany, North Korea is the evil twin of a successful regime just across its border. It must fear its eventual demise from the sheer power and pull of South Korea. Pyongyang, too, has little to gain and everything to lose from engagement in the international economy. The development of WMD thus provides the destructive way out for Kim Jong Il.

President Kim Dae Jung of South Korea is attempting to find a peaceful resolution with the north through engagement. Any U.S. policy toward the north should depend heavily on coordination with